The Recovery
of Virtue

The Recovery of Virtue

The Relevance of Aquinas for Christian Ethics

Jean Porter

Westminster/John Knox Press
Louisville, Kentucky

Book design by Steve Buren

First edition

Published by Westminster/John Knox Press
Louisville, Kentucky

PRINTED IN THE UNITED STATES OF AMERICA
9 8 7 6 5 4 3 2 1

Library of Congress Cataloging-in-Publication Data

Porter, Jean, 1955–
   The recovery of virtue : the relevance of Aquinas for Christian ethics / Jean Porter. — 1st ed.
        p.   cm.
   Includes bibliographical references.
   ISBN 0-664-21924-1

   1. Thomas Aquinas, Saint, 1225?–1274—Contributions in Christian ethics. 2. Christian ethics—History—Middle Ages, 600–1500. 3. Virtues—History. I. Title.
BJ1217.P67 1990
241'.042'092—dc20   90-32954
                                                                              CIP

For my parents
June H. Newton
and
Frank W. Porter
and in loving memory of my grandmother
Audrey M. Heidelberg
January 1, 1908–October 22, 1988

*Non est inconveniens si obligatio
gratitudinis interminabilis sit*
(*ST* II-II.106.6 *ad* 2)

Contents

Acknowledgments

I wish that I could thank everyone who has contributed in some way to this project. I am well aware of how deeply my colleagues and friends have shaped my thought on the subjects of this book, and I am aware, too, that I am not fully conscious of all that I owe them in this regard. But I would like at least to thank those who have contributed in more direct ways to the completion of this book.

In the first place, I wish to express my appreciation to Vanderbilt Divinity School for allowing me a sabbatical during the academic year 1988–1989, during which time I completed this book. The Association of Theological Schools and the Vanderbilt University Research Council generously provided funding that made it possible for me to avail myself of that sabbatical. And the Institute for Ecumenical and Cultural Research, in Collegeville, Minnesota, provided the space and support so important to sustained work. Jacqueline Cox, Arliene Dearing, and Judy Matthews Taylor offered invaluable help in preparing the final version of the manuscript.

A number of colleagues and friends have commented on one or more drafts of this project, including Margaret Farley, John Gurrieri, Patrick Henry, Andrew Hoyal, Justus George Lawler, and Raymond Pedrizetti. I learned a great deal from discussions with colleagues at the Institute for Ecumenical and Cultural Research; during a Junior Scholars' conference sponsored by the Association of Theological Schools, I had the opportunity to present a proposal for this project and to receive many helpful suggestions. My patient and indefatigable editor, Davis Perkins, and an anonymous reader for Westminster/John Knox Press suggested a number of changes, most of which I have incorporated. My copy editor, Hank Schlau, offered a number of very helpful suggestions that have improved the style and clarity of my prose. Karen Spear prepared the index. Jane Barr and Idit Dobbs-Weinstein reviewed my translations of Aquinas with me in some detail and saved me from many infelicities and outright mistakes; of course, I take full responsibility for any remaining errors. Finally, Alasdair MacIntyre deserves a special word of thanks. Not only did he read and comment on portions of the manuscript, but I believe that if I had not had the opportunity to learn from him while we were both on the faculty of Vanderbilt University, this book could not have been written. I am deeply grateful to all of these persons. Of course, I am responsible for the flaws that undoubtedly remain.

Portions of chapter 5 are adapted from my essay "Moral Rules and Moral Actions: A Comparison of Aquinas and Modern Moral Theology," *The Journal of Religious Ethics* 17/1 (Spring 1989), 123–49, and portions of chapter 6 are adapted from my essay *"De Ordine Caritatis:* Charity, Friendship and Justice in Thomas Aquinas' *Summa Theologiae,"* *The Thomist* 53/2 (April 1989), 197–214. Both essays are used by the kind permission of the editors of the journals in which they appeared.

Finally, I want to acknowledge a different kind of debt to the many dear friends and family members who have supported me through this process. It would be impossible to name them all, but at least I can mention the members of my local church, the Catholic Cathedral of the Incarnation in Nashville, Tennessee, and the many friends of the late Father Philip Donnelly (you know who you are!) who have been my mainstay for over seven years now. Above all, I want to express my gratitude to my parents and to my late grandmother, to whom this book is lovingly dedicated.

Introductory Note

The interpretation of Aquinas' theory of morality to be developed in this book is based on his *Summa Theologiae,* which he began in 1266 and which remained incomplete at his death in 1274. In order to assist those readers who are unfamiliar with Aquinas' works, in the following paragraphs I will sketch the overall plan of the *Summa Theologiae* and will offer an explanation of the form of the citations from it.

The *Summa Theologiae* is divided into three volumes, and the second volume is further divided into two parts. These four divisions of the work are usually referred to by their Latin names: the *Prima Pars,* the *Prima Secundae* and the *Secunda Secundae,* and the *Tertia Pars.* At his death, Aquinas had completed the first ninety questions of the *Tertia Pars.* The remainder of that volume was then compiled by others on the basis of his earlier writings.

Within each volume, the materials are arranged according to certain questions, which are sequentially ordered in each separate part of the *Summa.* (In other words, the *Prima Secundae* and the *Secunda Secundae* each begin with a question 1, as do the *Prima Pars* and the *Tertia Pars.*) These questions address general areas of inquiry: for example, the nature of happiness. They are in turn divided into separate articles, each of which is stated in the form of a particular query: for example, whether happiness consists in wealth. These articles, finally, are subdivided into the following: a number of objections, which defend one answer to the query of the article; the *sed contra,* "to the contrary," which states the opposite view and cites an argument or a traditional authority on which it rests; Aquinas' response, which interprets, defends, and sometimes modifies the view stated in the *sed contra;* and his responses to the objections enumerated in the beginning of the article.

For example, the first question of the *Prima Secundae,* "On the final end of the human person," is divided into eight articles. The first of these, "Whether it is proper to the human person to act for an end," begins with three objections, which give reasons why it is not proper to human beings to act for an end. Then, in the *sed contra,* Aquinas cites an argument from Aristotle showing that, on the contrary, it *is* proper to the human person to act for an end. In his response, he explains and defends that claim and then, on that basis, replies to the three initial objections.

The method of citing texts from the *Summa Theologiae* which is followed in this book consists of giving the volume in Roman numerals, followed by the question and article in Arabic numerals. Each part of the second volume is cited separately: The *Prima Secundae* is cited as I-II, and the *Secunda Secundae* is cited as II-II. If nothing further is noted, the citation should be taken as referring to the article as a whole. However, Aquinas' response to a particular objection is sometimes cited, and in that case, *"ad* x" is added to the citation. More rarely, an objection is cited, if the particular point in question is not denied by Aquinas later in the article. In that case, the citation would read, *"obj.* x, not denied."

For example, the first article of the question on the end of the human person—that is, *Prima Secundae*, question 1, article 1—would be cited as I-II.1.1. Aquinas' specific response to the second objection in that article would be cited as I-II.1.1 *ad* 2, and a reference to the objection itself would read, "I-II.1.1 *obj.* 2, not denied."

In preparing this book, I consulted two editions of the *Summa Theologiae:* the Latin text published by the Biblioteca de Autores Cristianos (Madrid, 1961), and the English translation by the Fathers of the English Dominican Province (New York: Benziger Brothers, 1947). All translations of Aquinas' writings in this book are mine unless otherwise noted, and I take full responsibility for any errors that may be present.

1

The Purpose of This Study

In this book, I will attempt to reconstruct the moral theory of Thomas Aquinas' *Summa Theologiae* in the light of the problematics of contemporary Christian ethics, Protestant as well as Catholic. In so doing, I hope to contribute to the contemporary discussion of those problematics as well as offer some insight into the work of Aquinas itself.

Admittedly, this will strike many of my readers as an unpromising program. The unprecedented problems of our own age have led many to conclude that theology must branch out in entirely new directions if it is to respond to the challenges of our time.[1] Furthermore, if there is a theologian whose moral thought in particular is likely to strike most of us as outmoded, it is surely Thomas Aquinas. Nor will this impression be lessened when it becomes apparent that, as I read him, Aquinas does indeed affirm many of the theses with which he is traditionally associated, and which seem most seriously problematic today, including the necessity of a metaphysical theory of goodness for moral theory, the existence of a hierarchy of being, and the claim that some kinds of actions are never morally permissible. An examination of Aquinas' moral theory is certainly still of historical interest, but what relevance can it have to contemporary Christian ethics?

In order to answer this question, it is not necessary to attempt an elaborate theoretical account of the (initially obscure) affinities between Aquinas and contemporary Christian ethicists, because in fact many of the latter have acknowledged their indebtedness to his work. Catholic moral theology since the Second Vatican Council has been profoundly influenced by essays on Aquinas written by John Dedek, Germain Grisez, and Louis Janssens.[2] But leading Protestant thinkers have also acknowledged their debt to Aquinas. James Gustafson invites us to consider the work of Aquinas as one of the benchmarks by which his own work should be considered,[3] and he elsewhere says that "I do not think that my *basic* move in drawing from the sciences . . . is essentially different from that of Thomas Aquinas or Schleiermacher or others."[4] Stanley Hauerwas draws heavily on the work of Aquinas to develop his theory of Christian ethics as an ethic of virtue, since, in his view, Aquinas and his predecessor, Aristotle, offer a "still unsurpassed analysis of how the virtues are acquired and form the self."[5] Alan Donagan, in his philosophical analysis of Christian love, cites Aquinas as one of those who holds that "humanity is to be loved as such."[6] Of course, none of these authors appropriates Aquinas uncritically or relies on him as the sole, or even the primary, source for his own work. But it is clear that, for better or worse, Aquinas' theory of morality is highly relevant to contemporary Christian ethics. For this reason, a study of that theory in the context of the problematics of contemporary Christian ethics may be expected to shed some light on the work of our contemporaries, while at the same time enabling us to appreciate the significance of Aquinas' own work in a fresh way.

Moreover, there is a more specific reason why a study of Aquinas' theory of morality can contribute to contemporary Christian ethics. In spite of the acknowledged common indebtedness to the Thomistic tradition of many of its practitioners, there is remarkably little collaboration or even mutual appreciation among today's Christian ethicists. To the contrary, it is impossible to escape the impression that the field of Christian ethics is made up of thinkers who not only disagree but who consider one another's approaches to be radically wrongheaded.

At one time, this absence of a common conversation might have been traced to the broad differences between Catholic and Protestant approaches to the moral life, but that is no longer the case. To be sure, as Gustafson notes in a recent article, "there is no longer much interest in developing ecumenical consensus, per se, between Protestant and Roman Catholic ethics."[7] But at this point, there is also no consensus on the correct interpretation of the Christian moral tradition among either Catholic or Protestant ethicists. For almost thirty years now, Catholic moral theology has been dominated by an intense and sometimes acrimonious debate between those who follow Grisez and John Finnis in asserting that there are some determinate kinds of actions that are never morally justified, and those, sometimes called proportionalists, who disagree. Grisez insists that "proportionalism is not false but absurd, literally incoherent."[8] On the other hand, Richard McCormick, who is a leading expositor of proportionalism, has nothing to say about the work of Grisez and his followers in his recent survey of moral theology since 1940, beyond the bare acknowledgment that they oppose proportionalism.[9] On the Protestant side, we find Hauerwas asserting that he cannot follow Gustafson in the latter's turn to nature, as interpreted by science, as a source for moral norms, because he, unlike Gustafson, believes that "we must continue to begin with the 'particular,' with the historical . . . because that is where God begins."[10] Gustafson, in turn, replies that "I find that sentence, even in context, to be ludicrous."[11] At the same time, they do agree that the tradition of Kantian liberalism, which dominated much of Protestant ethics earlier in this century, is fundamentally flawed and must be excised from Christian ethics.

In a response to his critics, Gustafson remarks on how odd it is that his work is so badly misunderstood and unappreciated by the Catholic McCormick, when his moral theory is so similar to that of Aquinas.[12] Without attempting to decide whether Gustafson is right to object that McCormick has misread him, we may generalize his point to include most of the field of Christian ethics, at least in this country. When so many of its leading practitioners are significantly indebted to one figure, it is very surprising, at first glance, that the field is as divided as it is.

Yet, on reflection, this phenomenon is not so surprising after all. We know that the fragmentation of contemporary Christian ethics is not unique. The same divisiveness may be found in secular discussions of moral matters, both practical and philosophical. I suggest that the roots of the fragmentation of Christian ethics are similar to those that Alasdair MacIntyre has identified for secular moral discourse.[13] Like their secular counterparts, today's Christian ethicists have seized on fragments of what was once a unified moral tradition as the basis for their interpretations of Christian ethics. The Catholic moral theologians mentioned above have attempted to construct a moral theory on the basis of accounts of human goods and their relation to human action, and Protestant thinkers have attempted to develop theories of Christian ethics out of some account of Christian love, an appeal to the goodness of nature, or a reflection on the virtues. But unfortunately, while those fragments once fitted together and made sense as a part of one unified theory of morality, none of them on its own seems to be adequate as a basis for a convincing, contemporary theory of morality. If this line of analysis is correct, then no one of these theories will have the cogency to be fully adequate on its own terms, much less to convince those who adopt different starting points in their interpretations of the Christian moral tradition. Hence, we would expect to see what we do see in the field of Christian ethics, namely, either interminable debate or a frustrated suspension of all attempts at conversation.

If something is fragmented, then the obvious solution to the difficulties caused by its brokenness is to put it back together. But of course, that is easier said than done. For this reason, it can be very tempting to abandon the current field of Christian ethics, with all its confusions, in order to take up one of the unified moral theories of the past. And Aquinas' moral theory would seem to be an excellent candidate for such a reappropriation, since it offers one of the most unified and cogent interpretations of the central concepts of the Christian moral tradition ever developed. The reader may suspect that that is what I plan to advocate.

But in fact, we cannot simply reappropriate the moral thought of Aquinas, or any other thinker, however formidable. Our philosophical and theological starting points, and the complex of ideas within which we reflect, are bound to be different in important respects from Aquinas' own. In order to restore a basis for common conversation in the field of Christian ethics, we must rethink the interconnections among the central concepts of the Christian moral tradition in the context of our own convictions and problematics.

At the same time, a careful consideration of Aquinas' moral theory can aid us in our own constructive task. For as I shall try to show in what follows, Aquinas does succeed in developing a unified theory of morality which holds together the different motifs found in Christian ethics today, and which is cogent, given his starting points. Even though we, with our different starting points, may not find that moral theory ultimately persuasive, nonetheless we can learn from it. It can suggest interconnections among basic concepts that we might not have considered, and it can call attention to difficulties that we might otherwise overlook. That at least is the presupposition of this book.

In the remainder of this chapter, I will offer a fuller account both of the state of contemporary Christian ethics and of the scope of this book.

Dominant Ideas in Contemporary Christian Ethics

We have already observed that certain central concepts of the Christian moral tradition which figure prominently in Aquinas' work also figure prominently in contemporary Christian ethics—but as fragments of competing theories, rather than as unified elements of one moral theory. In this section, I will expand upon this observation by offering a critical survey of the work of leading Christian ethicists. My purpose in this survey is to develop at least a prima facie case that the lack of productive dialogue in Christian ethics is indeed due to the fragmentary character of the most important work being done today.

I am well aware that a critical survey of this sort should be offered in an apologetic tone of voice, or its literary equivalent, and so it is. It would be impossible to do full justice to the thought of any one of the movements or authors mentioned below in a discussion this brief, and I do not want to give the impression that I believe that I have developed definitive critiques of their thought in a paragraph or two. Generally, I have limited myself to a very compressed account of the thought of each, together with a summary of what seem to me to be the most salient criticisms that have been directed to the work of each author. These criticisms are recounted simply in order to point to the limitations of these moral theories, limitations that remain present even if one grants the premises of each theory.

Human goods and human actions: Catholic moral theology since Vatican II. Since the Second Vatican Council called for a renewal of moral theology, work in this field has been largely aimed at breaking free of an excessive legalism that has dominated Catholic moral theology since the Counter-Reformation. At the same time, contemporary moral theologians, like their predecessors, have focused on the question of how we determine what counts as a morally good action, given that all human actions are directed in some way to a moral or premoral good. Soon after Vatican II, two sharply divergent answers to this question began to develop. One is contained in a radical reinterpretation of the traditional doctrine of the natural law, developed by Grisez in close collaboration with Finnis and others. The other is contained in a moral theory commonly called revisionism or proportionalism, which is represented in Europe through the work of Joseph Fuchs, Bruno Schüller, and Louis Janssens, among others, and which has McCormick and Charles Curran as its leading representatives in the United States.

The groundwork for the Grisez/Finnis reinterpretation of the natural law was laid in an influential article by Grisez, but it has since been developed far beyond the lines suggested by that article, and is no longer considered by Grisez and Finnis to be a representation of Aquinas' own conception of the natural law.[14] This reinterpretation takes its starting point from a general account of practical reason, which is then narrowed down into a theory of moral action, interpreted as action that is rational in the fullest possible sense. What is

required for an item of behavior to count as minimally rational, that
is, as an action? Following Aquinas (so far), Grisez and Finnis assert
that a true human action is necessarily directed toward some good.
That is, it accords with the first principle of practical reason, "The
good is to be done and pursued; the bad is to be avoided."[15] Hence,
the first principle of practical reason is not a moral precept, but serves
as the necessary starting point of all practical reasoning.

It will be evident that so far, Grisez and Finnis have characterized practical reasoning in a very formal way. The distinctiveness of
their theory of morality becomes more apparent when we ask the
next logical question: How do we know what counts as a true human
good? Both Grisez and Finnis insist that it would be a mistake to
conclude that the answer to that question must depend on some
metaphysical theory of goodness or some specific anthropology.
They accept the dictum, which was indeed almost universally accepted among Anglo-Saxon moral philosophers until relatively recently, that it is logically impossible to derive any conclusions about
what is good or what ought to be done from premises containing any
sort of empirical or metaphysical claims about the way things are.
Nonetheless, we do have substantive knowledge of those desiderata
that are true human goods. This knowledge is self-evident to us. It
is not innate in the sense of being present prior to all experience,
because it does depend on the experience of desiring those things
toward which all persons are naturally inclined. But once we have
had such experiences, it becomes evident to us that these goods are
desirable in and of themselves, although not everyone may be able
to say so in those terms. Specifically, there are seven such goods, of
which the first three are substantive (they exist prior to our choices)
and the rest are reflexive (they depend on our choices): human life,
knowledge and aesthetic appreciation, skilled performances of all
kinds, self-integration, authenticity/practical reasonableness, justice
and friendship, and religion/holiness.[16] According to Grisez and Finnis, all our actions are ultimately motivated by the desire for one or
more of these goods.

What, then, is the basis for specifically moral reasoning? Grisez
and Finnis reply that moral action is rational in the fullest possible
sense, whereas immoral action is irrational in some respect, although
it retains sufficient rationality to count as an action. We have already
observed that a putative action is truly such only if it is aimed in some
way at securing one or more of the basic goods. But because each of
these basic goods is immediately self-evident, they are incommensurable, and therefore stand in no intrinsic ordering to one another.
Hence, an action that aims at one basic good while arbitrarily slight-

ing others is irrational to the extent that it turns from a basic good without adequate reason, even though it retains sufficient rational intelligibility to count as an action.

Admittedly, we cannot aim at all the basic goods all the time. Even so, we can act in such a way as to remain open to those basic goods that we do not actively pursue in a given action. Only in this way will our action be fully rational, that is to say, morally good. Hence, the first principle of morality is, "In voluntarily acting for human goods and avoiding what is opposed to them, one ought to choose and otherwise will those and only those possibilities whose willing is compatible with a will towards integral human fulfillment."[17] Note that integral human fulfillment does *not* mean the attainment of some determinate ideal of human existence, over and above the fullest possible enjoyment of the basic goods. Grisez in particular is very careful to make this point clear.[18] Integral human fulfillment is nothing other than the complete enjoyment of all the basic human goods. What that would look like in principle cannot be determined, since the basic goods are open-ended and transcend their specific instantiations. Clearly, we will never attain this ideal by our own efforts, but a truly moral will is one that is directed toward it nonetheless, as a rational ideal.

The first principle of morality is translated into a set of criteria for evaluating the moral goodness of human actions by means of what Grisez refers to as eight modes of responsibility, which are (apparently) self-evident specifications of that principle: "Each mode of responsibility simply excludes a particular way in which a person can limit himself or herself to a quite partial and inadequate fulfillment."[19] Space does not permit an extended discussion of these eight modes. Suffice it to say that each one directs us to stay open to all the basic goods, and not to prefer one to another arbitrarily, that is to say, on the basis of emotion rather than reason, or to foreclose the possibility of attaining some good out of hostility or an arbitrary preference for another good.[20] But we should note that this interpretation of the first principle of morality leads Grisez and Finnis to conclude that some kinds of actions are never morally permissible. Specifically, any sort of action that would involve a direct attack on a basic good, for example, direct homicide, deliberate contraception, or lying, could never be morally justified.

It is at this point that the proportionalists part company with Grisez and Finnis.[21] Apparently, they accept at least the main lines of the Grisez/Finnis account of practical reasonableness and the theory of basic goods that gives that account its specific force.[22] However, they emphatically do not agree that no action that involves a direct attack on a basic good can be moral. This claim, they contend, reflects an arbitrary absolutizing of finite human goods. To the Grisez/Finnis claim that it is self-evidently true that one ought never to act against a basic good, the proportionalists offer a supposedly self-evident principle of their own: One must always act in such a way as to bring about the greatest possible balance of goods over evils, even if that means acting against some premoral good. As McCormick puts it: "Now in situations of this kind [conflict situations], the rule of Christian reason, if we are governed by the *ordo bonorum* [order of goods], is to choose the lesser evil. This general statement is, it would seem, beyond debate; for the only alternative is that in conflict situations we should choose the greater evil, which is patently absurd. This means that all concrete rules and distinctions are subsidiary to this and hence valid to the extent that they actually convey to us what is factually the lesser evil."[23]

Hence, the proportionalists' version of the first principle of morality might be formulated, "Always act in such a way as to bring about the greatest possible balance of premoral goods over premoral evils, given that you can do so without directly bringing about moral evil."[24] The negative corollary to the first principle of morality, as the proportionalists understand it, is, "Never act in such a way as to bring about a premoral evil, unless such an action is necessary to bring about or preserve proportionately greater premoral goods."

The application of these principles to the evaluation of particular actions would seem, on first glance, to be straightforward enough. One simply determines whether a particular action secures the best possible balance of premoral goods over premoral evils. If it does so, the action is morally licit, and if not, it is not. Hence, proportionalists insist that it is inaccurate to describe a particular action in terms that imply moral judgment without first carrying out such an assessment. Terms such as *murder, theft,* and *lying* refer to the wrongful (that is, unjustified) infliction of particular kinds of harms, and therefore, only an action which brings about premoral evils without a proportionate reason should be described by a term of this sort. Of course, the success of this program for moral analysis requires a convincing standard of commensuration by which we can determine which of a number of possible concrete outcomes really does count as the lesser evil or the greater good. The proportionalists are (wisely) reluctant to adopt the utilitarian strategy of analyzing all benefits and harms in terms of a single standard of well-being, but they have not come up with a convincing alternative, or even one single alternative that is acceptable to most proportionalists themselves.[25] Until they do, proportionalism must be seen as at best a program for constructing a theory of morality, rather than as a moral theory in its own right.

Nonetheless, the proportionalist critique of the Grisez/Finnis reinterpretation of the natural law is well-taken. It is hardly self-evident that we can never act against the basic goods, even to prevent an even greater destruction of these goods. Indeed, the proportionalists might have gone further in their critique, because as more than one critic has noted, there are a number of ambiguities in Grisez's and Finnis' accounts of the basic goods and their relationships to one another and to derived goods.[26] But at the same time, at least one of Grisez's criticisms of proportionalism is equally well-founded: Without a convincing standard of commensuration for comparing pre-moral goods and evils, a program for moral assessment that depends on commensurating them is meaningless.[27]

The interminableness of this debate in moral theology now becomes easier to understand. Each side insists that it has reformulated moral analysis on the basis of self-evident moral truths. But the first principle of morality as Grisez and Finnis understand it is hardly self-evident, and the same can be said of the list of basic goods which gives that principle concrete meaning. On the other hand, the first principle of morality as the proportionalists understand it is empty, since they offer no plausible account of the commensuration of goods.

Christian love as equal regard: **Gene Outka.** Is there a distinctively Christian form of love which requires the Christian to take on special duties, or to adopt a distinctive attitude, toward others? Until fairly recently, this was one of the key questions—if not *the* central question—in Protestant ethical reflection. In his *Agape: An Ethical Analysis,* Gene Outka analyzes the different interpretations of Christian love, or agape, to be found in this literature in the late nineteenth and twentieth centuries. His analysis ranges over a number of authors, including Anders Nygren, Søren Kierkegaard, Karl Barth, Reinhold Niebuhr, and Paul Ramsey, and touches on most of the issues that recur in discussions of Christian love, including the legitimacy of self-love and special relations and the relationship between Christian love and justice. In his view, there are three accounts of agape to be found there: agape as equal regard, as self-sacrifice, and as mutuality. In addition, he argues that Christian love, as such, should be understood as being primarily equivalent to equal regard, although such love will also incorporate elements of self-sacrifice and mutuality under particular circumstances.

What is meant by characterizing agape as equal regard? Equal regard, Outka explains, is "the regard for the neighbor which is independent and unalterable, and which applies to each neighbor qua human existent."[28] Hence, agape, so understood, extends to each person simply in virtue of his or her humanity, regardless of whether the neighbor who is loved is attractive or unattractive, virtuous or wicked, regardless of whether this regard is returned in kind or even acknowledged by its recipient. Because agape as equal regard does not depend on any of the particularities of the neighbor, it is independent of changes in the particular state of the neighbor and is therefore permanently stable. It regards the neighbor as irreducibly valuable, simply in virtue of being a human individual. Hence, Outka endorses the Kantian dictum that no human being should ever be treated as a mere means, but always as an end in himself or herself.[29]

Furthermore, Outka attempts to show that agape understood as equal regard incorporates the core insights of those who claim that the central meaning of Christian love is self-sacrifice or mutuality.[30] An interpretation of Christian love that required everyone to be self-sacrificial all the time would either encourage the sinful tendencies toward greed and selfishness on the part of those who disregard the imperative to love, or else it would be self-defeating, since if everyone sacrificed her interests in every situation, no one could go forward with a course of activity which required her to accept the sacrifices of others. On the other hand, equal regard will often call upon us to sacrifice ourselves, but it also provides criteria for determining which sacrifices are necessary, and which would be supererogatory or even pernicious (for example, because by sacrificing my desires to you, I encourage you in your selfish greed). Similarly, if Christian love were viewed solely in terms of mutuality, it would be limited in scope to those who return one's love, or at least are aware of it, and it would be subject to alteration as the neighbor alters her responses to the one who loves. Equal regard, on the other hand, provides a framework for all special relationships of mutality which safeguards them from the vicissitudes of inadequate response and change, at least by ensuring that even if mutuality should no longer be possible, the fundamental respect that persons owe one another as human beings will not thereby be jeopardized.[31] And equal regard, unlike mutuality, extends even to persons who are personally unknown to us, and for this reason equal regard, unlike mutuality, can provide a direct justification for work on behalf of social justice.

Recently, the claim that Christian morality is grounded in a commitment to equal regard has been rejected by leading Protestant scholars. As we will see in the next section, Gustafson holds that any interpretation of Christian ethics which places duties to other persons at the center of the Christian moral life is fundamentally wrongheaded. And according to Hauerwas, any attempt to equate Christian morality with Kantian liberalism is necessarily mistaken. He flatly asserts that "the kind of life Christians describe as faithful is substantively at odds with any account of morality that makes autonomy the necessary condition and/or goal of moral behavior."[32]

It is open to Outka to respond that neither Gustafson nor Hauerwas has grasped what is central to the Christian moral tradition. But at the same time, it is possible to raise questions about Outka's interpretation of Christian love as equal regard that represent a more serious challenge to that program from the point of view of its own premises. Indeed, Outka himself suggests some of these questions.

What does it mean to love another? Presumably, whatever else it means, to love another means to wish that person well and to refrain from harming him. But what counts as wishing another person well, or harming him? As Outka acknowledges, the answers to these questions are not as obvious as they appear.[33] There are some events which, when they befall a person, do seem to be obviously harmful, for example, death, injury, or substantial loss of relationships with others or of material goods. But it is possible to doubt whether any or all of these sorts of events are *true* harms, in general or in particular cases. The question of what counts as truly benefiting a person is even more difficult to answer. If it is possible to doubt that death, injury, and so forth are true harms, then it is possible to doubt whether we have truly benefited another by helping her to avoid such things. In what way, then, are we to express love for another? By supporting her own projects? But those projects may turn out to be harmful to her—or worse, success in them may reinforce negative or vicious tendencies in her. Should we bracket such questions and simply honor and support her own freedom? But how do we know that the exercise of freedom is truly good for this individual or any individual? How indeed, without some account of that in which true human good consists?

Correlatively, it is not immediately clear what is meant by loving others *equally*. The justification and exact meaning of a normative commitment to equality have been widely debated among moral philosophers, precisely because it is not clear what this commitment presupposes and demands.[34] Everyone agrees that a normative commitment to equality does not imply that everyone is equal in every respect, or that everyone should be treated equally. But in what respect *are* all persons equal? Or if there is no such respect, does that fact make a difference for our commitment to normative equality? These questions are closely related to the practical question of what, concretely, a commitment to equal regard requires. It would seem to be possible in principle to consider all equally, and yet to treat individuals differently. At least, everyone agrees that relevant differences in need should lead to differences in the way that individuals are treated (although the question of what counts as a genuine need has not received the attention it deserves in this discussion). But what other differences among people can justify differences in treatment? This question is very difficult to answer without a more definite account of the rationale for a commitment to equality than either Outka or the authors that he discusses have been able to provide.

The return to nature: James Gustafson. Gustafson's theological/ethical program is summed up in the title of his two-volume work, *Ethics from a Theocentric Perspective.* [35] In that work, he calls for a conscious turn away from what he describes as the anthropocentric orientation of traditional Christian thought, which has led us to assume that the well-being of the human race, or of some individuals, is of primary concern to God as well as to us, and that the rest of creation exists for the sake of human beings. In his view, these assumptions are dangerous because they can lead us to act in ways that imperil the ecosystem on which we depend for survival. And what is even more serious, they have been vitiated by the theories offered by modern science:

> Focus on man, and on man within very limited time-spans of life, leads to a distortion of the place of man within the universe. As physicists and astronomers have developed explanations of the origins of the universe, we see that even the most rudimentary preconditions for the evolution of the most primitive forms of life took millions of years to develop. There were contingencies of natural events that made development of life possible on our planet in a way that it has not developed elsewhere even in our solar system. . . . As astrophysicists and others assess the possibilities for the long-range future of our planet and its place in the universe, it becomes clear that in one way or another there shall be a *finis,* a temporal end, to life as we know it. If it were not for that knowledge, one might live contentedly with the traditional Western assurance that everything has taken place for the sake of man; that man is the crown of the creation.[36]

What, then, shall we do? Gustafson advocates that we turn to the Reformed tradition for resources out of which to shape a theocentric piety. Of course, he does not advocate an uncritical appropriation of the Reformed tradition, which in his view shares the liability of all theological traditions, in that it has traditionally held that God directs events for the sake of human persons. Nonetheless, if we free ourselves from that assumption, the Reformed tradition has three important resources to offer to modern piety: "1) The sense of a powerful, sovereign God who stands over against the creation; 2) an emphasis on the centrality of religious affections—dependence, respect, gratitude, obligation, remorse—within the religious life; 3) and the ethical imperative that we relate ourselves and all things in a manner appropriate to their relations to God."[37] This third resource calls for special emphasis, because it is the foundation of Gustafson's ethical program. What a theocentric piety demands, according to Gustafson, is a sustained attempt to act in accordance with God's purposes and not our own, even when those purposes may conflict with our own interests as individuals and as a species: "What we judge to be good for man, or for a human person, or some human group, may not be in accord with the ordering purposes of God, insofar as they can be discerned. The chief end of man may not be salvation in a traditional Christian sense; it may be to honor, to serve, and to glorify (celebrate) God (as the Calvinists have always said but not always believed and practiced)."[38]

Clearly, the mandate to relate to all things in a manner appropriate to their relations to God presupposes that we are able to determine just how creatures *are* related to God. How is that to be done? Gustafson warns us that the discernment of God's purposes can never be done perfectly, or with final certainty, but that is no excuse for not doing the best we can to determine what God's purposes are in a given situation. Moreover, he cautions us that in order to attain even limited insight into God's purposes, we must respond to the circumstances of our lives out of a fundamentally religious point of view. Above all, we must bring to our discernment an attitude of piety, which is characterized by awe and respect for God's purposes insofar as we can discern them, together with a fidelity which always attempts "an alignment of persons and communities with the 'coercive and persuasive powers' that order life."[39] But once we begin to act out of piety, we are enabled to discern at least something of God's purposes by discerning systems of order which sustain all human life, namely nature, history, culture, society, and the self. If we are committed to responding actively to all these forms of ordering out of piety, we can be sure that we will not stray too far from an alignment with God's purposes.

In the second volume of *Ethics from a Theocentric Perspective,* Gustafson attempts to show how his program might be applied to specific issues. He selects four issues for extended discussion: marriage and the family; suicide; population and nutrition; and allocation of biomedical research funding.[40] A few summary observations are in order for the present discussion.

First of all, it should be noted that Gustafson's theocentric perspective does not always lead to a sharp rejection of the tradition. For example, his analysis of marriage does not lead to any strikingly new normative conclusions, and he pronounces the existing guidelines for allocating funding for biomedical research to be quite adequate. As he himself points out, there is no reason to expect theocentric ethics to lead to a rejection of the tradition in every respect.[41] But, second, there are a number of points at which he does depart significantly from what he sees as the anthropocentric tradition. He argues that in some cases, suicide might be a justifiable response to circumstances in which an individual is forced to undergo pointless, unbearable, and unrelievable suffering. We must recognize that "the powers that bring life into being do not always sustain it but can lead to its untimely and tragic destruction."[42] Infanticide may be a permissible choice for an individual family faced with extreme scarcity of resources, although he does not believe that a social policy of infanticide can be justifiable.[43] Abortion is morally justifiable in some circumstances, although it remains a tragic choice.[44] The use of contraceptives is not only morally justifiable, but "little short of an imperative,"[45] given the realities of world overpopulation. Most strikingly, perhaps, he admits that at some point, the use of coercion to limit family size might be morally justified, although only as a last resort.[46]

These conclusions suggest that Gustafson has indeed replaced normative individualism with a limited, cautious, but definite preference for preserving the well-being of communities or the species as a whole. At the same time, the larger goods that he seeks to foster are all, as far as I can determine, human goods, in the sense that they are goods of communities or of the species itself. Gustafson gives us no examples of a situation in which the appropriate response to God's purposes would call upon us to disregard or act against any and all forms of human good, including that of the species.

One further observation is in order before we look at the criticisms that have been lodged against Gustafson's moral theory. As we noted above, nature is only one of the orderings toward which a theocentric piety directs us. However, Gustafson's insistence that an adequate theology must take account of the deliverances of natural science tends to result in a greater emphasis on nature in the subsequent discussion, and both he and his critics tend to focus on his appeal to the normative significance of nature in assessing his work. Nor is Gustafson alone in his appeal to nature as a source of moral norms. Feminist theologians, both Protestant and Catholic, have likewise advocated a renewed attention to, and respect for, the normative demands of the natural order.[47] More surprisingly, the neo-orthodox theologian Oliver O'Donovan admits that nature may offer a limited but real source of moral guidance.[48] It would be rash to claim that "nature" means exactly the same thing to all these authors, or that they all understand its normativity in the same way. Nonetheless, it does seem that the motif of the goodness of the natural, broadly understood, is making a comeback outside of traditional Catholic circles.

Criticisms of Gustafson's thought have tended to focus on the adequacy of his theology as a construal of the Christian tradition. It is argued that his radical revisions of traditional Christian doctrines lead him to a vision of human life in the world that is admirable, perhaps, but not Christian.[49] This line of criticism is obviously of the first importance to an overall assessment of Gustafson's work, but it is not so directly relevant to our purposes as a second line of criticism: Even after reading the discussions of specific questions in the second volume of his work, we are still uncertain as to what it means, concretely, to relate to all things in a manner appropriate to their relationships to God.[50] How, out of all the possible construals of the complex forms of ordering in the world, are we to pick out which ones are normative, even with the help of piety?

Gustafson never does provide an adequate answer to this question. As we have seen, his departures from the mainstream Christian views on specifics are apparently determined by a normative preference for the good of the community or the species, over that of the individual. Even his claim that suicide may sometimes be permissible seems to be determined by this preference, since he notes that an individual whose life is still of value to the community may be forcibly restrained, if necessary, from self-destruction.[51] This turn from individualism is certainly significant, but it is difficult to see how it is theocentric, even when theocentrism is viewed on Gustafson's own terms. The human good, now construed as the good of the community, or of the human race as a whole, is still at the center of moral concern. Gustafson might answer that the turn from individualism is only one part of his moral program, which becomes theocentric when it is placed in the context of a still wider commitment to relate to all things in a manner appropriate to their relations to God. But that only brings us back to the fundamental, and unanswered question: What, concretely, does that mean, over and above a general policy of giving priority to the well-being of human communities over that of individuals?

In search of the virtuous community: **Stanley Hauerwas.** In spite of their obvious differences, Grisez and Finnis, their Catholic critics, Outka and the authors he discusses, and Gustafson would all agree that the criteria for adequacy for an interpretation of the Christian moral tradition include some criteria that are external to that tradition. That is, they would agree that a successful interpretation of Christian ethics must meet wider standards of reasonableness and plausibility. The work of Stanley Hauerwas is characterized by an uncompromising denial of that claim. He insists that Christian ethics must begin with the particular, the historical, and specifically with God's unique self-revelation in Jesus Christ, in order to determine what God as revealed in Jesus demands that we do and be. Even more important, he insists that Christian ethics must remain with the particular, in the sense that the criteria for adequacy for Christian ethics are internal to the Christian tradition itself.[52]

At the same time, Hauerwas shares Gustafson's rejection of the individualism that lies at the core of so much of Christian moral reasoning. But instead of turning to the natural or to comprehensive communities as an alternative focus for moral reflection, he looks at a particular community, the church, and asks what sort of community it should be in order to be truly the church of the God revealed in Christ. Or to put the question in the form that Hauerwas prefers: How can the church be a truthful community, in which the story of Jesus can be remembered, recounted, and put into action? This question raises another, which is of central importance to his work: What sorts of persons must we be, what virtues must we have, in order to participate in and sustain the life of the church as a truthful community?

The notions of narrative, community, and virtue are thus central to Hauerwas' thought, and in order to understand his account of Christian ethics, it will be necessary to see how they fit together. Throughout his works, Hauerwas argues for the primacy and the interrelatedness of narrative and community, not only in the Christian tradition but for any moral tradition. Following MacIntyre, he argues that all moral traditions are context-bound, in the sense that they are intelligible only within the context of a particular community that has been shaped by foundational narratives and continues to display them.[53] For this reason, Hauerwas adds, the Enlightenment's project of justifying a morality for all times and places, based on the exigencies of universal reason, was doomed to fail. *All* moralities are necessarily relative to a particular community and its traditions. Hence, we should not let the Enlightenment's false ideal of morality distract us from pursuing the true task of Christian ethics, which is to reflect ever more deeply on what is distinctive to the formative narratives of the church: "Under the spell of Kantian accounts of rationality, there lingers the fear that if we recognize the historic nature of our moral convictions we will have to acknowledge them as arbitrary and possibly even false. But such fear is ill-founded, as there is no other basis of moral convictions than the historic and narrative-related experience of a community."[54]

What, then, are the distinctive features of the church as a moral community? First of all, the church is the community that is grounded in the stories of the life, death, and resurrection of Jesus of Nazareth, which it testifies to be truthful accounts of the way in which God has chosen to relate to the world. The first moral task of the church is to strive to be faithful to these stories in its common life, and to form individuals who have the skills necessary to be faithful to those stories, even in the midst of the sometimes conflicting demands of everyday life. Hence, it is incumbent upon the church to be a community of virtue, since the virtues are "specific skills required to live faithful to a tradition's understanding of the moral project in which its adherents participate."[55] These virtues can be acquired only through participation in "the embodiment of the story in the communities in which we are born,"[56] and so the individual can form a true Christian character only by participation in the life of the church.

At the same time, by participating in that common life and passing it on to strangers and especially to their children, Christians sustain the life of the church and perpetuate the tradition of witnessing to the formative stories of Jesus. It would be inaccurate to say that the church has nothing whatever to do with the world outside the church. But its primary responsibility to that world is to witness to its own foundational story and to invite others to respond to that story. The church should not expect to convert the world as a whole to a universally persuasive Christian way of life.

And what, concretely, does the way of life that is proper to the church look like? No one can accuse Hauerwas of avoiding that question. The Christian community is shaped by its awareness that its life is both a gift from God and a trust to be handed on to others—to inquirers, to the stranger in its midst, above all to those most mysterious of strangers, the children born into it. Hence, the Christian community should foster and sustain marriage and the bearing and raising of children, for these are activities of the greatest public significance for sustaining the life of the church itself. Hauerwas insists that sexual ethics and the question of abortion must be seen, from within a Christian perspective, in the context of this

public dimension of marriage and sexuality. Viewed from this perspective, he adds, the liberal and romantic visions of sexuality as a
source of private pleasure are unrealistic and inadequate, and abortion appears as a tragic choice which should be justified for only the
gravest of reasons.[57] He also argues that the church has a special
responsibility to reach out to, and provide care for, those who are cut
off from the mainstream of society because of their illnesses or
disabilities.[58]

Finally, he argues that the church should be, in the words of one
of his books, "the peaceable kingdom," committed to nonviolence in
all the relationships of life, public as well as private.[59] Because the
church knows itself to be a community under God's care, he argues,
it is altogether inappropriate for it to practice or advocate the defense
of oneself, others, or even one's ideals by violent means. Hence, the
church itself must practice strict nonviolence and provide a witness
for pacifism to the wider society.

Criticisms of Hauerwas' work have tended to focus on his contention that Christian ethics must always proceed within the particular frame of reference set by the Christian story. Thus it has been said
that this way of proceeding is antirational or sectarian. As Gustafson
says, Hauerwas' God is "the tribal God of a minority of the earth's
population" and his ethics therefore forfeits any relevance to a wider
society.[60] Of course, Hauerwas can simply respond that such criticisms reflect a wrongheaded attachment to the Enlightenment's ideal
of a universal morality. But more telling criticisms, even by Hauerwas' own criteria, have also been offered.

The first of these criticisms points to ambiguities and tensions
in Hauerwas' own account of Christian ethics which call certain
features of that account into question, and yet which appear to be
incapable of resolution on Hauerwas' own terms. For example, Outka
has pointed out that a tension between commitments to the community and to the individual runs throughout Hauerwas' work. Hauerwas argues that the formative narratives of a community are
foundational for the identity of individuals, and yet he also insists
elsewhere that each individual must become a self-determining person of character.[61] Hauerwas accepts this criticism and admits that he
does not know how to resolve it, although he does hold out the hope
that the tension to which Outka points would be resolved in practice
as one attempts to live out a narrative with fidelity.[62]

There is a still more serious ambiguity in Hauerwas' writings
that he does not address. It is never clear exactly what he means by
expressions such as "a truthful narrative." At some points, Hauerwas
seems to imply that the truthfulness of a narrative can be evaluated

only in terms internal to the way of life that it fosters.[63] If this is his meaning, then we have no reason at all to prefer the Christian narrative, except that it is ours. The narratives underlying the individualistic, libertine, bloodthirsty mainstream American way of life to which Hauerwas objects so strenuously are just as truthful, for those formed in those narratives, as the narratives of Jesus are for the church.[64] On the other hand, Hauerwas does sometimes seem to imply, and more so in his more recent writings, that the central narratives of the church are true in the sense of somehow conveying the actual character of reality.[65] But if that is what he means, then it would seem to follow that, potentially at least, there are standards for evaluating Christian ethics that are not purely internal to the Christian tradition.

It has also been argued that Hauerwas' depiction of the church, and the way of life appropriate to that church, is highly selective.[66] Most notably, not every Christian community is pacifist. Does it follow, then, that those Christian communities that are not pacifist are not truly part of the church? Of course, Hauerwas could reply that they are not, and so much the worse for them. But this response would not address an underlying question: By what criteria does Hauerwas adjudicate among conflicting interpretations of the central Christian story within the Christian community? If there are *no* criteria of adequacy by which a narrative-informed way of life can be evaluated except those that are internal to that way of life, then how can we make comparative evaluations of the different ways of living out the Christian story? Taken to its extremes, Hauerwas' position would seem to leave no room at all for constructive Christian moral reflection. The only moral task, for any of us, would seem to consist in living out the particular form of Christianity that we happen to inhabit, with no hope of real conversation even with other sorts of Christians, much less with the world.

The Scope of This Book

The point of this survey has been to suggest that the work of the leading representatives of contemporary Christian ethics is fragmented and therefore unsatisfactory, even given the premises of the authors themselves. But is there an alternative? What would a moral theory that incorporates the central concepts of contemporary Christian ethics into a unified theory look like?

It is my contention that the *Prima Secundae* and the *Secunda Secundae* of Aquinas' *Summa Theologiae* together offer just such a moral theory. Aquinas' theory of morality is grounded in a theory of the human good that gives content to the fundamental norms of love of neighbor and nonmaleficence and provides criteria by which to evaluate the goodness both of actions and of states of character. The specifics of this theory of the human good lead Aquinas to a particular account of what it is for a community to be a good, that is, a just community in which the equality of all persons in certain fundamental respects is preserved. At the same time, his theory of the human good is itself grounded in a general theory of goodness, which rests upon a particular theory of nature. Hence, the concepts that provide very different and even incompatible starting points for current interpretations of the Christian moral tradition fit together in a mutually illuminating way in Aquinas' moral theory. For that reason, his theory may have something to offer to our own reflections.

At the same time, while I hope that a study of Aquinas will shed light on our current debates, I also hope that current debates will illuminate Aquinas' thought in a new way. Hence, I have freely allowed Aquinas to be challenged by the questions of our contemporaries. Even though it would often be anachronistic to expect him to have anticipated those challenges in our terms, it is possible to reconstruct what his answers to them would have been, and the process of doing so serves to deepen our understanding of his work and its relevance for us.

It should be noted that the scope of this book is very modest. I have not attempted to reconstruct Aquinas' overall theory of morality. The only text that I consider systematically is the *Summa Theologiae*, which I take to contain Aquinas' mature theological synthesis. (In this book all references to Aquinas' works, unless otherwise indicated, are to the *Summa Theologiae*, hereafter referred to as the *ST*.) Nor have I attempted to discuss all of the enormous secondary literature on Aquinas' thought. Because my aim in this study is to understand Aquinas' moral theory in the context of a specific discussion, I have limited myself to addressing the secondary literature that is most relevant to that discussion.

Moreover, I have not attempted a complete account of the moral theory even of the *ST*. Rather, what I offer in this book is a reconstruction of the more strictly philosophical components of that theory, and I have generally bracketed its more properly theological components. My rationale for limiting the scope of this study in this way is contingent on the specific aims of this study. It simply happens that the aspect of Aquinas' moral thought that is most illuminating to contemporary Christian ethics is his conception of the natural end, or good, of the human person, seen in relation to his theory of goodness in general.

In the next chapter, I will examine Aquinas' general theory of goodness. In subsequent chapters, I will reconstruct the account of the natural human good that he derives from that theory, and we will see how he takes this account as the basis for a unified theory of moral virtue and the particular virtues. We will then be in a position to reflect on how Aquinas' theory of morality might contribute to the recovery of an integral account of natural goodness and human virtue.

2

The General Theory of Goodness in the *Summa Theologiae*

"Because, as Damascene says, the human person is said to be made in the image of God, insofar as through 'the image' is signified 'the intellectual, both [as having] freedom of judgment and [as having] the power of self-movement,' consequently, having spoken of the exemplar, that is, God, and of those things which proceed from the divine power in accordance with his will, it remains to consider his image, that is, the human person, insofar as he also is the originating principle of his works, as if he had free judgment and the power to originate his works." In these words, the introduction to the *Prima Secundae* of the *ST,* Aquinas sets out the aim of his theory of morality and places it in the theological and philosophical context of the *Prima Pars.* The point of his theory of morality will be to discuss the human person considered as the active agent of his own actions. But what, exactly, does that mean? As we have already been told, the human person is said to be the origin of his own actions in that he acts on the basis of an intellectual apprehension that the object of his action is in some way good, unlike the animals, who are determined by a natural instinct to act for the particular ends that are suitable to them; that is to say, the human person has free will (I.83.1; cf. I.103.5 *ad* 2, 3). Hence, the proper object of a theory of morality, as Aquinas sees it, is the human person considered as a creature that acts in accordance with an intellectual apprehension of the good. But immediately another question arises: What is meant by acting for the good? The whole of Aquinas' theory of morality may be taken as an extended answer to that question.

In order to answer the question, "What does it mean to act for the good?" Aquinas begins by asking what it means for persons to act for an ultimate end, and then proceeds to ask how we are to determine which, among the many seeming goods that persons pursue, is the true good that can alone satisfy all human desires (I-II.1–3). In doing so, he presupposes the general theory of goodness which was developed in the *Prima Pars*. Admittedly, this is not immediately obvious. It is sometimes assumed that the human person, as a spiritual being, is so radically different from the subrational creation that Aquinas either did not intend his general metaphysical theory to apply to the human person, or should not have done so, if he did. But for better or for worse, Aquinas clearly indicates that the inclination of the human person toward the good (whatever that will turn out to mean) cannot be understood apart from a general theory of goodness. We are told that the inclinations of the rational creature are to be understood in terms of the analogous inclinations to be found in creatures without reason (I.60.5). The most fundamental of these inclinations, in turn, is the inclination of all creatures to seek the good (I.5.4). Furthermore, when we turn to a more detailed examination of Aquinas' account of the natural inclinations of the human person toward her own specific good (that is to say, the good proper to her as a creature of a particular species, or kind of creature), we will find that this account cannot be adequately understood except in terms of Aquinas' general theory of goodness.

Accordingly, in this chapter, I will examine Aquinas' general theory of goodness as he presents it in the *ST*. In the next chapter, we will see how he employs this theory as the basis for his account of the specific good of the human person.

The General Theory of Goodness in the *Summa Theologiae*

"Good," it has been said, is the most general term of commendation.[1] True enough; but what can we say about the reality in virtue of which this commendation is bestowed? Does "good" refer to some one, self-evident desideratum, for example, pleasure, as the utilitarians assert? Or shall we follow G. E. Moore in arguing that "good" names a simple, indefinable property of good things, just as "yellow" names a simple, indefinable property of yellow things? Neither of these answers seems very persuasive, and so it is not surprising that moral philosophers early in the century began to argue that our uses of "good" are not grounded in any reality at all, beyond that of language itself. And so a new question about goodness arose: What is the correct linguistic analysis of our use of "good" and its cognates? But this revised question about goodness proved to be as hard to answer as the old-fashioned version had been.[2]

Perhaps because of these philosophical difficulties, Christian ethicists in this century have generally not appealed to a general theory of goodness as a basis for Christian ethics. Certainly, none of the authors discussed in the last chapter does so. Both Grisez and Finnis, and Hauerwas, for different reasons, deny the possibility of developing a general theory of goodness that could serve as the basis for a theory of morality, and Outka does not raise the question of whether a commitment to Christian love, understood as the foundation of Christian morality, presupposes a general theory of goodness. Only Gustafson seems even to hint that his theory of morality presupposes a general theory of goodness, but in his writings such hints remain only that. He, too, does not develop an explicit theory of goodness.

For Aquinas, on the other hand, there can be no theory of moral goodness without a theory of goodness in general. And as we would expect, his answer to the broad question, "What, or how, do we mean by 'good'?" is importantly different from any of the answers mentioned above. It is easy to minimize this difference by assuming that Aquinas presupposes our sharp dichotomy between ontological and linguistic analyses. This assumption can slip into even the most traditional Thomistic exegesis, through the widespread assertion that Aquinas holds that goodness, like being, unity, and truth, is a transcendental: that is, that it is a concept of a certain sort.[3] This assertion is true enough, so long as we do not take Aquinas to be saying that being, goodness, unity, and truth are mere concepts in some modern sense, that is, broadly speaking, expressions of the way in which we apprehend or order reality. Rather, Aquinas holds that we have concepts of being, goodness, unity, and truth which operate in a certain way, because beings exist in a certain complex way that only these interlocking concepts can capture.[4] That is why, in his discussions of these concepts, he moves back and forth between ontological and analytic considerations in a way that must seem confusing and perhaps confused to us (for example, see I.5; I.11; I.16). But Aquinas is not confused. He is simply presupposing a realism that has become foreign to much of our philosophy. If this is kept in mind, we can usefully employ the doctrine of the transcendentals as a way of getting at Aquinas' understanding of goodness and its relation to the other fundamental aspects of reality.

What does it mean to say that Aquinas considers being, goodness, unity, and truth to be transcendentals? To say that goodness is a transcendental is to say that it is a concept of such ubiquity and generality that it can be applied to anything whatever, in any category of real existence (I.5.1-3; however, logical entities, for example, those employed in mathematics, are neither good nor bad [I.5.3 *ad* 4; I.16.4]). The relevant contrast is with concepts that can be applied only within particular categories of supposits, as for example notions of colors can be applied only to visible objects. Unlike concepts of this sort, the concept of goodness can be applied to anything whatever, insofar as it exists in some way. Hence, my pen, my desk, and I myself can all be described as good insofar as we are actually existing beings. That is, *goodness* is convertible with *being*; it can be asserted whenever, in whatever way, and to whatever degree existence can be asserted of something (I.5.3).

Or can it? Suppose that my pen refuses to write, my desk is rickety, and I am a sick and ignorant embezzler. Can these things then be called *good* in any meaningful sense? Aquinas is of course aware of this objection, and his answer is instructive because it indicates the way in which goodness is notionally, if not really, different from being. He argues in this way (I.5.3): In its most proper sense, "goodness" applies to *perfected* being, to whatever is, insofar as it is what it ought to be. A good pen is a pen that writes well, a good desk is sturdy and even, and a good woman is healthy, wise, and virtuous.[5] Hence, to be good without qualification is to be perfect, that is, to exist in the fullest degree of actuality possible to a creature of this given kind (I.5.1, 5). But in a secondary, but nonetheless valid sense, goodness can be applied to anything whatever, insofar as it exists, since to exist at all is to be in act and therefore to possess some degree of perfection (I.5.1 *ad* 1). Correlatively, evil always has the character of a deficiency, since something is said to be evil because it lacks some perfection that a creature of its kind ought to have (I.48.1). Moreover, because evil is parasitical upon good in this way, nothing that exists can be wholly evil (I.48.3, 4). I may be the most wretched woman alive, but if I did not actually possess some of the qualities of a human being, I would not *be* a woman at all. Correlatively, the very fact that you can identify me as a very poor excuse for a woman presupposes that there is something recognizably human in me.

If goodness and being are convertible in this way, are we to conclude that these concepts are more or less interchangeable? Aquinas responds that they are not, because the concept of goodness introduces a note of desirability that does not properly belong to the concept of being: "The notion of the good consists in this, that it is in some way desirable. Hence the Philosopher says (*Ethic.* i): *The good is what all things desire*" (I.5.1).

At this point, a difficulty arises. The thesis that all things *seek* the good is distinct from the thesis that all things *are* (in some degree) good.[6] It is not immediately obvious how we are to reconcile these two claims. For taken together, these two theses would seem to suggest that all creatures are desirable, and that is hardly obvious: By whom, or for what, are all creatures desirable?

The answer to this question becomes apparent once we realize that Aquinas takes the two claims, that all things *are* good and all things *desire* the good, as two mutually interpreting ways of understanding the goodness that is proper to every creature in and for itself.[7] His understanding of the way in which these two claims fit together is most clearly evident in his discussion of the character of evil. We read: "We have said above that the good is everything which is desirable [I.5.1]. And so, since every nature desires its being and its own perfection, it is necessary to say that the being and perfection of any nature has the character of goodness [I.48.1]." In other words, the tendency of every creature to maintain itself in existence indicates that for every creature, its existence is a good (cf. II-II.64.5). And, since no creature exists at all except insofar as it instantiates some determinate kind of nature, however imperfectly (I.50.2 *ad* 1), it follows that perfection in accordance with its own nature is the primary good that all creatures necessarily desire and seek.[8] Aquinas frequently asserts that all creatures seek their own perfection (I.5.1; I.6.1; I.22.3 *obj.* 2, not denied; I.60.3, 4; I.62.1). Moreover, since by "perfection" he means full actuality of existence, in accordance with one's potential as a member of a given species, we are not surprised to read that the being of a thing is its own good (I.6.3 *obj.* 2, not denied; I-II.18.1); that everything naturally desires to preserve its own nature (I.63.3); and that the most fundamental good to which every creature is ordered is the perfection of its own proper act of existence (I.65.2). At the same time, this orientation of each creature to its own perfection does not exclude further orientations to wider goods, a point to which we shall return (again, see I.65.2).

Now that we have the main lines of Aquinas' general theory of goodness before us, we must ask how that theory fits into his wider theory of being. Otherwise, it would be too easy to dismiss his theory of goodness as a simple projection of notions such as purpose and desire onto inanimate creatures, or onto the universe as a whole. But in fact, Aquinas' general theory of goodness is an integral part of his wider account of what it is for a creature to exist and to exercise causal force. As such, the credibility and force of Aquinas' theory of goodness depend on the cogency of his overall account of what it is for a creature to exist.

As Étienne Gilson has argued, Aquinas holds that those things which are most fully real, which hold ontological priority in his universe, so to speak, are actually existing individuals (as opposed to the intelligible forms or ideas of the universal kinds of things).[9] That is, Aquinas holds, in the familiar phrase, that existence is prior to essence (I.3.4). But at the same time, he also holds that in order for any creature to exist at all, it must exist as something of this or that specific kind (I.5.5; I.50.2 *ad* 1). This is a necessity in the order of existence, but at the same time it is manifested by a parallel necessity in the order of knowledge: Unless we can identify at least in a general way what kind of a thing something is, we would not be able to recognize it as an individual existing creature at all. In other words, the species to which a thing belongs provides the criteria for its individuation, both in reality and in our knowledge of it. This point calls for further expansion, because it will provide the key to understanding how Aquinas' theory of goodness fits into his wider theory of being.

What is involved in recognizing that we have before us an individual, *one* individual and not many individuals or none at all? It is apparent that the judgment that this is an individual is first of all a judgment of unity. Here is *one* thing, maintaining an independent existence. In turn, a judgment of that sort presupposes that we have some idea, if only a very general one, of what kind of independent existence this thing is maintaining. Otherwise, we would have no criteria by which to pick out this one thing from its surrounding environment, or else to recognize it as one thing which has a number of constituent parts. In other words, a judgment that something is indeed one thing presupposes that we know, at least in a general way, what sort of thing it is. Any judgment to the effect that here is an individual something will always take the form, "Here we seem to have a so-and-so." If one should come across a hard little lump of something in the road, recognizing it as a something will necessarily be inseparable from recognizing it as a hard little lump.

This claim may seem implausible at first. Surely we can recognize that this lump of something *is* a something, without knowing *what* kind of something it is? We can indeed, but only within very narrow limits. That is, we can perceive that something exists without knowing *exactly* what it is, or what it *truly* is (I.85.3). Even so, unless we have at least a plausible general idea of what it is that we are perceiving, we cannot perceive that there is something there at all. An existence that is finite and yet not qualified in any way is inconceivable and *therefore* not perceivable. And so, we must have some idea that what is before us is, let us say, a solid object, somewhat resembling a stone, in order to recognize that here is something, we don't know what, that we might examine further. We examine; we reflect, evaluate, compare, and judge; and if our mental processes are working correctly, we form a more or less accurate idea of the essential form of the thing, as it is revealed in the causal dynamisms of its ongoing existence.[10] If it cuts glass, that lump may be an uncut diamond, but if it dissolves in water, it probably is not.

Hence, a judgment of existence always necessarily involves an evaluation of what sort of thing a creature is. Moreover, this evaluation will necessarily involve a normative component. In other words, if we are to learn *that* something exists, we must know, at least in very general terms, *what* it is, and as this knowledge is perfected, we will also necessarily come to know what it would be for this creature to be good, in accordance with the ideal proper to its species. And that is why, for Aquinas, goodness is convertible with truth, or intelligibility, as well as with being, for all save purely logical entities (I.16.4).[11]

This normative component will be most obvious in the case of living creatures, since the concept of a living creature of a certain kind, if it is complete, will necessarily include a notion of what counts as growth and health for that sort of creature.[12] But a normative component will likewise be present in judgments concerning inanimate creatures. In order to know what sort of thing a particular creature is, it is necessary to be able to do more than just identify it at a given moment. It is also necessary to be able to recognize that one and the same creature is persisting over time, through the vicissitudes to which everything material is subject.[13] And this sort of judgment presupposes that we know what counts as a normal development or neutral alteration for a creature of that sort, and what counts as its corruption or destruction. In order to identify a homely rock for what it is, we need to know, among other things, that a change in color is neutral to the existence of rocks (in themselves), whereas crazing and chipping corrupt the existence of rocks, and pulverizing into sand destroys them. The sorts of judgments that we are required to make are no different in principle, and no less normative, than our judgments as to what counts as health, sickness, or death for a plant or an animal. But because living creatures enjoy more complex and sharply delineated existences, the normative character of our judgments is clearer in the case of living creatures.

Note that our knowledge of what kind of creature an individual instantiates is dependent in part on our observations of the ways in which it interacts with its environment. This suggests that Aquinas' theory of goodness, considered as a part of his overall theory of being, cannot be completely understood without some examination of his account of causality. We now turn to that account.

According to Aquinas, causality is grounded in—is of a piece with—the ordered act by which creatures exist as individuals of this or that kind (I.5.4; cf. I.115.1, 2). According to him, whenever any-thing exercises efficient causality, it communicates something of its intelligible being by introducing a new quality, or a new ordering, into the configuration of events surrounding it. Hence, efficient cau-sality can be spoken of as purposive, since any act of efficient causal-ity is also necessarily an act of formal and final causality: Through its exercise of efficient causality, an agent introduces a (relatively) new form into the world around it, and in turn, this form can be said to be the aim (that is, *finis*) to which this act of causation is directed.

Aquinas is fond of citing the effects of fire as an instance of efficient causality: Fire, or something that is heated by fire, is capable of communicating the form of heat, that is, of heating something else (for example, see I.115.1). Note that this is a very simple form of causality. The fire in my fireplace will heat, and in most cases, even-tually burn, whatever comes in contact with it, but it cannot be said to take any sort of active role in its own propagation. It will not seek out combustible material, or move away if I pour water on it. It can be said to strive to maintain itself in being, but only in the limited sense that by its own natural dynamisms, it maintains its form and communicates it to whatever comes near it. This very simple mode of causal activity is characteristic of inanimate creatures. But note that even at this level, the processes of efficient causality may be seen to have an intrinsically normative dimension. Fire acts in such a way as to communicate what is distinctive to its own existence, namely, heat, which is to say that it acts by communicating its own form. And because we can characterize the proper mode of the action of fire by pointing to what it achieves, we may say that the aim, or *finis*, of the action of the fire is its self-perpetuation by communicating heat to its surroundings.

Living creatures engage their environment in still more active and complex ways (I.18.1, 2), which reveal the normative component of causality still more clearly. Living creatures are distinguished from nonliving creatures in that the former are capable of moving them-selves in some way. That is, living creatures actively engage their environment in the course of their efforts to maintain themselves in existence, to mature, and to reproduce themselves. Plants take in elements from the soil and air, and with the energy that they absorb from sunlight, they transform these elements into their own sub-stance. In other words, they act on elements of inanimate nature by incorporating them, thereby informing them with a new identity: wood-of-oak, crisp-tasty-flesh-of-fungus, or whatever. In the pro-cess, they grow, mature, turn their leaves to the sun (in the case of the higher plants), and reproduce themselves. In short, they move in pursuit of whatever will promote their continued existence. Animals are still more aggressive in their relations to the external world. Guided by some sort of apprehension of their environment, they actively take in whatever it is that they need in order to survive and grow, transforming it by natural processes into their own substance. In addition, many kinds of animals involve themselves actively in the processes of generation and the rearing of their young. In all these ways, the activities of living creatures are directed toward a twofold aim: to thrive as individuals, in accordance with the ideal of their species; and to communicate that specific ideal to new creatures by reproducing themselves.

Hence, as we move through the gradations of creatures, from stones to the highest forms of animal life, we see an increase in the scope and power of causality. In other words, we observe that there is a natural hierarchy of being, ordered in accordance with the degree of causal efficacy to be found at each level (I.47.2).[14] At the bottom of this hierarchy are beings that are so fragmentary that it is hard to say whether they are distinct individual existences at all. (What *one* creature is this runny lump of mud?) It moves up through the grades of coherence and active engagement in one's own continued existence, through us, the highest of the corporeal creatures, and past us to creatures that are not subject to corruption, and therefore have no need to strive to maintain their existence. (These are the angels; for Aquinas, God, as Creator, is wholly outside this hierarchy.) Hence, the hierarchy of being is also a hierarchy of goodness and intelligibility in that higher creatures are more distinctly individuated and more fully intelligible than lower creatures. It should be noted, by the way, that this is the only sort of hierarchy of being that Aquinas recognizes. He does not assert a hierarchy of being *within* the human species (or any other species), in virtue of which some have authority to dominate others (I.109.2 *ad* 3).

This line of analysis has an often-overlooked corollary that will prove to be of the first importance for understanding Aquinas' moral theory. If the actions of living creatures, and specifically rational creatures, offer the highest instances of natural processes, it is no less true that these processes must be understood as analogously the same processes. To take Aquinas' own example, all creatures may be said to love something, but each does so in accordance with its proper mode of being. Rational creatures do so through the will, sentient creatures do so through the sensitive appetite, and nonsentient creatures do so through their natural dynamisms toward the perfect attainment of the way of existing proper to their own specific kind.

(Again, see I.60.1; note that Aquinas explicitly applies this line of analysis to pure spirits, as well as to the different grades of corporeal creatures.) And since it is easier to understand the simpler processes of inanimate creatures and the lower living creatures, we would expect to find that a study of their processes would illuminate our own more complex analogues of the same processes. That is in fact what Aquinas does say: "The natural inclination in those things devoid of reason makes manifest the natural inclination belonging to the will of an intellectual nature" (I.60.5). There could hardly be a stronger assertion of the fundamental continuity between human beings and the varied world of creatures within which we move.

The main lines of Aquinas' general theory of goodness and its place in his wider metaphysics, as these are developed in the *ST,* are now before us. It will be obvious that this theory raises numerous philosophical and theological questions. While it would be impossible to address all of the criticisms that might be directed against Aquinas' theory of goodness from any point of view whatever, it is possible to identify those questions which arise with special urgency from within the perspective of contemporary Christian ethics, and to begin, at least, to address them. In the remainder of this chapter, we will examine some of these questions, both in order to see how Aquinas' theory of goodness might be relevant to some of our contemporary concerns, and also to draw out the implications of that theory more fully.

The Dreadful Chasm: Deriving "Ought" from "Is"

If we accept the main lines of Aquinas' theory of goodness as they have been sketched so far, then it follows that there is nothing mysterious or even distinctive about our knowledge of good and evil. Indeed, our knowledge of what is good for a thing is of a piece with our knowledge of what that thing is. To the extent that we know what something is, we can judge how nearly it approaches to the ideal of its kind of creature, and in which ways it falls short of that ideal. If we know enough about the creature and its usual mode of existence, we can even offer suggestions about what would promote its nearer approach to the ideal state of existence proper to its specific kind, and conversely, what would be harmful to it. If we know what an oak tree is, then we can recognize both defective and flourishing specimens of oaks, and we can even offer some advice to the grower on what will be good for his oak and what will harm it. Surely there is nothing in this to excite our philosophical suspicions.

But let us be clear on what our advice to the oak grower implies:

So far from there being a gap between fact and value, there can be no real understanding of the facts that is not also simultaneously a knowledge of values. For this reason, there is in Aquinas' theory of goodness no gap to be bridged between "is" and "ought."[15] If we know what something *is,* we know what it *ought* to be. Indeed, knowing what something ought to be, in accordance with the ideal of its species, is the only way of knowing what it is.

Moreover, this observation is as true of us as it is of any other sort of creature. Our knowledge of what we ought to be, which includes moral knowledge, is a necessary component of our knowledge of what we are. Hence, according to Aquinas' theory of morality, the moral "ought" cannot be separated from the anthropological "is."

This reading of Aquinas contradicts the interpretation developed by Grisez in his 1965 article, "The First Principle of Practical Reason," and subsequently adopted by Finnis in his *Natural Law and Natural Rights.*[16] According to this interpretation, Aquinas holds that both the first principles of practical reason, and the knowledge of the basic goods that give substantive content to those principles, are self-evident and therefore underived (although not innate, in the sense of being known prior to all experience). Hence, according to Grisez and Finnis, Aquinas holds that moral knowledge does not presuppose factual knowledge or metaphysical theories of any sort whatever, but can be derived entirely from self-evident principles and our knowledge of the basic goods, which is also self-evident to us. Although Grisez and Finnis do not claim to be following Aquinas in their later works, they do continue to hold that on this fundamental point, at least, he is correct and deserves to be followed.

Obviously, the Grisez/Finnis interpretation raises important exegetical and philosophical questions that must be addressed if the account of Aquinas' general theory of goodness developed in this chapter is to be defended. Since that interpretation is grounded exegetically in an interpretation of I-II.94.2, I will postpone a discussion of the exegetical issues at stake until the next chapter, when I will have occasion to discuss I-II.94.2 in some detail. In this section, I will attempt to address what I see as the major philosophical question raised by the Grisez/Finnis reading of Aquinas: Is it legitimate to move from claims about the way things are (broadly construed) to claims about the way that things ought to be (broadly construed)? Grisez and Finnis insist that such a move is not legitimate, whereas Aquinas holds that adequate knowledge of what a thing is necessarily includes some knowledge of what it ought to be.[17]

Why do Grisez and Finnis insist so strongly that there is no way to derive a moral "ought" from a theoretical/factual "is"? Grisez in particular seems to insist on this claim in part to correct earlier readings of Aquinas which represent him as holding that moral norms are derived by means of deduction from statements about human nature or God's will.[18] And so far, Grisez is correct.[19] However, this reading reflects more than a recognition that Aquinas does not hold that the primary form of moral reasoning is deductive. It is founded in a conviction that *any* sort of move from "is" to a moral "ought" is illegitimate. What is the basis of that conviction? Grisez and Finnis both treat it as an undeniable tenet of pure logic, which stands in need of no defense. Since Grisez refers to David Hume as one of the first to articulate this principle,[20] we may allow Hume to state the claim more fully:

> In every system of morality, which I have hitherto met with, I have always remark'd, that the author proceeds for some time in the ordinary way of reasoning, and establishes the being of a God, or makes observations concerning human affairs; when of a sudden I am surpriz'd to find, that instead of the usual copulations of propositions, *is,* and *is not,* I meet with no proposition that is not connected with an *ought,* or an *ought not.* This change is imperceptible; but is, however, of the last consequence. For as this *ought,* or *ought not,* expresses some new relation or affirmation, 'tis necessary that it shou'd be observ'd and explain'd; and at the same time that a reason should be given, for what seems altogether inconceivable, how this new relation can be a deduction from others, *which are entirely different from it* [the last instance of emphasis is mine].[21]

Hume is not merely objecting that moralists have failed to make explicit the premises by which they draw moral conclusions from factual premises. That would be easy enough to do: If "I am a daughter" and "I ought to take care of my mother in her old age" will not do as a complete argument, then it will be easy enough to make explicit what is clearly presupposed as the major premise—"All daughters should care for their elderly mothers." Hume's real objection is contained in the phrase underscored above: Because claims about what ought to be are wholly disparate in character from claims about what is, our observations on the latter point can never provide us with any information, directly or indirectly, on the former point. The logical argument that nothing can be introduced into the conclusion of an argument that was not first in the premises is dependent for its force in this context on this claim about the meaning of factual statements.

This claim has been repeated so many times that it has taken on the status of a truism. Nonetheless, our analysis of Aquinas should serve to indicate that the complete disparity between "is" statements and "ought" statements cannot be taken for granted. Aquinas' analysis of the general notion of goodness presents us with an alternative account. By his analysis, things exist in accordance with rational principles that are intrinsically normative, and therefore, our knowledge of what things are carries with it an intrinsically normative dimension as well. How might Hume respond to this analysis?

It is often assumed that Hume argues that factual and normative statements are disparate in character, in that the former are objective, whereas the latter are dependent on sentiment and are therefore subjective. But as MacIntyre points out, Hume could not have drawn the line between factual and normative statements in that way, because for him, factual statements no less than moral statements are dependent on sentiment and feeling:

> When for example in the *Enquiry Concerning Human Understanding* he wishes to distinguish between factual belief and the mere entertainment in imagination of some fiction, he writes that "It follows, therefore, that the difference between *fiction* and *belief* lies in some sentiment or feeling, which is annexed to the latter, not to the former, and which depends not on the will, nor can be commanded at pleasure." Again a little later Hume writes that "it is evident that belief consists not in the peculiar nature or order of ideas, but in the *manner* of their conception, and in their *feeling* to the mind."[22]

Why, then, does Hume place a dreadful chasm between "is" and "ought"? To quote MacIntyre again:

> Moral judgments cannot be factual, so Hume argues, on quite other grounds. They are not factual, because factual judgments cannot move us to action. Factual judgments are not practical, whereas this is the central function of moral judgments. Reason is concerned either with relations of ideas (as in mathematics) or with matters of fact. Neither of these impels us to action. . . . When Hume says that not reason but the passions move us to act, he may be read as asserting that from any number of premises of the form "Such-and-such is the case," where some relation of ideas or matter of fact is asserted, no conclusion of the form "So I ought to do so-and-so" or even of the form "So I will do so-and-so" follows. For such a conclusion to follow from such premises we need an additional premise of quite another

kind, namely one presenting us with a prospect of pleasure or pain, one appealing to the passions.[23]

In other words, Hume holds that factual and moral statements are disparate in character because of their disparate relations to action. Only the latter can move us to act.

It would not be quite accurate to say that Aquinas addresses this line of argument, even implicitly, because again, a modern dichotomy, in this case between factual and motivational considerations, simply does not arise within the framework of his metaphysical system. For Aquinas, every creature necessarily seeks its own good, in the sense explained above. The human quest for happiness, which is nothing other than the enjoyment of a mode of being in accordance with the ideal of specific perfection proper to humanity, is only one instance of a universal and necessary dynamism of all creatures (I-II.1.7, 8). But unlike subrational creatures, we can only attain happiness in and through actions that follow from a reasoned grasp of that in which happiness consists (I-II.1.2). It follows that there is a motivational link between at least one sort of factual or theoretical knowledge and action: If anyone perceives that a particular course of action is necessary to her attainment of happiness, she is rationally committed to following that course of action, and correlatively, to the degree that her actions are fully rational, they will admit of explanation in terms of her beliefs about happiness (I-II.1.6, 7; I-II.5.8; I-II.10.1).

Even so, it might be argued that, at most, on Aquinas' premises there is no gap to be bridged between factual statements and what might be called the imperatives of self-interest, that is, statements of the form that one ought to do so-and-so in order to attain one's own good. But how can we justify the further claim that there is no gap to be bridged between factual statements and moral imperatives? It would seem that this claim can be justified on Aquinas' terms only if he also holds that moral behavior is always ultimately in one's own self-interest.

As I read him, that is indeed Aquinas' view. For him, there is no final distinction between what an agent ought (morally) to do and what is in that agent's true self-interest. Hence, he says that no one commits serious sin, except through ignorance, error, or lack of consideration concerning the proper way in which to seek what is good (I.63.1 *ad* 4; I-II.78.1. Note, however, that since everyone is capable of knowing the fundamental principles of morality, ignorance or error concerning them does not excuse from sin [I-II.6.8; I-II.76.2]). This equivalence may seem strange to us, accustomed as we are to drawing a sharp dichotomy between morality and self-interest, but it follows naturally from Aquinas' general theory of goodness. For if all creatures, ourselves included, necessarily seek their own good, then at the very least it follows that no creature acting out of its own proper dynamisms of action can act toward something harmful to itself as such (I.49.1).[24] This general principle implies that no sentient creature, ourselves included, knowingly chooses what is harmful to itself, considered simply as harmful, although of course we can and do choose what is incidentally harmful in some way, if the harm to be endured is the necessary concomitant to enjoying some good (I.5.2 ad 2). Hence, on Aquinas' terms, the norms of morality would not be rational if they prescribed what was contrary to the well-being of the individual, and, of course, it would be absurd to deny the rationality of the norms of morality. That is why, for Aquinas, moral claims have motivational force even though they are grounded in truths about human nature. Anyone who understands that his own true good lies in acting in accordance with these claims will necessarily be motivated to act upon them. Of course, someone who does not understand that will not be so motivated, but most moral theories recognize that moral imperatives do not have motivational force for those who do not accept them.

It may seem at this point that we have addressed one philosophical difficulty only to raise another one. Certainly, the claim that it is always in one's ultimate self-interest to act morally cannot be passed off as obvious. Nonetheless, as I read Aquinas, this claim plays a central role in his moral theory. We turn to a fuller examination of it now.

Self-love and the Moral Order

"The human person is said to love himself in that he loves himself in accordance with his spiritual nature . . . and accordingly, the human person ought to love himself more than anyone else after God" (II-II.26.4). This claim is likely to seem scandalous to many. As Outka notes, "A fairly prevalent impression exists that theologians have only dour and condemnatory things to say about self-love. While . . . this is untrue *simpliciter,* the impression obviously has some basis."[25]

It is already clear that Aquinas would not agree that self-love has no place in moral considerations, much less that it is necessarily morally evil. In addition to the statement just cited, we will see that he holds that two of the cardinal moral virtues, temperance and fortitude, are primarily concerned with the well-being of the agent herself (I-II.60.2; II-II.58.10). And yet, in these same questions he also says that there is another moral virtue, namely justice, that is intrinsically other-regarding. Furthermore, he asserts that each individual naturally loves the common good more than her own individual good, even with reference to the love of self proper to charity (II-II.26.4 *ad* 3). Is it possible to reconcile these claims with the reading of Aquinas, suggested above, that on his view, moral action is always ultimately aimed at one's own good? In my view, such a reconciliation is possible, but it presupposes that we understand the sense that Aquinas gives to the notions of love, beneficence, and harm.

On the one hand, if Aquinas were committed to the view that seeking one's own good is a wholly disparate activity from seeking the good of another, there would be no way to reconcile the reading of Aquinas proposed above with his understanding of justice as being necessarily an other-directed virtue, or his strong statements that the common good is always more lovable to the individual than his own particular good. On the other hand, Aquinas might simply intend to equate the good of the individual with the good of others or (more plausibly) the common good. Such a move would permit us to say that moral behavior is always ultimately in the agent's own self-interest, but only at the cost of emptying either the notion of one's own good or the notion of the common good of any distinctive content. But in fact, the relation between individual good and the good of others as Aquinas understands it is more complex than either alternative would suggest. In order to understand this relation, it will be necessary to turn once again to his general account of goodness.

In our previous examination of Aquinas' notion of goodness, we noted that when Aquinas says that every creature seeks the good, his primary meaning is that every creature is oriented toward its own goodness, that is, its fullness of being in accordance with the ideal of its species. However, this analysis of goodness does not rule out the possibility that in a secondary sense, creatures may be said to be directed toward a wider good. As we have already noted, Aquinas does in fact hold that beyond its orientation toward its own specific perfection, each creature is oriented toward wider goods in two senses: Lower kinds of creatures exist for the sake of higher kinds of creatures (although it does not seem that we exist for the sake of the angels), and all creatures are oriented toward the good of the universe as a whole (I.65.2). At the same time, we are also told that the universe has been arranged in such a way that the good of the creatures of lower kinds is promoted through the activities of creatures of higher kinds (I.64.4). In other words, Aquinas' universe is a web of creatures bound together by relationships of mutual benefit, in which each is oriented to the good of some others, and all together, in their ordered interrelationships, are ordered to the good of the whole.

Like all other creatures, the human being is oriented toward goods beyond that of her own individual existence. Indeed, in addition to the diverse sorts of orientation toward wider goods just noted, she is oriented toward a wider good of a specifically human sort, namely, the common good of her community (I-II.92.1 *ad* 3; II-II.47.10 *ad* 2). And yet, her relation to all these wider goods is necessarily more complex than that of lower sorts of creatures. The human being is "an individual substance of a rational nature"—that is to say, a person—and as such, she enjoys an individual and distinctive existence in the highest way possible to a creature (I.29.1, 3). For this reason, the good of an individual person cannot simply be subordinated to any wider good in the way that the individual goods of lesser creatures can be.[26] As we shall see in chapter 5, Aquinas' theory of justice is spelled out in such a way as to protect the individual from complete subordination to the community.

Hence, Aquinas holds both that the human individual is oriented toward wider goods, and that she is oriented toward her own irreducible good as an individual. The question before us is how Aquinas manages to reconcile these two strands of his thought. A full answer to this question must await our discussion of Aquinas' theory of justice in chapter 5, but it is possible even at this point to trace the outlines of his answer.

We must first note that Aquinas is committed to the view that no human person can deliberately inflict harm per se on himself (I-II.29.4). He is well aware, of course, that persons do harm themselves in various ways, but he argues that whenever a person harms himself, he does so in order to obtain some real or supposed benefit which he believes can be achieved only at the price of incurring some harm (I.5.2 *ad* 3). Even suicides act in order to attain some benefit, for example, release from anxiety or pain, even though in doing so, they foolishly prefer what is objectively a greater evil to an objectively lesser evil (II-I.64.5 *ad* 3). Furthermore, Aquinas insists that each person has a moral obligation not to inflict genuine harm on himself. This is the negative corollary of the positive injunction truly to love oneself, which Aquinas takes to be the most fundamental human obligation after our obligations to God (II-II.26.4; II-II.64.5).

But of course, the normative bite in those injunctions lies in the qualifications implied in Aquinas' theory: *genuine* harm and *true* self-love. What counts as truly loving oneself or genuinely harming oneself? As we saw in our discussion of Outka's analysis of agape, the answers to these questions are not as obvious as they may at first seem to be, because they depend on an account of what is in one's true self-interest, therefore on an account of the true human good. And it is at this point, in his substantive account of the true human good, that Aquinas attempts to reconcile individual and communal good. To anticipate what will be spelled out in more detail in subsequent chapters: Aquinas does indeed finally equate the true good of the individual and the common good in such a way that the highest natural good of the individual consists in participation in a just community. However, this equation cuts both ways, since he understands the good of a community in such a way that a community that violates the well-being of its members in certain fundamental ways thereby destroys its own common good. In other words, the natural orientation of the human person toward the common good is not antithetical to the orientation of the individual to her own private good, because the common good to which she is oriented has as part of its own intrinsic nature the promotion of the well-being of the individual members of the community.

It will be clear by now that Aquinas' equation of morality and self-interest depends on his persuasive definitions of well-being and harm, and stands or falls on whether those definitions actually persuade. It may seem that this is a tendentious procedure, but our discussion of Outka's work would suggest that it is a procedure that no moral theorist can avoid. What counts as harming a human being depends ultimately on what counts as human well-being, and that is by no means self-evident; it calls for a theory. The details of the theory that Aquinas offers will be presented in the following chapters. At this point, we must continue with our examination of possible objections to Aquinas' general theory of goodness.

Can the Notion of an Intelligible Universe Be Defended Today?

A number of objections might be raised against Aquinas' claim that there is an intrinsic intelligibility in things themselves, distinct from and prior to any ordering scheme that we may impose on them. In order fully to defend Aquinas' theory of goodness against all the objections of this sort that could be raised, it would be necessary to defend a certain account of nature, science, and ultimately rationality itself over against many contemporary views. While I believe that task could indeed be done, I do not intend to undertake it here. But even though a full defense of Aquinas' theory of goodness against these sorts of objections is not possible here, it is possible to identify and discuss certain of these objections that are especially relevant to the work being done in contemporary Christian ethics, in particular those that are raised by Gustafson and Hauerwas.

Let us take a very straightforward objection first. In the course of a generally sympathetic treatment of Aquinas' moral theory, Gustafson argues that Aquinas' claim that every creature is an intelligible instantiation of a specific kind depends on a particular understanding of creation—that is, presumably, some version of creationism according to which each species of creature was brought about directly by God in its immutable form in the original act of creation. Hence, he suggests that the theory of evolution seriously calls into question the claim that there is a fixed human essence which can serve as the basis for morality.[27] By implication, the general claim that all creatures are intelligible instantiations of some species of creature is likewise undermined by the theory of evolution and our knowledge of the way in which the universe came into being.

But Aquinas is in no way committed philosophically to the view that the specific kinds of creatures that now exist are themselves immutable, nor, more generally, to any particular view as to how existing species of creatures came to be. What he is saying is this: Every creature that now exists, did exist, or will exist belongs to some species, or to put it another way, has the rational character (ratio) of this sort of being and no other (I.86.1, 4). To the extent that we grasp the ratio of something (and we will often, perhaps always, fail to do so perfectly), then we have a concept of what it is to be a creature of that sort, by which we not only know what it is but can also recognize other members of the same species. Now that concept is immutable in the same way that any well-formed concept is. (We are speaking here of an ideal case, in which we actually do have a correct and complete concept of a certain kind of thing. In fact, most of our notions fall short of this ideal, and are therefore subject to development and revision.) That is, we can apply such a concept wherever and whenever the conditions for applying it are adequately fulfilled, and we can also recognize situations in which it does not apply, even though perhaps we expected at first that it would. It does not follow that the class of actually existing creatures that instantiate this concept is itself immutable. There may well have been a time when the concept was not instantiated, and there may come a time when it will no longer be instantiated. That fact, in itself, does not have anything to do with the fact that this creature here and now instantiates a given species, such that any other creature having the same specific characteristics will necessarily instantiate the same species. Nor does Aquinas' concept of a species imply any particular view as to how actually existing kinds of creatures came into existence. It may well be that a given kind of creature emerged by a process of random selection from a different kind of creature. Moreover, the same processes, over time, may well replace this sort of creature with another sort, so that this particular species of creature will no longer exist. In no way does that possibility change the fact that here and now, this particular creature instantiates a particular species.

Similarly, Gustafson argues that Aquinas' claim that all creatures came from God and will return to God can no longer be sustained, given what we know about the probable end of the universe.[28] As I noted briefly in the last chapter, Gustafson is deeply impressed with the conclusions of many modern scientists that the earth, and even the universe as a whole, are fated to come to an end someday. For this reason, he argues, neither the general Christian hope for an eschatological renewal of all things, nor Aquinas' belief that all creatures, including human beings, are oriented toward an ultimate fulfillment, can be sustained.

In order to address this objection, it is necessary to distinguish, as Gustafson does not, between the natural and supernatural senses in which creatures may be said, according to Aquinas, to return to God. Like most other Christian theologians up until modern times, Aquinas did indeed look forward to a supernatural fulfillment of the human person and of all creation at the general resurrection. But neither he nor any other premodern Christian theologian (to my knowledge) anticipated that this fulfillment would come about as the result of natural processes. To the contrary, as the medieval hymn *Dies Irae* puts it, "death and nature will be stupefied" at the renewal of all things. Hence, on the one hand, Gustafson's argument against the Christian hope for an eschatological renewal of all things is not persuasive. On the other hand, applied to Aquinas' argument that all creatures may be said to return to God in a natural sense, Gustafson's objection misses the point. For Aquinas makes it clear that naturally speaking, creatures return to God insofar as they attain perfection in accordance with the ideal of the specific kinds of the creatures that they are. In other words, all creatures may be said to love God, and to attain God, insofar as they strive toward and attain the good proper to them as members of a particular species (I-II.1.8; cf. I-II.109.3). In turn, this interpretation of the dictum that all creatures return to God depends upon a theology of creation according to which all created existences participate in their degree in God's goodness (I.4.3; I.6.4). This interpretation does *not* depend on holding that all creatures will necessarily attain their ultimate good, since the imperfections of creatures contribute to the supreme created good of the universe as a whole (I.47.2; I.49.2). Nor does it depend on the view that the universe as a whole will last forever, since a good that comes to an end is a good nonetheless.

A more fundamental objection to Aquinas' general theory of goodness is suggested by contemporary work in the philosophy of science, rather than by any specific scientific theory. Granted, it may be argued, that Aquinas' concept of a species does not depend on any particular account of how actually existing species came to be; nor is it called into question by any particular account of how they will cease to be in the future. Nonetheless, it does at least presuppose that the world as it presents itself here and now is arranged into recognizable kinds of creatures, prior to any efforts at classification on our part. But that assumption does not stand up to close scrutiny. It is true that the world as we perceive it is an orderly place, which lends itself to classificatory schemes. But contacts with other cultures, and our growing awareness of our own history, have forced us to realize that other times and places divide the world up in accordance with quite different classificatory schemes. Moreover—and this is critically important—there is no way to show that one scheme is simply wrong, without presupposing the foundational beliefs of another scheme. That is, there is no neutral standpoint from which to evaluate different schemes, on the basis of which we could decide which one offers the correct classification of things in the world. In that sense, the rival schemes are incommensurable. Hence, it would appear that the specific kinds that are so important to Aquinas are grounded in the particular conceptual scheme that he brings to things, and not in the nature of things themselves. At the very least, the burden of proof is on Aquinas (or more precisely, his present-day defenders) to prove otherwise.[29]

The thesis that there are genuinely incommensurable conceptual schemes is both complex and controversial. The reader will recognize that Hauerwas sometimes appears to defend one version of this thesis, which we may call the incommensurability thesis, and for that reason alone he would have difficulty in accepting Aquinas' general theory of goodness.[30] In my view, Hauerwas' particular version of this thesis is not persuasive. But it is possible to make a better case for the incommensurability thesis than Hauerwas does, and let me say at once that I do accept a version different from his.[31] Nonetheless, I will argue that this thesis does not undermine Aquinas' argument for the intrinsic intelligibility of things, in accordance with their various ways of instantiating specific kinds. The existence of genuine incommensurability not only does not exclude a generally agreed upon body of knowledge of species of creatures—it presupposes it.

In the last section, we saw that in order to make a judgment that here we have one unified individual (of whatever sort), it is necessary to judge that this individual instantiates a particular kind of creature. Moreover, that judgment will implicitly include the criteria by which to evaluate how good a representative of its kind it is. That is, the most basic sort of judgment to the effect that here is an individual of such and such a kind will necessarily imply the Thomistic transcendental judgments of unity, intelligibility, and goodness. But at this point, the impatient reader may wish to point out that the subject at hand is incommensurability. Even granting that judgments of unity, intelligibility, and goodness interact as Aquinas says they do, it may still be the case that proponents of different conceptual schemes will categorize individuals in different ways, that is, will categorize the world in accordance with different species. Hence, even though we may admit that all judgments concerning the actual existence of an individual imply judgments of unity, intelligibility, and goodness, that would be a formal similarity only. Incommensurability of substantive categorical schemes is quite consistent with this sort of formal similarity of judgments.

It is true that a diversity of categorical schemes is consistent with the presence of formal similarity of judgments of the sort just desribed. My point is rather that if a diversity of substantive judgments were possible at every level of reflection and explanation, there could be no incommensurability at all, because there would be no recognizably identical individuals about which to propose incommensurable theories. In order for two interpretations of a thing to be genuinely incommensurable, they must refer to the same thing, and the proponents of the different views must recognize it to be the same thing. For example, theories about the nature of owls and the nature of my Kaypro computer are not as such incommensurable; they are simply two different explanations of two different kinds of things. And since every judgment to the effect, "Here's a something," must also be a judgment, however general, as to what sort of something this is, then if proponents of rival schemes of thought are to identify the same things, they must share a common classificatory scheme at some level, however basic. Incommensurability still remains, but it enters in at the more advanced level of reflection at which people begin to develop interpretative and explanatory theories about things.

One of the advantages of this argument is that it explains why it is that in spite of the existence of profoundly incommensurable views of the nature of the universe and of the place of the human person within it, there does seem to be universal agreement that things in the world are divided into the broad categories of inanimate objects, plants, and animals, and nearly universal recognition of most of the specific kinds within those categories. For example, there is probably no human culture that does not possess the categories of water, air, fire, flowering plants, trees, dogs, cats. . . . Of course, many, perhaps all, cultures develop diverse interpretations of these categories, in the very process of offering explanatory theories about the things that fall within them. And this process of interpretation may well lead a particular culture to judge that a given category is illusory, or insufficiently descriptive, or too general or too specific. Nonetheless, even these processes of interpretation presuppose that everyone can agree upon the fundamental categories of description, by which to identify what it is that is being interpreted. Those of us who move within the tradition of Western science will all agree that water is not really a simple substance, but a complex of oxygen and hydrogen. But unless we all know water when we see it, *prior to* learning that it is really H_2O, this theory would make no sense.[32]

If this argument is sound, it shows that Aquinas' claim that the creatures of the world are divided into intelligible specific kinds is consistent with the incommensurability thesis. Hence, his general theory of goodness, which depends on this claim, is not invalidated by that thesis. It follows that his theory of morality is not invalidated by the incommensurability thesis, at least insofar as that theory depends on his general theory of goodness.

It is tempting to conclude further that Aquinas' theory of morality escapes the constraints of incommensurability altogether, that is, that it can be shown to be universally valid even to those who do not accept its starting points. Aquinas himself thought that at least the central tenets of morality are knowable to all (I-II.94.4–6). Nonetheless, nothing in the preceding argument serves to establish that Aquinas' theory of morality would be rationally compelling to anyone, operating from within any conceptual scheme whatever. To the contrary, there is good reason to believe that it would not be. Even though Aquinas' theory of morality is directly dependent on his general theory of goodness, it also presupposes the whole structure of his philosophical and theological beliefs in a variety of complex ways. For example, I will argue in chapter 5 that his theory embodies a limited but definite commitment to normative equality. That being the case, it would not be necessarily compelling to someone whose starting points implied the denial of normative equality, for example, a classically oriented Hindu.

On the other hand, neither does it follow that Aquinas' moral theory is "only true for us," or more generally, that it is necessarily irrelevant or unconvincing to those who do not share his starting points. As MacIntyre has shown, the general assumption that the incommensurability thesis necessarily implies either relativism or perspectivism reflects an untenable view of rational discourse as necessarily perspective-free.[33] He argues to the contrary that both rationality and truth are embedded in tradition-constituted inquiry, in such a way that this inquiry is capable of both self-assessment and genuine critique by others. Let me say, briefly, what I believe the implications of his analysis to be for the issue at hand: Any effort to commend Aquinas' particular account of morality to those whose starting points are not his own would have to find some starting point from within those others' own tradition, on the basis of which Aquinas' account of morality could at least be rendered plausible. How do we know that some such starting point would necessarily exist? We cannot be certain that it does, at least not on philosophical grounds. But I believe that both Aquinas' theology and the central tenets of Christianity give us reason to hope that such a starting point could always be found, sooner or later. The dialogue in this century between Christianity and Hinduism, which took its starting point from, among other things, the commitment to nonviolence found in some strands of each tradition, might provide one example of a fruitful conversation between two very differerent intellectual and moral traditions.

Given some version of the incommensurability thesis, it would be natural to assume that any moral theory of the natural law must necessarily flounder, because such a theory would be committed to defending an account of the nature of the human person, held to be universal in scope, from within the standpoint of a particular tradition.[34] However, if the preceding analysis is correct, it follows that such an undertaking, although it may seem paradoxical, is not absurd. Modern scientists, too, offer theories about the world and human persons which are intended to be universal in scope, yet which are developed within the framework of a particular tradition. And if MacIntyre's theory of rationality is correct, they are not self-deluded in proposing their theories as possible candidates for a description of The Way Things Really Are. Admittedly, there is no guarantee that they will be able to prove their theories to all challengers, *even if* they are in fact correct. The same may be said about a Thomist, or any other, theory of the natural law. The fact that it is developed from within a particular historical framework does not necessarily invalidate its claims to truth. Of course, Aquinas himself would not have defended his theory of the natural law in this way, but I believe that it could now be defended in this way.

We have not yet considered one particular aspect of Aquinas' general theory of goodness that is both especially problematic to contemporary thought and especially important to his theory of morality, namely, his defense of the claim that there is a hierarchy of being. We turn to this claim now.

The Hierarchy of Being

As we saw above, Aquinas holds that the hierarchy of being is comprised of the ordered grades of causal efficacy into which creatures naturally fall. Hence, living creatures have a greater causal efficacy—are a higher kind of creature—than inanimate objects, animals are a higher kind of creature than plants, human beings are higher than irrational animals, and angels are higher than human beings. And so far, it would seem that Aquinas is right, waiving the normative implications of the language of higher and lower. Plants do engage the world more actively, and exercise a wider causal force, than do stones, and so on through the list. What has been said here that is not implicit in the fundamental claim that the creatures of the world instantiate the familiar species of creatures?

There is something more, and that something more is contained in the implications of the language of higher and lower, which on Aquinas' view cannot be waived. As I read him, Aquinas interprets the hierarchy of being as an ordering from lower to higher, or lesser to greater, because only in that way can he view the universe itself as an ordered and hence unified whole, which in its own way instantiates one of the notes of goodness, namely, order (I.5.5).[35] (The notions of mode and species as applied to the universe as a whole would be unintelligible.)

But why should the universe as a whole be taken to be an intrinsically unified existence? It seems to me that Aquinas does so because he believes in a creator God, whose most proper work of creation is held, on theological grounds, to be the universe, considered precisely as an ordered and unified whole. It is true that Aquinas believes that he can prove the existence of God from the orderliness of the universe. As I read them, all five of his well-known proofs for the existence of God are variants of a proof from the reality of order in the universe (I.2.3). Without at all claiming to adjudicate among the extensive arguments that have surrounded Aquinas' proofs, I would suggest that it is nearer the mark to say that the existence of a creator God and the claim that the universe is itself a unified whole mutually imply one another in the framework of Aquinas' thought. At the same time, Aquinas' claim that the universe is a unified whole is not merely an imposition of theological doctrine onto the recalcitrant data of experience. The evidences of ordering and gradation among the specific kinds of creatures in the universe may not be sufficient to establish that the universe itself is a unified whole, but they are amenable to such an interpretation. And, although we cannot pursue the point here, it could be argued that this interpretation has proved to be fruitful for further efforts to investigate the nature of our world, since it is one of the presuppositions of modern science.

At this point, we must consider two objections to the notion of a hierarchy of being that are important to contemporary Christian ethics. The first of these holds that this idea is morally problematic, because it gives rise to a mind-set in which the dominion of one class of people by another seems to be justified, even inevitable.[36] This objection must be taken seriously. It is certainly true that concepts and imagery drawn from the claim that there is a hierarchy of being have been used to justify the subordination of certain groups of people, notably women, and it is probably true that the subordination of women and class stratification have existed in all the societies in which a belief in a hierarchy of being is widespread.

Nonetheless, there is no necessary connection between asserting that there is a hierarchy of being and defending social stratification, such that anyone who defends one must defend the other, on pain of incoherence. As was noted above, the hierarchy of being that Aquinas defends is an ordered gradation among different species of creatures. There is no such hierarchical ordering *within* a particular species, and therefore Aquinas denies that there is a natural precedence among human beings of the sort that exists among creatures of different species (I.109.2 *ad* 3; Aquinas is here contrasting our situation with that of the angels, who are hierarchically ordered precisely because each one belongs to a species of one [cf. I.50.4]). It is true that Aquinas defends the subordination of some members of society to others, notably of women to men, but as we will see in chapter 5, his rationale for doing so is not based on his doctrine of the hierarchy of being.

But if there is no necessary link between a belief in a hierarchy of being and a social structure marked by the subordination of some to others, then why do we find these beliefs linked throughout our history? It is important to put this question into context. Nearly every society, ancient and modern, has been characterized by the subordination of some to others on racial, class, and especially gender lines. We would expect to find some rationale for these stratifications in terms of beliefs widespread in the culture in question, whatever it may happen to be, and that is in fact what we do find. In the ancient and modern societies from which we descended, a belief in a hierarchy of being of some sort was widespread, and so naturally social stratification in those societies was often justified by appeals to a hierarchy of being. But in the more recent past, we have also seen social and gender stratification defended on the grounds that it has been scientifically validated, for example by Darwinism taken as a social theory, or by the work of Sigmund Freud. Even the reverence for nature that is often commended by these critics of the notion of a hierarchy of being has been used to justify limiting women to a narrow social role, in order to preserve woman's supposed closeness to nature.[37]

My point in offering these examples is that it would seem that social stratification can be justified in the terms of any worldview whatever, by those who are minded to do so. It does not follow that any of these worldviews must necessarily have oppressive consequences which render them fatally problematic. Any complex tradition will include within itself possibilities for tendentious justifications of existing social structures, but it will also contain within itself possibilities for the correction of such abuses. I would argue that Aquinas' treatment of the notion of a hierarchy of being includes an implicit critique of the abuses of that notion that its critics rightly deplore. At any rate, we will see that it is not inconsistent in his own mind with a commitment to normative equality.

Gustafson poses a still more radical objection to Aquinas' claim that there is a hierarchy of being, with its implication that lower creatures naturally serve higher creatures.[38] This theory was plausible in Aquinas' day, he concedes, because at that time our capacities to alter the natural order were very limited. But now, due to our far more extensive abilities to modify the natural order to suit our own purposes, we can no longer take the permanence of the natural order for granted. Hence, it is better to see our relation to that order as one of interdependence, rather than sheer dependence.

This objection is based on an understandable but nonetheless serious misunderstanding of the sense in which Aquinas holds that the creatures of the world are hierarchically ordered. The order of creation, as Aquinas understands it, cannot be identified with what might be called the local orderings of particular ecosystems, which we can indeed alter to suit our purposes. As we have seen, the hierarchy of being as Aquinas understands it is an ordering that is displayed in and through the orderly array of the fundamental species of things, which have ascending capacities for active involvement with their surroundings. And it is difficult to understand how the human person could alter this ordering without either destroy-

ing one broad class of beings (all the plants, for example), or con-
cocting a kind of creature that is off the continuum of the hierarchy
of being altogether. The former possibility seems remote, and
would clearly be disastrous if made actual, and I am not sure that
the latter is really even a conceivable possibility. Furthermore,
Aquinas' understanding of the ordering of creation leaves more
room for acknowledging the interdependence of all creatures than
is commonly thought. It is true that Aquinas holds that lower creatures are ordained to serve the higher, although each creature exists
for the sake of its own proper good first of all (I.65.2). But he also
says that God wills to preserve the lower orders of creatures
through the actions of the higher orders (I.64.4), and the good of
the universe as a whole is the supreme created good (I.65.2).

Before we leave this subject, it is worth noting that Aquinas'
account of the hierarchy of being presents a challenge, and perhaps
a corrective, to Gustafson's theocentric ethic. As we saw in the last
chapter, Gustafson holds that we are obliged to relate to all things
in a manner appropriate to their relations to God. If our actions are
guided by this norm, he adds, we will avoid the traditional an-
thropocentrism which is no longer credible. But we also noted
that Gustafson has some difficulty in saying what the relations of
creatures to God are, or even how we would go about determining
what they are. The challenge that Aquinas' general theory of goodness presents to Gustafson's moral theory is this: Aquinas does
have a persuasive theory of the way in which creatures are ordered
to God and one another, and it is precisely that theory that provides the basis for what Gustafson would call Aquinas' an-
thropocentrism.

How so? It is obvious that on Aquinas' account of the hierarchy
of being, it is appropriate to place subrational creatures at the service
of the human person (II-II.64.1). But that is only one aspect, and the
less interesting aspect, of the moral significance of the ordering of
creation as Aquinas understands it. Aquinas also holds that there are
higher creatures than we are (namely, the angels), and as we have
noted, he holds that the good of the universe as a whole is greater
than the good of any particular creature, however exalted (I.47.1, 2).
Aquinas takes the supreme goodness of the universe as a whole very
seriously, even to the extent of explaining predestination as necessary to the good order of the universe (I.23.5 *ad* 3). And yet, even
though he clearly acknowledges that human existence is not the
greatest sort of created good, Aquinas also clearly holds that concern
for human well-being is central to the moral life. Indeed, he goes
further than that: He asserts that a proper love of oneself should take

precedence over love of the neighbor (II-II.26.4), and we are obliged to love those who are more closely connected to us more than strangers (II-II.26.6; Aquinas is speaking of the love of charity in these passages, but he explicitly says at II-II.26.6 that the order of charity corresponds to the order of reason).[39]

What is his rationale for these remarkable assertions? It may be found in the same passage (II-II.26.6): Aquinas argues that the natural inclinations of the human person are manifestations of the divine wisdom, which bestows inclinations and principles of motion on every sort of creature in accordance with its own species (indeed, that bestowal *is* the creation of a being with a specific nature). And since the inclinations of rational creatures are to be understood by analogy to the inclinations of subrational creatures (again, see I.60.5), we may infer the order of our obligations by inquiring into the general principles of unity and connectedness that are displayed throughout creation. Indeed, Aquinas' discussion of the order of charity is informed by just this sort of analysis (II-II.26, esp. 26.4–12; for other examples of the same sort of reasoning, see I.60.3, 4; II–II.64.5).

My point is this. The ordering of the universe, for Aquinas, includes not only what we might call a macro-ordering of all creatures into an array of species. It also includes the fundamental ordering of all creatures toward the attainment of their own proper good and the exercise of their own proper causality. It is this aspect of the ordering of creatures which provides Aquinas with his most fundamental justification for what Gustafson would call his anthropocentricism. Even though we recognize that our own existence, as individuals or as a species, is not the greatest created good, nonetheless, it is only right—that is, in accordance with the ordering of ourselves and all other things by God—for us to be concerned first of all with our own well-being, rather than with the good of the universe as a whole. The good of the universe is God's proper concern, and although we are obliged to conform our wills to God's formally, God is not so unreasonable as to expect us always to will concretely what he wills in his capacity as the governor of the whole universe (I-II.19.10).[40]

We must consider one final argument before turning to an examination of Aquinas' account of the human good. According to this line of argument, Aquinas' general theory of goodness, while intrinsically sound, is finally irrelevant to his theory of morality, because according to him, the final end of human life cannot be understood in philosophical terms at all. We now turn to a consideration of this argument.

Natural and Supernatural in Aquinas' Moral Theory

The reading of Aquinas' moral theory to be developed in subsequent chapters presupposes that Aquinas takes the naturally attainable specific perfection of the human person to be the proximate norm of the moral life. And so he does. But that is not immediately obvious, because he also clearly holds that the true ultimate perfection of the human person is not natural, but supernatural in character.

Near the beginning of his moral treatise, Aquinas raises the question, "What is happiness?" This question is equivalent to asking, "What, substantively, counts as human perfection?" (I-II.3; cf. I.2.1 *ad* 1; I-II. 1.5, 8). But nothing in our analysis so far has prepared us for his answer: True happiness consists in God, perceived in his essence through that beatific vision which can alone satisfy the rational creature's longing for intelligibility (I.12.1; I-II.3.5, 8). The attainment of this goal is totally beyond not only our own natural powers, but the natural powers of any creature, the highest angels included. It can be bestowed on us only through a supernatural transformation of our capacities for knowledge and love, which begins in this life through grace, and culminates in the glory of the blessed (I.12.11–13; I-II.5.5; I-II.62.1, 2; I-II.67.6; I-II.109.5).

Aquinas' assertion that the true end of human life is supernatural rather than natural has led a number of commentators to conclude that he holds that the human person has no natural end, as subrational creatures do.[41] According to some, the only end toward which we are directed is the direct vision of God. Others hold that we do have natural inclinations to finite ends, but these are directed toward a plurality of goods, and not to a unified state of perfection that would count as a true end. To the objection that according to Aquinas, all created natures are inclined toward that determinate state of perfect fulfillment which he describes as their end, it is said that this dictum applies only to subrational creatures. The human person is a spiritual creature, and as such he is not oriented toward a determinate fulfillment, as material creatures are. In the words of Anton Pegis, "Natures *qua* natures are closed only in the sense that they are not subject to more or less. There are, to be sure, closed natures, but they are closed, not because they are natures, but because they are material. If there are creatures with spiritual natures, they are open because they are spiritual."[42]

As Kevin Staley points out, the difficulty with this line of interpretation is that "it is quite evident on textual grounds alone that Thomas does allow for a determinate form of happiness which both

(a) corresponds to human nature and (b) is an end proportionate to its native potencies."[43] Indeed, not only does Aquinas repeatedly assert that the human person is directed toward a natural, as well as a supernatural, form of perfection (I-II.5.5; I-II.62.1), he says the same thing about those pure spirits, the angels. At I.62.1, "Whether the angels were created in happiness?" we read that

> by the word "happiness" [*beatitudine*, the same word used of human happiness] is understood the highest perfection of a rational or intellectual nature; hence, that is what is naturally desired, since everything naturally desires its highest perfection. However, the highest perfection of a rational or intellectual nature is twofold. There is a perfection which can be attained by the power *(virtute)* of such a nature, and this is called happiness or felicity in a certain sense. . . . But beyond this felicity is another felicity which we expect for the future, that is, that "we shall see God as he is" (1 John 3:2). This latter is beyond the nature of every created intellect, as has been shown above [I.12.4]. . . . Thus, it ought to be said that as regards the first sort of happiness, which the angel could attain by its own natural power, the angel was created blessed. . . . But the angels did not have immediately from the beginning of their creation that ultimate beatitude, which exceeds the faculties of their nature, because such beatitude does not belong to their nature, but rather is the end of nature.

I have quoted this passage at some length in order to make the point that for Aquinas, *every* creature is oriented toward an end proportionate to its own determinate potentialities. It is true that the rational or intellectual creature is "open" by nature, in the sense that such a creature is capable of knowledge by a kind of assimilation of the forms of things (in our case, through discursive thought rather than through direct intuition [I.85.1, 2]). In other words, a spiritual creature as such is not determined to one form in the way that subrational creatures are (I.75.1). Nonetheless, the spiritual creature remains a creature, and as such it instantiates "a determinate degree of being" (I.50.2 *ad* 1). For this reason, the fundamental metaphysical principles by which we understand created natures in general are to be applied to spiritual natures as well. That is why Aquinas says, as we noted above, that the inclinations of spiritual natures are to be interpreted by analogy with the inclinations common to all other sorts of natures (I.60.5). Hence, we should not be surprised to find that human beings, as well as angels, are oriented by nature toward a connatural mode of perfection, which we may describe as natural happiness.

How are we to reconcile this conclusion with Aquinas' clear statement that "highest and perfect happiness can be nothing other than the vision of the divine essence" (II-II.3.8)? Staley argues convincingly that for Aquinas, the human person is actually directed toward only one end, which is attained in a twofold manner, natural and supernatural. "Imperfect as well as perfect beatitude both respond to man's desire for goodness as such, though in differing degrees of completeness."[44] Indeed, both aspects of beatitude have the same object, that is, God, attained, however, in radically different ways. Through natural happiness, the human creature attains God in the same manner as any other creature does, that is, by created participation in God's goodness (I-II.1.8), but in supernatural happiness, she attains God as he is in himself, and not merely as the principle of her created existence. Hence, Staley concludes, while Aquinas holds that happiness in the fullest sense can consist only in the beatific vision, he also uses the word analogously to refer to the natural happiness that can be attained in this life (I-II.3.2 *ad* 4; I-II.5.3, esp. *ad* 3, 5).

But in what sense can the imperfect happiness that we can attain in this life be described as an end which perfects the human person and satisfies all her desires? Natural happiness is the end of the human person in the same sense that the specific ideal of what would count as perfection for any other sort of creature may be said to be the end toward which that creature is naturally inclined. That is, it is an ideal state toward which we are directed by the constitutive inclinations of our human nature, and which is therefore intrinsic to the intelligibility of that nature. Nonetheless, although we are really inclined toward natural happiness and can only be understood as so inclined, there is no guarantee that we will attain it. Indeed, all our experience points toward the conclusion that we will not attain it completely, even though some of us may come very near to doing so. The same may be said of any other sort of creature. It must also be said that although natural happiness is the natural end of the human creature in the sense of being her fulfillment, it is not likely to be her end in the sense of being temporally the last stage of development that she attains.[45] Like all creatures, we are subject to decay and dissolution. Moreover, there is every reason to suppose that the separated soul would in no sense be happy, apart from the beatific vision.

To prevent confusion, it should be noted that I use the expressions "the end of the human person, the ultimate goal of life, happiness, natural perfection," and the like to refer to the natural happiness of the human person, unless otherwise noted.

Even if it is granted that Aquinas holds that the human person is oriented toward a natural as well as a supernatural perfection, we must still ask how the natural and supernatural components of the end of human life are brought to bear on moral reflection. The first point to note in attempting to answer this question is that on Aquinas' own premises, the natural and supernatural ends of human life cannot function in precisely the same way in moral reflection. The supernatural end of human life as such cannot be the subject of direct knowledge for creatures such as ourselves, since it consists in direct union with the God who is utterly inaccessible to our conceptual knowledge.[46] For this reason, it cannot directly serve as the goal by which we evaluate our actions, since we cannot orient our practical reason by a goal that we cannot conceive. We can know something about the moral content, so to speak, of the life of grace. Otherwise, Aquinas could not have detailed the moral qualities associated with the theological virtues as he does. But that knowledge is based on our observation of graced lives, interpreted in the light of doctrine and natural moral wisdom, and does not—could not—derive from our knowledge of the qualities of the beatific vision toward which the graced life is directed.[47]

At the same time, Aquinas' theological convictions would never permit him to conclude that the natural specific perfection of the human person is contradicted, or rendered otiose, by the life of grace. It is a truism of Aquinas scholarship, and no less true for being such, that Aquinas consistently affirms the integrity and goodness of creation, even though he also insists on the infinite distance between creature and Creator.[48] Certainly, he holds that there is a radical qualitative difference between even the complete natural rectitude that would have been possible to our first parents, and the life of those who are justified by grace (I-II.109.1–4). Moreover, contrary to what is often assumed, he insists that moral rectitude is not even partially sufficient for the bestowal of sanctifying grace, which God bestows without regard to any prior conditions whatever. The naturally just individual who lacks grace is objectively as far from salvation, according to him, as the worst of sinners (I-II.109.5; I-II.112.2, 3). Nonetheless, in his view it would be absurd to suppose that the God of grace and the God of nature could be so radically at odds that the imperatives of grace might call for the actual destruction, rather than the subordination and transformation, of natural human happiness (cf. I.60.5). The absurdity of this assumption becomes even clearer when we recall that objectively, the end attained through the beatific vision, and the end that would be attained by those who achieve natural happiness, if that were the highest goal possible to us, is in fact the same end, God, although at the same time there is an infinite qualitative difference between these two modes of attaining God (I-II.109.3, esp. *ad* 1).

In my view, the only interpretation that makes sense of everything that Aquinas says about the final end of human life, and its relation to morality, is this: The natural end of human life, that is, the attainment of specific perfection as a human being, is not rendered otiose or irrelevant by the fact that we are actually directed toward a supernatural end. The specific natural ideal of humanity remains the proximate norm of morality. That is why Aquinas insists that while the theological virtues transform the cardinal virtues, they do so in such a way as to leave intact the rational structure of the latter (II-II.26.6), which is itself derived from their orientation toward the natural human good (I-II.62.1; I-II.63.2), that is, natural perfection in accordance with the specific kind of humanity (I.62.1). At the same time, the theological virtues do add something to the moral life, beyond a new motivation for moral behavior. It is only through the theological virtues, and especially charity, that women and men are enabled to achieve that inner harmony and unity of life that all things naturally desire (II-II.29.1, 2). Moreover, the life of grace does add at least one new quality to the cardinal virtues, namely patience, which is one aspect of infused fortitude (II-II.136, esp. 136.2).[49]

Because the specific ideal of humanity is the proximate norm of morality, it is legitimate to attempt a reconstruction of Aquinas' understanding of that ideal. But it should be kept in mind that what we are attempting here is indeed a reconstruction. In the *ST,* Aquinas does not directly address the question, "In what does our natural perfection consist?" except in passing (for example, at I.62.1), and then he generally just repeats Aristotle's view that our highest natural happiness consists in contemplation. And yet, when Aquinas considers the contemplative life in detail, it becomes apparent that the ideal, as he sees it, would be a life that strikes an appropriate balance between activity and contemplation, in accordance with the temperament of the individual (II-II.182.4 *ad* 3; cf. I-II.3.5; I-II.4.5; I-II.5.5).[50] In other words, the specific ideal of humanity, as he sees it, is not a life spent in contemplation alone (as if that were possible), but a life that incorporates other sorts of activities as well. Hence, we must examine his moral theory in more detail in order to attain a more complete view of the notion of natural perfection—that is, specifically human perfection—that underlies that theory.

So far, we have been laying the necessary groundwork for a Thomistic account of morality through an examination of the most general philosophical presuppositions of that account. As a result, we are now in a position to understand what it means for Aquinas to speak of the human good, and what, on his terms, an account of the human good can be expected to yield for a theory of morality. For everything that has been said about the goodness of creatures in general applies to human beings in particular. We, too, are members of a particular species, and our good consists in approaching perfection, as nearly as may be, in accordance with the ideal of that species. Certainly, there is a fundamental difference between us and subrational creatures with respect to the way in which we approach our own specific ideal. We can do so only on the basis of a reasoned apprehension of that ideal, whereas subrational creatures do so instinctively or automatically, as it were (I.103.5 *ad* 2; I-II.1.8; I-II.93.5). But this difference is grounded in the distinctive character of our species, and is no more mysterious in principle than the distinctions among the ways in which inanimate creatures, plants, and animals approach their diverse sorts of specific ideals.

Hence, Aquinas' general theory of goodness provides a foundation for a theory of morality that grounds moral norms in an account of the natural human good. Once we have some notion of what the specific ideal of humanity is, we can begin to discern what sorts of actions and habits would promote the attainment of that ideal, and which would be inconsistent with it. And that, I will attempt to show, is the procedure that Aquinas does indeed follow. In the next chapter, we will examine his theory of natural human goodness. In subsequent chapters, we will see how he develops his theory of the virtues on the basis of his understanding of the human good.

3

The Human Good

At the end of the last chapter, it was suggested that Aquinas' theory of morality presupposes an account of the natural human good, which serves as the proximate norm for morality. If we are to reconstruct his moral philosophy, we must therefore examine his understanding of the natural end of the human person, that in which natural happiness consists (or would consist, if it were still completely attainable under present conditions [see I-II.109.2]). At the same time, in our efforts to understand Aquinas' view of the natural good of the human person, we must keep the main tenets of his general theory of goodness in mind. As we would expect by now, Aquinas' conception of the natural human good is dependent on his general theory of goodness, so much so that his account of the natural human good may be taken as a specification and elaboration of his general theory of goodness with respect to human beings. And yet, this account is not derived from his general theory of goodness without reference to the data of experience. His general theory puts those data into the order of a theoretical account, but at the same time, those data give his account of the natural human good substantive content and practical force. In this chapter, we turn to a reconstruction of that account.

Human Action and the End of Life

As Ralph McInerny has noted, the key to Aquinas' theory of morality is the concept of action.[1] For Aquinas, the point of disciplined moral reflection is to enable the individual to *act well*, that is, to act in accordance with a reasoned grasp of the exigencies of human nature. The centrality of the concept of action for Aquinas' moral theory may not be readily apparent, since so much of the *Secunda Secundae* is taken up with discussions of law or virtue. But as we examine the specifics of these discussions, it will become apparent that an account of action is the common thread running through them all. The moral virtues are the enduring traits of character that persons must possess if they are to be able to sustain a course of activity, and correlatively, the moral laws are comprised of the ordering principles that a community must embody if its members are to be able to act in concert while each also seeks his or her own good as an individual.

Like all creatures, the human person is good and approaches perfection to the extent that she actively exists (I-II.3.2). But because the human person is naturally the origin of her own actions, in a way that even the higher animals are not, the perfection-in-action proper to her has a dimension that is not found in the lower creatures. A human being who approaches perfection in accordance with the specific ideal of humanity is not only in act in the general metaphysical sense of instantiating the perfections proper to her specific kind, she is also in act in the more familiar sense of being in action, of securing and enjoying her well-being through her own deliberate choices. Indeed, there is no other way in which a human being could attain perfection, since if it is proper to a given sort of creature to originate its own actions, then the capacity to act well will be a component, and not merely a disposable means, toward the perfection of that sort of creature (I.26.1; I-II.5.7). Hence, Aquinas can say that the natural perfection of the human person consists in acting in accordance with virtue (I-II.5.5), or alternatively, in being in accordance with the norms of reason, which is of course the precondition of virtuous action (II-II.47.6; cf. I-II.57.5; I-II.58.2). At the same time, that goodness of action in which human perfection consists cannot be understood in purely formal terms. It requires that the person acts and sustains activities in accordance with a (roughly) correct understanding of what it means to be a good human being (I-II.1.2, 7; I-II.3.2). And so, Aquinas also speaks of human perfection in terms of the object of human happiness, whether that be God as attained in the beatific vision, or, in the case of natural happiness, God as attained in and through an existence that participates in God's own goodness by attaining one's own specific goodness as nearly as possible (I-II.3.1; I.4.2; I-II.1.8; I-II.109.3). Hence, when Aquinas speaks of the perfection or happiness of the human creature, he sometimes emphasizes that this good is necessarily attained in and through human action, while at other times he emphasizes the object attained through that action.

Because Aquinas' account of human perfection may be construed, in the sense just indicated, as an account of what it means for the human person to act well, it is necessary to have some understanding of his theory of action in order to make sense of that account. Aquinas' theory of action takes its starting point from the distinction that he draws between human action and animal behavior. At I-II.1.7, he observes that animals move toward those goods that are appropriate to them by natural instinct or conditioning, whereas mature humans are free to 'choose this or that (seemingly) good thing, whether it is helpful and appropriate to them or not (cf. I-II.1.2 *ad* 3; I-II.10.1, 2; I-II.13.2). Negatively, he says that the human will is not determined to any particular good or class of goods (except God, who is not directly present to us in this life anyway [I-II.10.2]). Positively, he says that the human person (in contrast to a subrational animal) chooses among the array of seeming goods on the basis of a rational apprehension of what is truly good for human beings, on the basis of which she determines (correctly or not) which seeming particular goods are truly such (I-II.1.6; I-II.8.1; I-II.9.1).

In other words, what Aquinas is saying is that we are distinguished from subrational animals by the fact that we, unlike they, do not automatically seek out the goods that will promote our growth and flourishing. Left to its own devices, my male parakeet will seek out the sorts of fruits and seeds that it needs to be healthy, the kind of environment in which it can make a safe, comfortable nest, and the kind of bird, namely a female parakeet, that will make a suitable mate for it. Significantly, any healthy parakeet will do so, which, Aquinas would claim, indicates that the parakeet acts in accordance with the bent of its nature, and not through an intellectual consideration of what the good for parakeets requires (II-II.47.15 *ad* 3). In contrast to my parakeet, I do not automatically choose the sorts of things that will promote my healthy functioning. For example, left to my own desires I may well choose to live primarily on fast foods and chocolate, rather than selecting the healthier diet that would in fact be readily available to me. If I am to select those things that will really promote my healthy functioning as a human being, it is first of all necessary for me to know what that means, concretely. Even then I must still bring that knowledge to bear on each particular situation, and choose accordingly (and as we will see in chapter 4, I may well fail to do so). Hence, my will, unlike animal impulses, is never oriented by natural necessity toward any particular finite good. (Or to be more exact, *I,* considered as a volitional creature, am never so directed. Aquinas does not hold to a faculty psychology of the sort that some of his followers later made notorious.)

Given this account of what is distinctive to human action, we
can see the point of saying that a successful human life is a life spent
in acting in accordance with a (roughly) correct concept of the human
good. That is, this statement should be taken as a shorthand reminder
of what is involved in the successful pursuit of a distinctively human
life. Such a life calls for deliberate activity guided by knowledge of
what is truly good for human beings, and what is not. But of course,
this raises the questions of what, precisely, "the truly good for the
human person" might be, and how we come to know what it is.

We are now approaching one of the most difficult issues in
Aquinas' moral theory. The difficulty is of course that Aquinas begins the *Prima Secundae* with two claims that are hardly obvious: Every
human action is aimed, directly or indirectly, at the attainment or
preservation of some one good which the agent believes will perfect
him as a human being, that is, render him happy; and there is in fact
one end, and one only, in which human happiness truly can be found
(I-II.1.6; I-II.2.8). Although these claims are usually discussed together, and Aquinas does combine them into one theory, they are
independent claims. It would be possible to assert that everyone acts
for some final end or other without going on to assert (as Aquinas
in fact does) that there is only one final end for which we all should
act, whether we do so or not. We will examine the first of these claims
in this section, reserving a discussion of the second for the next
section.

"It is necessary that all things which a person desires, he desires
on account of a final end" (I-II.1.6). This is not necessarily *the* one true
end of human life (so to say, the objective end of life), Aquinas goes
on to explain, but whatever the individual may believe to be the
proper goal of human life, or of this particular individual's life (his
subjective end, so to speak). Even though we have bracketed the
question of whether there is indeed objectively one end of human
life, the claim that all our actions are aimed, directly or indirectly, at
some one goal is problematic enough. For surely our own experiences
plainly contradict it? Not many of us have the self-possession, or the
fanaticism, to shape our whole lives around devotion to some one
object, cause, or ideal. And even those few of us who do cannot be
said literally to direct all our actions toward one end. Even the most
dedicated individuals indulge in an ice-cream cone or a joke once in
a while. Indeed, even if it were possible to direct all one's actions
toward one goal, who would want to do so? The individual who, as
we say, lives for one thing only, is more likely to seem fanatical than
saintly to us. As John Rawls says, "Surely it is contrary to our considered judgments of value, and indeed inhuman, to be so taken with

but one of these ends [that persons may seek] that we do not moderate the pursuit of it for the sake of anything else."[2]

Let me say at once that if Aquinas does indeed claim that each person *always* directs *all* her actions and activities toward some one goal or ideal, then I do not see how that claim could be defended. Admittedly, the passage just quoted seems to say just that. Nonetheless, when this passage is taken in the context of other remarks in the *ST,* it becomes apparent that Aquinas does acknowledge that in fact, persons do act out of aims that are not derived from the ultimate goal of their lives. Elsewhere, he discusses a type of sin that consists precisely in acting in a way that is not in accordance with the overall (good) end of one's life (that is, venial sin [I-II.72.5; cf. I-II.18.9]). Moreover, Aquinas, like Aristotle before him, devotes some attention to the case of the individual (usually described as the incontinent person) whose overall conception of the human good is sound, but who is led by passion of some sort to act contrary to what that overall conception would prescribe (II-II.156).[3] How, then, are we to interpret his comments at I-II.1.6?

In my view, Aquinas' remarks at I-II.1.6, that we desire all that we desire for the sake of whatever we take to be the true end of our lives, should be taken as a metaphysically informed analysis of rational action, which still leaves room to admit that some behaviors which do not meet this ideal can still be said to be rational, and hence true human actions, albeit in a derivative sense. In any case, this weaker claim is all that Aquinas needs as the foundation of his moral theory.

Is there evidence elsewhere in the *ST* that would support the claim that I-II.1.6 should be taken as an ideal statement of that in which fully rational, and therefore fully human action consists? Yes—it is to be found in his account of the conditions that an item of behavior must fulfill if it is to count *minimally* as a human action (I-II.6). When we examine these minimal conditions, we find that they point toward the claim of I-II.1.6 as an expression of their fullest possible instantiation.

Aquinas is well aware that not every item of human behavior can be considered to be an action, and therefore early in his discussion he suggests guidelines for distinguishing actions from other kinds of behavior.[4] To begin with, Aquinas holds that in order to count as a human action at all, an item of behavior must proceed from the agent's desire for something (object, state of affairs, or whatever) that his reason judges to be good. That is to say, a true action must be voluntary, in that it proceeds from the agent's will (I-II.6.1). Seeming actions produced by violence are simply involuntary and therefore are in no sense true actions (I-II.6.5). In contrast, there are actions of a sort that Aquinas describes as simply voluntary, but involuntary in a restricted sense (I-II.6.6). These actions are the result of fear, for example, the act of a ship's captain who throws his valuable cargo overboard in a storm in order to keep the ship from sinking. Actions of this sort are voluntary, strictly speaking, because they are done knowingly, in pursuit of what the agent prefers, all things considered. However, they can be said to be involuntary in the restricted sense that the agent acts as he does only under the press of circumstances that he would have preferred to avoid. (Aquinas denies that actions are rendered even relatively involuntary by a great desire for pleasure, which, he says, rather increases their voluntariness [I-II.6.7].)

A third category includes those actions which are either nonvoluntary or involuntary under one description, and voluntary under another; these actions arise when the agent is ignorant of some relevant feature of the situation in which she acts (given that this ignorance is not itself voluntarily incurred [I-II.6.8]). For example, consider how we might describe the action of a hunter who shoots and kills what he thinks is a deer, but which is actually another hunter in (much too good) disguise. Described as shooting a gun, or even as shooting a gun at this target, the action is voluntary, but we nonetheless cannot say that the hunter voluntarily shot a man. It may be that if he had known that his victim was a man, he would have shot him anyway, if, for example, the victim had been seeing the hunter's wife, and the hunter had planned to shoot him sometime next week. In such a case, the action that falls under the description "shooting a man" is *non*voluntary. On the other hand, the hunter may be appalled by what he has done, and in that case, his action, described as shooting a man, is *in*voluntary.

Finally, there are those actions that we would call inadvertent or habitual actions, and which Aquinas calls acts of a human person, in contrast to human actions in the full sense (I-II.1.1 *ad* 3). These are the things that we "do without thinking," as the saying goes, like scratching or cracking the knuckles. Such behaviors are not really involuntary, since we could refrain from them if we thought about it, and yet they do not seem to reflect sufficient thought to count as fully deliberate human actions.

All these distinctions serve to draw out the implications of Aquinas' fundamental claim that if a putative action is to count as voluntary, therefore as a true human action, it must be directed by the agent herself toward the attainment or preservation of some state of affairs that she judges to be good. In particular, they indicate that if a putative action is to count as voluntary—and therefore as a true action—it must be intelligible in terms of the agent's reasons for action.[5] This is simply another way of saying that in order to be a true human action, an item of behavior must be rational, at least in a minimal sense.

But is the qualification "a minimal sense" really necessary? That is, beyond its fulfilling the minimal conditions for a voluntary action, is anything required for an action to be fully intelligible? As I read him, Aquinas' contention that fully rational action must be directed toward some one ultimate aim presupposes that an action that is only minimally voluntary is not fully intelligible. Full intelligibility requires that in addition to being able to account for this action in terms of the agent's desire to bring about a certain state of affairs, we must also be able to explain why this agent finds this state of affairs to be desirable, that is, considers it to be a good. Otherwise, the choice of this particular good remains unjustified, a rational surd, and the agent's action is so far unintelligible to outside observers and even to himself.

What form might such an explanation take? For Aquinas, there are only two ways in which we can account for the agent's judgment that such and such is a good. Either he believes that the attainment of this good will satisfy his longing for his own perfection as a human being—that is, he believes that his happiness consists in the enjoyment of this good—or he believes that the attainment of this good will serve as a means toward, or a component of, the attainment of his perfection, and therefore, his happiness (I-II.1.4, 5). Hence, in order for an action to be fully intelligible, and thus, to be a human action in the fullest possible sense, it must be directed toward the attainment or preservation of that good toward which the agent has directed his whole life, which he takes to be the object of his happiness, as we are told at I-II.1.6. And so, the claim of I-II.1.6, that all human action is grounded in some one goal toward which the individual orients his life, should be taken as a metaphysically based ideal of what human action should be, and must be if it is to be a human action in the fullest sense.

But of course, the validity of Aquinas' account of action and freedom is not secured simply by showing that it is meant as an ideal, which may never be fully instantiated. Even an ideal account of human action must necessarily have some recognizable bearing on what we actually do. Hence we must still ask whether this ideal makes sense of human behavior as we observe it. That is, granted that no ideal is ever fully realized, can we nonetheless see patterns or tendencies in human behavior that can be understood as directed toward this ideal? And correlatively, is this ideal plausible *as* an ideal by which we would really want to live our lives? It will be clear by now that not only Aquinas' moral theory, but by implication his metaphysics as a whole, will stand or fall with the way in which we answer these questions, since if they are answered negatively, Aquinas' metaphysics will be seen to have led to an unsatisfactory account of what it is to be human.

I shall argue that the answer to these questions (which are of course interlocking) is "yes": Aquinas' ideal of fully rational action does indeed make good sense of what we do, and strive to do, in the conduct of our lives, and at the same time it makes sense of our widely held beliefs as to what are better and worse ways of living.

One obvious objection to Aquinas' ideal of human action is that there is no need to offer an explanation of why we desire this or that, in terms of some overarching orientation toward whatever one takes to be one's supreme good. Our desires may indeed be based on some such orientation, but they may just as well be based on our simple emotional or sensual inclinations. After all, there are many things that are simply desirable to us in themselves, without reference to any wider good that they somehow promote: fine music, a life of service, chocolates, children, religious ecstasy, sexual ecstasy . . . the list is endless. If Aquinas is to maintain his account of what counts as fully rational action, even considered as an ideal which admittedly may not always be attained, then he must show that there is something problematic in acting just in order to attain something that is appealing to us, without reference to any wider aim. And it is initially difficult to see how he would go about doing that. After all, what could be wrong with this item of practical reason: I like chocolate ice-cream cones; here's a chocolate ice-cream cone; down it goes!

As we have already noted, Aquinas does admit that we do sometimes act contrary to our overall conception of the human good, simply because this or that is immediately appealing. An act of this sort must be said to be rational in the minimal sense that it proceeds out of a judgment of the intellect that this desideratum, perceived here and now, is indeed a good in itself, since otherwise, the putative action would not be a true action at all (I-II.6.7 *ad* 3). Nonetheless, Aquinas would argue that an action of this sort approaches, although it is not identical with, the mode of behavior proper to a subrational animal.

Like every other creature, we naturally strive for goodness in accordance with the ideal of the specific kind of creature that we are. Moreover, both the character of that ideal and our means of striving for it are set by the mode of causality that is proper to our species, namely the exercise of discursive rationality in thought and action. And if the argument of this section is correct, in order for an action to be fully rational in Aquinas' terms, not only the behavior itself but the agent's desire for this particular good must be intelligible. That is, it must admit of an explanation in terms of what the agent considers to be her overall good. We *can* desire and seek something simply because it is immediately appealing, without considering how it fits into our overall good, but in so doing, we are responding to what is immediately appealing in somewhat the way that a subrational animal would (I-II.13.2).

And what is wrong with that? It is one of the implications of Aquinas' general theory of goodness that no good can come of acting in a way that is not in accordance with one's own specifically proper mode of being. In this particular case, the difficulty with making beasts of ourselves is that we are bound to botch the job. Animals are directed by the exigencies of their nature toward the things and circumstances that are truly beneficial to them (I-II.13.2 *ad* 3). For example, my parakeet, as I mentioned above, is naturally oriented toward those things that are good for parakeets, so that it is safe for it to trust its urges. But any instinctive orientation of that sort that we may have is rudimentary, at best. And so we should not find it surprising that individuals who live their lives on the basis of pursuing what appeals from moment to moment do not lead notably successful lives, even on their own terms. In other words, while it is possible to act in a way that is more nearly bestial than human, that mode of action will constitute a breakdown in the ongoing process by which we become ever more fully the human beings that we are. This conclusion follows from Aquinas' general theory of goodness, but it is reinforced by a second set of considerations, which will follow upon the consideration of a second objection to Aquinas' ideal for rational action.

This second objection is grounded in a very natural misunderstanding of Aquinas' claim that ideally our actions are all directed toward whatever we take to be our true good. It is easy to assume that Aquinas holds that the good toward which one's life is directed must be some one determinate kind of good. In fact, Aquinas gives examples of determinate kinds of goods around which people do structure their lives: riches, honor, physical pleasure, and so on (I-II.2.1-6). We can readily agree that there really are people who only live for pleasures, or wealth, or power, or whatever, although fortunately there are probably not too many of them. And we are likely to agree with Aquinas that this sort of life is wretched. Think of the person who sacrifices leisure, friendships, the good of his family, and even his moral integrity, it may be with great remorse, in order to attain and keep political power. Yet it may seem that our reasons for this judgment are very different from Aquinas' own. He says that these kinds of goods are the wrong goods around which to structure a life. But is the problem not rather that once *any* particular good is taken as the basis for one's whole life, the individual will be forced to forgo many other good things, and even to violate the legitimate claims of others in order to secure the greatest possible measure of that one good? Even a life that is wholly devoted to some noble goal, for example, Aristotelian contemplation, is likely to strike us as somehow distorted and impoverished, in comparison to a life that is built around a balanced pursuit of a number of different kinds of goals.[6]

But it is possible to conceive of the ultimate goal of a human life in another way, as including a number of different sorts of goods, pursued and enjoyed in an orderly and harmonious way. For example, a woman may decide that for her, the best possible life would be one in which the joys of philosophical contemplation predominated, but which also included the cultivation of other abilities and interests, some participation in civic affairs, and the active cultivation of a relation with a higher power through frequent prayer and meditation. A life of this sort would be structured around some conception of the proper ordering and interrelationships of the diverse particular goods of human life, which would give it its unity. In other words, in a case of this sort, the goal around which an individual structured her activities would in fact be an ideal of a certain kind of life, rather than one determinate kind of good. To borrow terms from W. F. R. Hardie, her life would then be directed toward an inclusive end, to be fulfilled in and through the pursuit of a variety of goods in an ordered way, rather than toward the dominant end of one determinate good.[7]

And in fact, Aquinas does allow for the possibility that the goal of a human life might be an inclusive rather than a dominant end (although of course, he does not use that terminology). In his discussion of the question, "Whether it is possible for a person to have many final ends?" (I-II.1.5), he begins by quoting Augustine to the effect that some philosophers have held that the true last end of human life consists in the enjoyment of pleasure, leisure, natural goods, and virtue. In his response, he simply notes that for these philosophers, the final good of human life was conceived of as one perfect good comprised of these particular goods (I-II.1.5 *ad* 1). Similarly, in the next question he observes that the particular goods of the joker, or of the scientist, are sought by them as components of their overall good as individuals, thereby indicating once again that it is possible to direct one's life toward a comprehensive ideal that makes room for diverse particular goods (I-II.1.6 *ad* 1, 2). Hence, Aquinas holds open the possibility that the goal toward which an individual directs his life may be an inclusive—rather than a dominant—end. Moreover, he insists that no single determinate good, which in our terms would be a dominant end, can be an adequate goal for a human life (I-II.2.5–8). Indeed, as we will see in the next section, the natural end of human life, as he understands it, is indeed an inclusive end.

If we understand that the final goal of a person's life may be an inclusive—rather than a dominant—end, then Aquinas' claim that a human life can and should be structured around some such final goal begins to seem far more plausible. Indeed, it begins to appear that individuals must either adopt at least a tentative inclusive goal of this sort, or allow such a goal to be imposed upon them, if they are to function in society at all.

Much attention has been given recently to the importance of social roles in structuring our common life and giving content to many of our moral commitments.[8] This discussion raises complex and controversial questions that cannot be adjudicated here. But without attempting to pronounce on the merits of these questions, we may nonetheless recognize that this discussion calls attention to certain features of social life that are so fundamental that they are likely to be overlooked. To begin with the most basic of these, every society is structured around certain roles, which carry with them expectations about how they are to be lived out over time. Furthermore, MacIntyre points out that because any life will involve its subject in more than one role (unless it is a very short and simple life indeed), the social fabric must also include ideal narratives that tell how a typical human life, which incorporates more than one basic role, will be lived, thereby providing individuals with guidance as to how to harmonize the expectations of their diverse roles.[9] For this reason, Hauerwas is right to claim that every society is informed by narratives which provide it with its collective identity, although, as we saw in the last chapter, it does not follow that the particular narratives of a community cannot be subject to rational scrutiny from a standpoint external to them. Even the simplest society will find it necessary to provide more than one such narrative, and a complex society like ours will offer scores of them, with considerable room for improvisation. But the variety and complexity of these ideal narratives in our own society should not obscure the fact that we have them, and could not live together without them. They are presupposed in our institutions, they structure our expectations of ourselves and one another, they are

expressed in our entertainment, our worship, even our forms of eti-
quette. If we are to function as members of society at all, each of us
must make one of them her own, or it will be done for us, by the
informing pressures of the community around us.

My point is that these ideal narratives of typical kinds of human
lives are nothing other than schemata for inclusive life-plans; they
indicate how certain of the goods of human life are to be achieved
in an orderly way. And we must take one of these plans as our own
(or perhaps invent an entirely new one, if that can be done) if we are
to function as an active member of a society that calls upon us to
assume diverse roles. Certainly, any workable plan of this sort will
necessarily be flexible and open to some revision. For most of us, it
will emerge out of the choices that we make as adolescents and young
adults, rather than coming as the subject of a once-for-all decision.
Furthermore, most of us will probably not find it necessary to formulate our conception of the ideal life in so many words, which is not
to say that we could not do so, if asked. Finally, it is always possible
that an individual might adopt a plan of life that is destructive to
himself, others, or society as a whole. But as we will see in the next
section, Aquinas is hardly committed to the view that any plan of life
whatever will do. To the contrary, he carefully delineates what a
truly good plan for a human life must include.

But isn't it possible to go through life without adopting even the
most tentative and inchoate life-plan, by taking things as they come,
following the path of least resistance, following one's impulses, doing
what one is told, or taking some other stereotypical path away from
the burdens of assuming the active direction of one's own life? Undoubtedly it is; but it is significant that each of these alternatives
describes a stereotypical image for a life that is unsuccessful or unde-
sirable in some way. The drifter, the bum, and the profligate are all
objects of moral reproach, more or less severe as the individual is seen
to victimize others, or only herself. Those who always follow the
path of least resistance, or who allow others to run their lives, are not
so generally subject to moral condemnation, but they are vulnerable
to disaster when their external supports are taken away and they are
generally regarded as weak or foolish. The force of Aquinas' claim
that a (truly, adequately) human life must be structured around some
ideal of what our lives should be now begins to be felt.

We might place all these sorts of people, that is the drifters, the
timid, and the unthinking, under the heading of the feckless. It is not
good to be feckless, but there are worse things to be, and these ways
of failing in the conduct of one's own life indicate still more strongly
that Aquinas is right about what it means to succeed. Consider the

situation of those who are generally capable of lucid thought and action, but who exhibit a self-destructive lack of control in some area of their lives, for example, alcoholics and addicts of all kinds, those who are plagued by phobias, and those who suffer from obsessive-compulsive neuroses. What characterizes these individuals is their inability to sustain a consistent course of activity in accordance with an overall ideal of life, because they cannot (or perhaps will not) refrain from the self-destructive activities and ways of thinking that repeatedly disrupt their lives. The situation of the gravely insane is even worse. Such persons cannot live in accordance with the norms and roles of society at all, and must be cared for by others if they are to survive. It will be objected that these are examples of persons suffering from pathological disorders. Precisely so; we would expect a radical departure from Aquinas' ideal of fully rational action to express itself pathologically, if that ideal is indeed grounded in the realities of what it is to be human.

Recall that it is the argument of this section that Aquinas' claim at I-II.1.6, that a (fully) human life is structured around some final goal, is to be taken as expressing his ideal concept of fully rational action; I interpret this claim in this way on the grounds that this ideal can be understood as the completion of the conditions for minimally rational action expressed in his discussion of voluntariness. The negative examples presented above offer further confirmation of that argument, because they point to a sense in which those who cannot or will not regulate their actions by some final goal do not enjoy full freedom as rational agents. The feckless, and those who suffer from a pathological lack of self-direction, are certainly capable of voluntary action (at least, up to a point), but the course of their lives will necessarily be determined by the decisions of others, by external circumstances, and (sometimes) by the working out of their own pathologies. In other words, while they are capable of particular free actions, they are incapable of sustaining a course of activity that is fully their own. For this reason, their full development as free agents remains stunted.

On the other hand, those who do structure their lives in accordance with some goal can and do sustain a course of activity directed toward that goal. They thereby approach fulfillment as creatures who are the source of their own actions, and who direct themselves by those actions toward their own specific perfection. At first, it might seem that just the opposite is the case. What sort of freedom is available to the individual who must shape his life out of the social roles that are available to him? But as Martin Hollis has argued, this question reflects a misunderstanding.[10] The simple fact that our society provides us with roles in which to live out our lives does not, by itself, imply that we are determined by those roles in such a way as to be nothing more than the puppets of social forces, any more than the fact that we can only think (beyond a certain very basic point) by means of a socially structured language implies that *what* we think is heteronomously determined by our society. The free human being is not someone who is free of occupying any social role at all. That sort of freedom may be proper to an angel, but it is impossible to social creatures such as ourselves. Rather, the free human being is one who has made the roles that she occupies into a part of herself by her conscious choice to accept them, and who takes responsibility for the direction of her own life by fitting those roles together into an orderly life-plan that is the goal of her life. And by so doing, she fashions her life into an at least partial unity, which is intelligible as a whole in terms of the ideal of life that she strives to attain. That is, her life reflects and embodies that unity of aim that Aquinas holds to be essential to fully rational action.

Human Goods and the Human Good

Suppose that we now agree that a fully human life is one that is lived in accordance with a plan of life toward which all one's activities are directed, in some way or other. What more needs to be said? That is, have we now said enough to indicate what it is that a successful human life should be, and what the point of moral reflection is? More than one contemporary moral thinker would say that we have. It is significant that MacIntyre, who is one of the most prominent of the neo-Aristotelians, is also one of those who argues that human lives are stories with a natural dramatic unity out of which they can and should be lived.[11] Of course, MacIntyre is hardly the only recent thinker to insist on the importance of some notion of the unity of a life for moral or religious reflection, or to try to explicate that unity by appeal to the notion of narrative. For example, as we saw in the first chapter, Hauerwas introduces MacIntyre's notion of narrative unity into Christian ethics, although with some important modifications. But what is especially important about MacIntyre's argument, for our purposes, is that he proposes the notion of narrative unity as a substitute for Aristotle's account of the true end of human life; this narrative unity, MacIntyre suggests, can provide us with a basis for a reconstruction of an Aristotelian account of the virtues. "The good life for man is a life spent in seeking for the good life for man," he remarks, in what is no doubt meant to be a paradoxical summary of his views.[12]

In my view, this remark is not so much a paradox as it is an indication that an appeal to the idea of the narrative unity of a life taken by itself is inadequate as the basis for a reconstruction of an Aristotelian account of the virtues. In the first place, "narrative unity" is too imprecise a notion, as MacIntyre's summary remark should lead us to suspect. It says too little about what a good human life should be. History offers numerous examples of lives that are tragedies or melodramas or horror stories, but lives of these sorts, while arguably exhibiting a real dramatic unity, are surely not what MacIntyre wants to commend. (Or if lives of this sort fail to exhibit real narrative unity, then we need to be told why they do not. In other words, we should be told what substantive qualities must be present in a truly unified life.) Moreover, social unity grounded in shared virtues is rightly of much importance to MacIntyre, but if we are all engaged in our personal quests for the good, where are we to find the basis for such social unity? It would seem that the closing vision of *After Virtue,* of individuals banding together in little communities—or lifestyle enclaves[13]—on the basis of similar quests for the good, is itself a liberal/romantic vision which suffers from all the inadequacies of liberal programs that MacIntyre himself identifies.

Aquinas would suggest that what has gone wrong with MacIntyre's argument is that he refuses (in *After Virtue*) to entertain what he refers to as Aristotle's "metaphysical biology."[14] That is, he rejects the claim that for the human person there is such a thing as the objective good that serves as the organizing principle for the unity of a human life and gives content and structure to the virtues.[15] Aquinas, on the other hand, insists that in order for a human life to be truly successful, it is not enough that it be structured around some goal. The goal chosen must be the correct goal. Most properly speaking, this goal can only be the direct vision of God (I-II.3.8). But as we saw in the last chapter, Aquinas also holds that God is attained by the human person, in either a supernatural or a natural sense, in and through a life that approaches and, for the justified, transcends the constitutive ideal of the human species.[16] Or to be more exact, God is attained by us in and through our efforts to approach that ideal, and to live in accordance with it, since the actual attainment of natural (as opposed to supernatural) happiness will always be partially dependent on factors outside the control of the individual. Hence, even though Aquinas affirms that the true end of human life is supernatural, he takes the natural end of human life as the proximate norm for moral reflection.

But what is this natural end of the human person? If our analysis in the last section is correct, we would expect to find that the natural end of the human person is a certain kind of life which incorporates more than one sort of determinate good and does so in an orderly way that bestows an organic unity on that life and on the agent who leads it. (In just the same way, the natural end of my parakeet is to lead a healthy parakeet life which incorporates determinate avian goods in an orderly way.) And when we turn to Aquinas' scattered remarks on natural happiness, we find that this is indeed his understanding of the sort of life that fulfills the specific ideal of the human person. Hence, we read that since the happiness of any intellectual or rational creature consists most properly in an act of its intellect, the natural happiness of the human person, whose intellect is complex, consists in activity of both the speculative and the practical dimensions of that intellect (I-II. 4.5, 6). It would be easy to assume that Aquinas means that our natural happiness consists in speculation on matters practical and theoretical, but that would be a mistake. Since the practical function of the intellect is expressed in and through action (I.79.11), the activity of the intellect proper to natural happiness will necessarily result in good actions, as well as good thinking. And that is indeed Aquinas' view. Hence, we are told that the imperfect happiness of this life consists principally in contemplation, but also includes the active direction of human affairs that is the work of the intellect functioning practically (I-II.3.5). Elsewhere, Aquinas simply says that the happiness proper to this life consists in the operation of virtue, without mentioning contemplation at all (I-II.5.5). Thus, natural happiness requires an aggregate of goods, without which we cannot live well in this life (I-II.3.3).

It will be clear, on the basis of what has been said so far, that Aquinas' explicit account of the natural end of human life is somewhat sketchy. Nonetheless, it is possible to say more about the substantive account of the naturally good life that underlies his moral theory. The key to that account is found in what has become one of the most widely discussed questions in Aquinas scholarship, namely I-II.94.2, "Whether the natural law contains many precepts, or only one?" It may seem surprising to take this text as a summary account of the natural end of human life, but when it is read in the context of Aquinas' general theory of goodness, and then applied to the specifics of his moral theory, I believe that it becomes impossible to read it in any other way.

As we read through I-II.94.2, it becomes apparent that Aquinas wants to show that although there are indeed many precepts of the natural law, nonetheless, there is a sense in which they may be said to be one, because they reflect an internal principle of order. His explanation of the sort of order that these precepts display appears at first to be very simple. He begins by observing that just as there are first principles of speculative reason (most important, the principle of noncontradiction), so there is a first principle of practical reason, namely, "Good is to be done and pursued, and evil is to be avoided." Like its speculative counterparts, this first principle is self-evident and indemonstrable. It is necessary that it should be self-evident, since without some first principles that stand in need of no prior justification, no process of reasoning, practical or otherwise, can begin. But if we cannot deny the first principle of practical reason, neither does it get us very far, taken by itself. However, it does receive determinate content from the inclinations of the human person, to live, to reproduce himself, to live with others, and to know the truth about God. It is these inclinations which provide order as well as content to the precepts of the natural law, and therefore bestow on them a kind of unity: "Therefore, the order of the precepts of the natural law is in accordance with the order of the natural inclinations."

So far, Aquinas' exposition seems clear enough. And indeed it is. But as we examine this text more closely, it becomes apparent that it is clear only so long as his general theory of goodness is kept in mind.

Our first clue that there is more in this passage than meets the modern eye comes early in the body of the main article.[17] Immediately after observing that the first principle of practical reasoning is self-evident, Aquinas carefully distinguishes between what is self-evident in itself, and what is self-evident to us. That which is self-evident in itself, he says, is such because what is predicated of the subject is actually contained in the very *ratione subiecti,* that is, in the intelligible nature of the subject. Hence, anyone who grasps the *ratio* of the subject will immediately affirm the proposition, but someone who does not grasp that *ratio* will not find the proposition self-evident. And for Aquinas, it is quite possible to understand a term, to a degree sufficient for linguistic facility, *without grasping the* ratio *of what the term signifies* (I.85.3). For this reason, it is entirely possible that a proposition, self-evident in itself, can be discovered by us only after exhaustive research into, and reflection on, the true nature of a certain kind of thing. Indeed, there almost certainly are propositions that are self-evident in themselves, and that we believe to be true, which we nonetheless do not *know* to be true because we do not have a sufficient grasp of the *ratio* of the subject to enable us to recognize their self-evidential quality.

Why does Aquinas introduce this distinction between what is self-evident to all and what is self-evident only to the wise at this point? It would appear that he simply wants to make it clear that the first principle of practical reason is one of those principles which are self-evident to all persons, just as the principle of noncontradiction is. In any case, his general theory of goodness requires him to hold that the first principle of practical reasoning is self-evident to all. This necessity is grounded in the wider ontological necessity that all creatures, including us, act (in a wider sense of "act") in order to obtain or to hold on to some good. Hence, when Aquinas says that this first principle—that good should be done and evil avoided—is known to all, he is not necessarily saying that everyone could formulate it. What he is saying is that everyone necessarily acts upon it, since an item of behavior that does not enact this principle does not count as an action at all.[18] At the same time, it is of the first importance to recall that the good for which all creatures act, directly or indirectly, is the perfection appropriate to the species of each one. And so, when Aquinas says that all persons naturally seek the good, what he has in mind is not any good whatever, but the specifically human good, that is, a life that approaches the ideal of human perfection as nearly as possible. In other words, Aquinas' formulation of the first principle of practical reason is a restatement of what he has already said more than once: All persons naturally seek happiness, that is, the fullest possible enjoyment of the good(s) that each believes will perfect and fulfill him or her as a human being (I.2.1 *ad* 1; I-II.5.8).

We have already seen that anyone who may be said to act at all must be said to be acting for some good. Moreover, we have seen that anyone who may be said to act in the fullest sense will act in accordance with some overarching inclusive ideal of the good life that serves as the basis for the unity of that individual's life. But the claim that each individual acts in order to attain happiness, understood as the specific perfection appropriate to a human being, introduces another question. How can Aquinas say that all persons seek the specifically human good, by a kind of metaphysical necessity, when elsewhere he claims that most persons spend their lives in pursuit of a sham happiness (I.49.3 *ad* 5; cf. I.63.9)?

The answer to this question is simple enough: For most of us, our natural inclination toward the good fails to operate correctly. It must be operative on some level if we are to act, or even to exist as human beings at all. But it will not operate correctly if we are mistaken about that in which true human perfection consists, since we, unlike subrational creatures, can only direct ourselves toward our specific perfection on the basis of an intellectual apprehension of what that perfection would be. And in fact, many of us are mistaken about the true nature of specifically human perfection, and therefore spend our lives in pursuit of false ideals of human perfection while neglecting those things that really would make us happy (I.49.3 *ad* 5). In addition, as we saw in the last section, Aquinas also allows for the possibility of a still more serious breakdown in the human search for happiness, which is exhibited by one who is unable or unwilling to orient his life toward an overarching goal at all. Even such a person may be said to desire happiness, in the sense that she, too, desires that her will be satisfied (cf. I-II.5.8). But because she is either incapable of conceiving of that satisfaction in terms that take her beyond the impulses of the moment, or unable to act on such a conception if she can form it, her desire for happiness will not lead her to act in such a way as to attain overall satisfaction. (The movements of subrational creatures toward their specific perfection can also go awry, of course, but not in these particular ways.)

Aquinas' comparison of the first principle of practical reason with the principle of noncontradiction helps to clarify the sense in which all persons seek the human good. We cannot know something if we violate the principle of noncontradiction—because that thing *is,* it possesses unity and self-identity over time, and therefore cannot be and not be (in precisely the same respect) at the same time. For this reason, one must at least try to avoid self-contradiction if one's activity is to count as thinking at all, although of course it is still possible to think badly, to contradict oneself unknowingly, and to fail to attain true knowledge of the object of one's thought.

Just as we can think badly, while still thinking, we can act badly, out of a mistaken notion of that in which the true human good consists, and yet still be acting. The first principle of practical reason, which is self-evident to all, is sufficient to ground action. But if we are to act well, we must arrive at a correct notion of that in which true human good consists. At this point, we must recall Aquinas' distinction between what is self-evident to all and what is self-evident to the wise. It is clear that Aquinas holds the first principle of practical reason is self-evident to all, but it is not at all clear that the true nature of the human good, which alone can give this principle concrete meaning and practical force, is similarly self-evident to all. Indeed, it would seem that the true nature of the human good *cannot* be self-evident to all, since, as Aquinas often remarks, many persons are in fact mistaken about that in which true happiness consists (for example, see I-II.1.7). And yet, he also says in I-II.94.2 that the objects of the natural inclinations are naturally apprehended by the reason as being good. How are we to interpret this remark?

In order to answer this question, we must draw out the implications of Aquinas' claim that the human person is naturally inclined toward certain desiderata. His point is that these inclinations are a part of the specific dynamism of the human person, just as an inclination toward nesting is part of the specific dynamism of my parakeet (cf. I-II.10.1). But does it follow that every human being will necessarily feel inclined toward the objects of each of these inclinations? It does not. Nature sometimes fails, especially in the case of complex creatures like ourselves, and therefore, natural dynamisms may fail to function in a particular case (I.49.1, 2; cf. I.49.3 *ad* 5). Indeed, Aquinas specifically says that even though the human will is naturally inclined toward certain goods, such as life and knowledge, it is not *necessarily* determined to these, or to any other substantive good (I-II. 10.1 *ad* 2, 3). That is, while it is natural to the human person to desire life and the other goods enumerated in I-II.94.2, it is nonetheless possible that a certain individual might happen not to desire one or more of these goods. Such a person would be abnormal, on Aquinas' terms, but he would not be a logical impossibility. But if this is so, it follows that it is not self-evident to all that the objects of the inclinations are good, since, as Finnis notes, the natural apprehension that an object is good is dependent on actually feeling inclined toward that object.[19]

Nor may we conclude that Aquinas holds that it is self-evident to everyone that *only* the objects of the natural inclinations are good in themselves.[20] Aquinas is well aware that people are inclined toward all sorts of things, and at least some of these inclinations are just as ubiquitous as the ones to which he refers here. In some cases, it is possible to show that a particular desideratum (wealth, for example) is really only desirable as a means to other goods, but it is not obvious that it would be possible to do so in every case. (At any rate, the very fact that we must *argue* that wealth is not desirable in itself indicates that its derivative desirability is not *self-evident* to all.) It is not at all obvious that physical pleasure must always be sought as a means to something else, for example. On the other hand, it would be possible to come up with a plausible theory according to which some of the inclinations enumerated in I-II.94.2 are themselves sought as means toward an end. For example, it might be argued that life is valuable only as a precondition to the enjoyment of intellectual activity and human relationships. Such a theory would be mistaken, in my view, but the fact that it can be constructed at all calls into question the universally self-evident desirability of these goods.

Finally, it is important to recall that Aquinas' point in I-II.94.2 is that the precepts of the natural law, while many, nonetheless possess a collective unity because they are ordered to one another, in accordance with the inclinations of the human person.[21] Hence,

Aquinas' delineation of the order of the inclinations is the point of the passage. And yet, the order of the inclinations is clearly not self-evident to all, since Aquinas establishes it by an argument.

Recall that Aquinas' general theory of goodness implies that human inclinations are to be understood by analogy to the inclinations that are displayed by lower creatures (I.60.5). And in fact, in I-II.94.2 that is how Aquinas analyzes the fundamental inclinations of the human person. He argues that the human creature, which stands at the summit of material creation, will necessarily manifest a mode of operation proper to each lower level of creation, in addition to a mode distinctive to itself. This necessity is natural rather than honorific (so to speak); each level in the hierarchy of being manifests a level of perfection that must be maintained as a necessary condition for existing at a higher level (I.60.1). He accordingly interprets the recurring human inclinations in the light of the degree of perfection to be found at each lower level of being, together with what he takes to be distinctive about the human person, in order to discern which inclinations are truly constitutive of human nature, and to put them into a proper ordering with one another. As a result, he comes up with the list of I-II.94.2: We are inclined to *self-preservation* (as all creatures strive to maintain themselves in existence); we are inclined to *reproduce ourselves* through procreation (as all living creatures are); and we are inclined *to live in society* and *to know the truth about God* (as expressions of what is distinctive about us as rational creatures).

We are now in a position to understand the significance of Aquinas' appeal in I-II.94.2 to the existence of naturally known goods. Our common experience of the fundamental inclinations enumerated in that passage provides a widely held starting point for moral reflection. However, the goodness of the objects of these inclinations is not necessarily self-evident to all, and even more important, the significance of these goods for moral behavior is not self-evident even to those who recognize them as goods. In order to determine clearly what the fundamental inclinations are, and to see how they fit together in a good human life, it is necessary to interpret them in the light of an account of goodness in general. That is why the substantive meaning of the human good, which alone can give concrete content to the first principle of practical reason, is not self-evident to all, but only to the wise, who are able to develop the data of common human aspirations into a theory of the human good.

My contention is that Aquinas' account of the fundamental inclinations of the human person, including his account of their proper order to one another, should indeed be taken as his theory of the natural human good. What Aquinas offers in I-II.94.2 is an outline of what a human life should properly look like, what goods it will incorporate, and what relation those goods should have to one another. That is, he offers an inclusive life-plan, which, as we saw in the last section, can serve as the aim by which an individual can bring the diverse activities of his life into a unified whole.

A normative human life, as Aquinas' account of the inclinations indicates, is one in which the goods of all the inclinations (except, in some cases, procreation) are pursued in an orderly way, with the pursuit of the lower inclinations being subordinated to the pursuit of the higher inclinations.[22] Clearly, the natural end of human life, so understood, allows for considerable flexibility in the specific goods that are pursued, as well as allowing for considerable variety in the way in which these pursuits are combined into a complete life. At the same time, because the characteristic inclinations of the human person stand in an intrinsic order to one another, a life that is in accordance with the specific ideal of humanity will possess an intrinsic ordering and unity. In such a life, the pursuit of the lower inclinations will not be conducted at the expense of the higher inclinations, but will be subordinated to the pursuit of the higher inclinations. At the same time, the pursuit of the higher inclinations must not lead to such neglect of the objects of the lower inclinations that the individual becomes incapable of pursuing anything at all.

Hence, in the course of a naturally good human life, an individual will attempt to preserve her health and well-being, but health will not be an end in itself to her. She will eat to live, as the saying goes, and live in order to participate in the life of her family and community, and to attempt to gain some insight into the highest realities. The individual who lives to eat, or to jog, or to dress nicely, will fail to live a naturally good human life because he subordinates the pursuit of higher goods to the pursuit of lower goods, even if he does not actively do anything to cut himself off from the attainment of those goods. Similarly, the person who is attempting to live a naturally good human life will usually have children and raise them, but the point of raising children for her will not be to perpetuate her own family line or to pass on her genes, but to initiate those children into the wider life of their community and its constitutive traditions, and to educate them to be capable of some degree of intellectual contemplation of God. Or she may choose to forgo procreation altogether in order to devote herself more fully to participation in the life of her community or to intellectual contemplation, since procreation is not strictly necessary to the well-being of the individual (cf. II–II.152.2 *ad* 1). In any case, the individual who is pursuing a naturally good human life will participate actively in the life of her community, both drawing on and attempting to contribute to its sustaining traditions, and she will devote herself, to some degree at least, to the intellectual contemplation of God.

This last point raises an important question. It may seem that the inclination to seek the truth about God cannot play a role in natural human perfection, because it cannot be attained by means of unaided human reason but requires the theological virtues of faith, hope, and charity (I-II.3.8; I-II.5.5; I-II.62.1). However, Aquinas makes it clear that even without the assistance of grace, the human person is capable of knowing God as the first and preeminently excellent cause of all things (I.12.12), and can even recognize and love God as the good toward which the universe as a whole tends (I-II.109.3; note, however, that this latter capacity has been seriously vitiated by sin). Hence, we may infer that a naturally good human life will always include some form of intellectual reflection on the ultimate principles of reality, directed toward an ever-fuller appreciation of the first cause of all things. Moreover, we may infer that whatever form this reflection takes for a particular individual, he will pursue his reflections in a community of others who are engaged in similar sorts of reflections, since all intellectual activities presuppose an ongoing tradition of inquiry. This may be why Aquinas links the inclinations to seek the truth about God and to live in community: "In the third mode, an inclination to the good in accordance with reason, which is proper to him, belongs to the human person. Thus the human person has a natural inclination both to know the truth about God, and to live in society" (I-II.94.2). Correlatively, this inclination places an obligation on each society to sustain such traditions in inquiry, and more generally, to provide sufficient means, including some leisure time, for each person to incorporate speculative activity of some sort into her life.

If the analysis of this section is correct, we would expect to find that the norms of morality, as Aquinas sets them forth, take their concrete content from the account of the human good outlined in I-II.94.2. And that is indeed what we do find, as I will attempt to show in subsequent chapters. But before proceeding to Aquinas' substantive moral theory, it will be necessary to consider one final aspect of his account of the human good, namely, his analysis of what it means to say that a particular action is morally good.

The Human Good and Human Action

We are now in a position to ask what characterizes a morally good action, that is, an action that is good in every respect. The natural answer to that question would be that a good action is one that corresponds with the human good, but of course, such an answer would be too general to serve as more than a reminder of the point and subject matter of moral reflection. Hence, in I-II.18–21, Aquinas offers an account of those features in virtue of which an action is or is not in correspondence with the overall human good as that is discerned by the reason. In this section, we will examine that account.

As we noted in the first chapter, Catholic moral theology has traditionally had, and continues to have, considerable interest in the question of how one determines the moral value of particular actions. Interpretations of Aquinas' answer to this question have been very influential in the current debate among Catholic moral theologians over this question. Hence, before turning to my own interpretation of Aquinas' answer to that question, an examination of two of these interpretations that have had considerable impact on the current debate in Catholic moral theology will be in order.

The first of these, developed by Grisez and Finnis, will be familiar from our discussion of the moral theory offered by those authors, for on this point, both claim to be following Aquinas himself.[23] In their reading, Aquinas holds that not only the first principle of practical reason, but the goodness of the objects of the inclinations, are self-evident to all. Furthermore, they read Aquinas as saying that it is also self-evident to all that one should not act in such a way as directly to foreclose the possibility of enjoying a basic good. Therefore, they take Aquinas to be saying that actions are morally good insofar as they are fully open to the goods of the basic inclinations, and morally bad insofar as they involve acting against a basic good in some way.

It will be apparent that I disagree with this reading of Aquinas' analysis of the moral goodness or evil of particular actions. I have already argued for a different reading of I-II.94.2. In addition, it should be noted that according to Aquinas himself, the first principle of morality is the double precept of love of God and neighbor, including oneself (I-II.100.3 *ad* 1; I-II.100.11), which may be formulated negatively as the precept to do evil to no one (I-II.100.3, 5 *ad* 4). As Donagan observes, this principle, while it may often lead to conclusions similar to a prohibition against attacking basic goods, should not be taken to be identical with it.[24] And as we will see in chapter 5, Aquinas defines intrinsically morally evil kinds of actions in terms of the kinds of harm that they do to persons, and not in terms of the basic goods that they attack. Thus, the inclinations enumerated in I-II.94.2 provide the basis for substantive moral prohibitions only indirectly, in that they provide the basis for an account of the human good, which serves in turn to determine what, concretely, counts as harming a person.[25]

There is nonetheless an important element of truth in the claim that the inclinations enumerated in I-II.94.2 provide the content of moral obligation for Aquinas. For in fact, Aquinas holds that it is always moral to act *in accordance with* the inclinations, so long as one does so in a rationally appropriate way. For example, one may use lethal force in self-defense, or engage in sexual intercourse for the purpose of procreation (II-II.64.7; II-II.153.2). In other words, insofar as they do function as a direct basis for moral norms, the inclinations are fundamentally permissive in their effect. Only secondarily do they serve to ground prohibitions. Moreover, one's pursuit of the fundamental inclinations cannot licitly be impeded by other persons. No one can legitimately compel another either to marry or to remain celibate, for example (II-II.104.5). Because they mark out what is fundamental to human life, the inclinations indicate the parameters of individual freedom, which neither other individuals nor the state should cross (except when an individual forfeits certain of his claims on the community by serious maleficence).

A second reading of Aquinas' account of goodness in action was developed by Janssens in an influential article in 1972.[26] According to this interpretation, Aquinas holds that the moral goodness or evil of an action is determined solely by the end, that is, the ultimate intention toward which the agent acts. Correlatively, the proper definition of the action from the standpoint of moral reflection is determined by the end of the agent, since the specific kind of an action is determined in part by its moral goodness or otherwise. Hence, Janssens argues, the object of the action, that aspect of it that could be described without reference to the agent's specific intentions, does not enter into the formal description of the action or serve to determine its moral value, but is, as it were, the matter that is informed by the agent's intention. It might be objected that on this reading, Aquinas' moral theory implies subjectivism, but Janssens argues that that is not so, because the agent's end will be objectively either good or evil. If the agent intends to gratify a sinful passion, for example, her action will be evil, even if what she does is objectively good. For example, the action of a woman who gives alms out of vainglory is formally a sinful act of vainglory, even though the agent accomplishes a nonmoral good.

The difficulty with Janssens' reading is that Aquinas explicitly contradicts his claim that the object of an action does not enter into its proper description or its moral evaluation. To the contrary, Aquinas asserts that the object of an action is the first determinate of its specific kind and its moral goodness or evil. Moreover, his examples make it clear that by "the object of an action" he is referring to an aspect of the action that can be described without reference to the agent's ultimate intention in so acting (I-II.18.2; his examples are, "to make use of what is one's own" and "to take what belongs to another"). It is true that the moral goodness or evil of an action, and therefore its proper moral definition, may *also* be determined by the agent's intention, as Janssens points out (I-II.18.4). Might we not conclude that the object of the action is itself determined by the agent's intention? Aquinas himself raises this question, and answers it by drawing a distinction (II-II.18.7):

> The object of an exterior action can be related in two ways to the end of the will: In one way, it can be directed in itself to that end, as for example, to fight well is in itself directed to the end of attaining victory; in the other way, it can be directed accidentally toward that end, as for example, to take what is another's is accidentally directed toward the end of giving alms.

He goes on to argue that in the former case, the specific kind of the action is determined first of all by the end of the agent, and then by the object as a further specification (and so, the particular action suggested by his example might be described as attaining victory by fighting well, in contrast to attaining victory by, say, tricking the enemy). But in the latter case, neither the species of the action set by the agent's end nor the species of the action set by the object of the action is subordinated to the other. In a case of this sort, the individual action falls under two disparate specific kinds (I-II.18.7). Therefore, Aquinas goes on to say, we say that the person who commits a theft in order to commit adultery is guilty of a twofold malice in one action (cf. I-II.18.4 *ad* 3; I-II.20.2). The upshot of this article is clear: While Aquinas holds that the end of the agent is one of the aspects of an action that can determine its proper description, from a moral point of view, it is only one of the aspects of an action that can be so determinative.

In fact, Aquinas holds that the goodness or evil of an action depends on four aspects of the action, which may or may not be dependent on one another in a particular action (I-II.18.4). First of all, any action is good in the sense that any existing thing is good, "because as much as it has of action and being, so much it has of goodness" (I-II.18.4; cf. I-II.18.1). But like any other existing thing, an action can fail to be good simply speaking, if it lacks some of its proper perfections, and in the case of an action, this is equivalent to being morally evil. Specifically, if an action is to be morally good, it must be directed toward a good object, in appropriate circumstances, by an agent who is acting for a good end. An action that is deficient in any one of these respects will not be good simply, that is, will be a morally evil action.

Although Janssens' reading of Aquinas must be rejected, it none-theless calls attention to an important question. If the object of an action is an independent determinate of the species of the action, which cannot be assimilated to circumstances or to the end for which the agent acts, then how is this object itself determined? Aquinas answers that the object of an action is determined by its conformity, or otherwise, to the order of reason (I-II.18.8). And since it is proper to the rational creature to direct himself to his specific perfection by means of his reason, this answer is equivalent to saying that the object of an action is determined by its conformity to, or opposition to, the human good. Moreover, it must be noted that the human good, in this context, should be taken to include the good of the whole community, since the individual's attainment of his own good depends in part on his good relation with his community (II-II.47.10 *ad* 2). Hence, the object of an action is determined by ascertaining the way in which an action of this sort either promotes or hinders the well-being of individuals and the community.

At the same time, it is true that a particular action cannot be evaluated on the basis of its object alone. We must also take account of the end for which the agent acts, and the circumstances of the action, in order to evaluate an action fully. (This is true even of an intrinsically evil action, that is, an action that has as its object some-thing that is contrary to the order of reason. While such an action can be judged to be morally evil simply on the basis of its object, the degree and quality of its evil will depend also on circumstances and on the end for which the agent acted [see I-II.18.7, 10, 11].) Moreover, a fuller consideration of the circumstances and end of a particular action may lead us to modify or correct our assessment of its object. As we have seen, the end for which the agent acts may or may not subsume the object of the action in determining the proper descrip-tion of the individual action, depending on whether or not the object of the action has an intrinsic relation to the attainment of the agent's end. Furthermore, the circumstances of an action may introduce a new character of harm or beneficence, thereby changing the defini-tion of the action. Hence, what seemed at first to be an accidental circumstance may be assimilated into the object of an action as part of its proper description (I-II.18.10, 11).

If these distinctions seem confusing, it may be helpful to recast them in terms of the levels of description of an action.[27] Aquinas is well aware that an action may admit of more than one description, each of which is correct from a certain point of view. Indeed, his theory of action implies that we must be able to describe any putative action from more than one point of view, if we are to describe it as an action at all. For as we saw in the first section of this chapter, an action must necessarily be intelligible in terms of some good that the agent seeks to attain or preserve, and must therefore admit of description in terms of that good. But at the same time, an action may be harmful to others, or even in some respect to the agent herself, and Aquinas assumes that certain kinds of harmfulness are always relevant to a full description of an action, even when they do not render it morally evil.[28] Hence, any action, on Aquinas' account, will admit of different levels of description, in accordance with different ways of relating the nonmoral goods and evils that it effects to the wider contexts of individual and communal well-being.

On the first level, an action may be described in any terms that serve to delimit a particular item of behavior, without necessarily giving rise to a moral evaluation. The most satisfactory sort of description on this level would be one that rendered the action intelligible in terms of the nonmoral good that it accomplishes (toward which the agent's will may be presumed to be directed). The most obvious nonmoral goods give rise to natural (that is, nonmoral) species of actions, for example, sexual intercourse (I-II.18.5 *ad* 3). It is also possible to describe a putative action at this level in terms that do not point to any particular good, for example, picking up straws (I-II.18.8), or that indicate that the action involves an important kind of harm, for example, killing a human being (I-II.19.10). However, putative actions described in this way must be redescribable in terms of their orientation toward some good, if they are to count as actions at all. If the good that a particular seeming action obtains is very obscure, it may be necessary to construct an elaborate narrative accounting for some good that the agent hopes to attain or preserve, if we are to consider this particular item of behavior to be a true action.[29]

A description of an action at this level, which Aquinas refers to as the natural species of the action (I-II.1.3 *ad* 3), is not incorrect or even necessarily incomplete when taken in reference to a specific purpose. But this sort of description is not sufficient for the purpose of moral evaluation, which calls for an action to be described and evaluated in terms of its congruity or otherwise with the overall true human good. In order to describe an action from a moral point of view, it is necessary to redescribe it, considered as falling into a natural generic kind of action, since moral goodness and evil are specifying differences for actions. That is, if one action is morally good, and the other is morally evil, they necessarily belong to different moral species of actions, even though they may belong to the same natural species of actions. It is not the case that adultery and marital intercourse are simply two variants, one illicit and one permissible, of the same kind of action. Rather, adultery and marital intercourse are two different kinds of action, described from the moral point of view, even though they could be redescribed as the same kind of action from a natural, that is to say a nonmoral, point of view (I-II.18.5 *ad* 3). Hence, in order to offer a correct description of an action from a moral point of view, it is necessary to redescribe it, and while this redescription will generally assimilate the natural description of the act, it will not simply add a nonessential qualification to it.

How, then, is this redescription to proceed? We have already remarked that in order to describe an action correctly from a moral point of view, it will be necessary to describe it from the point of view of the overall human good. But at this point, we must introduce another distinction. For while the ultimate good of each individual necessarily includes a good relationship to a well-ordered community, nonetheless, that good relationship presupposes that the individual is able to maintain a good order in his own character and life. In order to act in concert with others, and even to seek knowledge of the highest things, the individual must be able to sustain a course of activity, and that capacity presupposes that he is able to integrate his passions into a unified character, out of which he consistently pursues the ultimate goal of happiness. Hence, it is legitimate and even necessary, from a moral point of view, to describe and evaluate actions in terms of what they both express and effect in the character of the individual agent. Is this the sort of action that would typically proceed from a person whose passions are integrated into a unified personality, or does it seem to reflect some disharmony between the agent's overall goals and his immediate desires or aversions? At this level, an action is described in terms of the affective virtues of temperance and fortitude. That is, it is described as an act of temperance or fortitude, or of one of the virtues associated with these two, or it is described as an act of one of the correlative vices.

While every action ultimately affects the community as a whole, there are many sorts of actions that immediately affect the agent alone, at least in most circumstances, for example, eating, drinking, and sleeping. There may be no practical need to further redescribe the object of actions of this sort in terms of their effect on the community, although it would always be possible to do so. But an action that directly affects other persons must always be described in terms of its effect on the community as a whole, if it is to be described adequately from the standpoint of moral evaluations. That is, the action must be described in terms of the virtue of justice, to which are assimilated all moral considerations involving other persons and even God. From the standpoint of justice, an action is described in terms either of the obligation or claim that it fulfills (including one's own claims over against others) or the sort of harm that it produces. Because Aquinas holds that some (not all) kinds of harms are never justifiable, he holds that some kinds of actions are morally intrinsically evil in their object and may therefore never be justified. (But as we shall see in chapter 5, it is necessary to use some care to determine exactly which kinds of harms fall within the scope of these absolute prohibitions.)

Do we now have a complete description of an action? If we have established that a particular action has as its object a kind of harm that is always prohibited, we have described the action sufficiently to establish that it is morally wrong, but even in that case, we do not have a complete description of the action from a moral point of view. Much less is a description of the object of an action sufficient to describe the action completely, if the object of the action is good or neutral from the moral standpoint. In order for an action to be morally good without qualification, the end for which the agent acts must also be good, and must therefore be described in terms of the ideals of temperance, fortitude, and justice. Moreover, the agent must pay attention to the particular situation in which she must live out these ideals, in order to choose the concrete actions that will truly instantiate them. (For example, a woman who gives a basket of food to her neighbor, simply out of the goodness of her heart, may still act in a blameworthy way if she presents the neighbor with the basket in front of his little daughter, thus shaming him in his daughter's eyes as someone who has to take charity.) At this point, our description of the action will introduce the norms of yet another virtue, namely the virtue of prudence, which attends to the particulars of a situation in order best to accomplish the good that is sought. Only when we have evaluated an action in accordance with the norms of prudence do we have a complete description of this particular action on which to base a moral evaluation.

It will be apparent that in the process of determining how we are to evaluate an action, we have begun to develop the outline of a theory of the virtues. And that outcome is what we should have expected, since as we will see in the next chapter, it is impossible to separate the moral evaluation of actions from an account of the virtues, or conversely, to describe a virtue without saying what sorts of actions are typical of that virtue. But at the same time, Aquinas' theory of the virtues goes beyond his analysis of the morality of actions—it goes on to include an account of what it means to be a good agent. In the next chapter, we will begin to examine that account.

4

The Affective Virtues

If the analysis of Aquinas' understanding of the goodness of actions developed at the end of the last chapter is correct, then we are on the way to an understanding of his theory of morality. But so far, we are only on the way. Guidelines for determining the kinds of actions that are in accordance with the true human good are not in themselves sufficient to translate a concept of the human good into substantive moral guidance. And why not? Because a humanly good life, unlike some of the other kinds of aims for which we act, cannot be attained solely by setting ourselves to perform determinate actions of the correct kinds, while avoiding other kinds of actions. If we are to live a humanly good life, we must maintain a course of activity of a certain sort over time, indeed, over the course of our whole lives. And while that course of activity will include discrete actions, and will also be characterized by the absence of other sorts of discrete actions, it will not be possible to describe it in those terms alone. Much less will we be able to carry out such a course of activity solely by setting ourselves to choose correct actions and to avoid incorrect actions, over and over again. In order to appreciate the distinction between a discrete action and a course of activity, it may be helpful to compare two sorts of goal-directed behavior, one of which can readily be broken down into discrete actions, and one which does not lend itself so readily to such analysis.

Consider first of all what is involved in baking a cake. In order to produce a perfectly adequate cake, it is only necessary to follow the guidelines on the back of one's box of cake mix, which will call for the performance of a few clearly delineated actions: Turn on the oven to 350 degrees. Open the box. Pour contents into a bowl. Break two eggs into a cup. Add eggs and half a cup of water to mix. Stir.

Grease a pan. Pour batter into pan. Bake for thirty minutes. If these actions are carried out in the right sequence, and the agent avoids doing any of the (generally well-known) things that are not conducive to the well-being of cakes, such as opening the oven door too soon, *voilà!* he has baked a cake.

On the other hand, if one wants to write a book, there is no similar recipe that the erstwhile author can employ to arrive infallibly at her goal. There are some kinds of actions that she must perform if she is to write a book at all. For example, she must either write, or make some other permanent symbolic record of her thoughts, directly (typing, reading the words into a tape recorder) or through an intermediary (dictating them). Moreover, there are some sorts of actions which are likely to be conducive to the attainment of her goal, for example, resolving to write a little every day, and other kinds of actions that would almost certainly be inimical to the attainment of that goal, for example, resolving to read everything on a large subject before ever beginning to write about it. But beyond truisms and very general guidelines like these, there is no definite formula of discrete actions for writing a book, as there is for baking a cake.

Moreover, what the agent does in the course of writing a book cannot readily be broken down into discrete actions. It is possible to count "writing this book" as *one* action for some purposes (for example, determining whether a contract to write a book has been fulfilled), but clearly, this is not the sort of thing that we ordinarily have in mind when we speak of performing a single action. What then *are* the discrete actions that go into writing a book? This question is not so easy to answer. Writing (or one of its equivalents) is likely to be the first answer that comes to mind. But when an author sits and writes for a couple of hours, is that to count as one action, or are we to count the writing of each word as a separate action, or perhaps each penstroke? When we attempt to characterize the many sorts of things that a writer really does, for example, staring into space, pacing, getting coffee, reading, scribbling notes, thinking, reconsidering, and more staring into space, it becomes still more difficult to identify the point at which one discrete action leaves off and another one begins.

It would be a mistake to assume that there must be some one correct description of the actions that an author performs, by which the above questions could be answered definitively. As we saw in the last chapter, actions are redescribable, and given our purposes, we might with equal validity describe what an author does as a single action ("writing a book"), or as a multitude of very brief individual actions (if for some reason we chose to count each penstroke as a separate action), or as anything in between. For the same reason, it would be a mistake to draw the line between baking a cake and writing a book too sharply. Just as the latter can be broken up into distinct actions, so the former could, for some purposes, be described as a continuous activity. Nonetheless, there does seem to be at least a relative difference between goal-directed behaviors that follow a definite formula (like baking cakes) and those that do not (like writing books). The former lend themselves readily to description in terms of a sequence of discrete actions, whereas the latter are more difficult to describe in those terms, and would not usually be so described except from some specialized standpoint. That is, a goal-directed activity of the latter sort is more naturally described as sustaining a course of activity directed toward a goal, rather than as performing a number of discrete actions directed toward a goal.[1]

It should be clear that the effort to lead a humanly good life is an example of the latter sort of goal-directed behavior. Indeed, this effort is an exemplary example of a kind of behavior that is best characterized as sustaining a course of activity, rather than performing a series of discrete actions. Of course, we do perform discrete actions of great moral significance in the course of attempting to live a humanly good life, or failing to do so. But a life that is humanly good without qualification cannot be characterized as simply the sum of morally praiseworthy discrete actions. Rather, such a life will be good in its entirety, including the individual's reactions and his overall style of living as well as his particular acts.

How, then, are we to sustain a course of activity, and monitor our reactions to events, in such a way as to achieve a morally good life? It would seem that in order to do so, it would be necessary to attend consciously to one's overall aim at every moment, so as to determine one's actions and reactions accordingly. But the claim that we ought to try to live our lives at this level of intentionality all the time appears to be very implausible. Wouldn't that sort of program for living destroy all of the spontaneity and joy of life, even if it were possible to carry it out?

Aquinas is aware of this problem, as we see in his response to the question raised at I-II.1.6, "Whether all things that the human person wills, he wills on account of a final end?" At I-II.1.6 *obj.* 3, he raises the objection that whoever is acting for a goal must be thinking of that goal, whereas the human person does not always think of the last end in all that she desires or does. In his response to this objection, he simply observes that it is not necessary to be thinking consciously of one's goal at every moment in order to be directing one's actions toward it (I-II.1.6 *ad* 3). For example, he adds, it is possible to make a journey without thinking of one's destination at every step. And this answer would seem to be persuasive, as far as it goes. We are all familiar with the experience of undertaking some activity that is familiar to us, even something very complex, and doing it automatically, so to speak.

Nonetheless, Aquinas' answer does not go as far as we would like. It still leaves us with the question, "How do we direct our activities toward the goal of living a humanly good life, even when we are not explicitly thinking of it?"

The answer to this question is implied in Aquinas' treatment of the moral virtues, which shape the human agent as a desiring creature in such a way that he spontaneously desires and seeks what is in accordance with the truly good life that he is trying to lead (I-II.55.4). And because human desire is grounded in both subrational passions of concupiscence and aversion, and the distinctively rational appetite—that is to say, the will—for what is apprehended by the mind as good, distinct moral virtues are needed to rectify these different aspects of human desire (I-II.56.4, 6; strictly speaking, prudence is an intellectual virtue, although there can be no moral virtue without it [I-II.57.4, 5; I-II.58.4]). Justice and the theological virtues orient the will toward goods that transcend the individual, without which orientation she could not achieve even her true individual good. Hence, these virtues direct her particular choices in such a way that she acts in accordance with her own good and the wider goods that she seeks (I-II.56.5; I-II.60.3).

In particular, the affective virtues of fortitude and temperance are both possible and necessary because of the special character of the passions that they rectify (namely, fear, desire, and anger [I-II.59.2, 4, 5; I-II.60.1]). What characterizes these passions is that they are not rational in the full sense, and yet they have a cognitive component that is amenable to rational direction. For example, fear is a visceral response, so to speak, to what is perceived to be harmful, and for that very reason it is possible to modify one's emotional responses so as not to fear what is not really harmful, given one's overall plan of life. The formation of the affective virtues consists precisely in the reeducation of one's emotional responses in this way. Hence, to the extent that this process has been successfully carried out, the individual's immediate emotional responses, his likes and dislikes, will accord with what his more considered rational judgments on the matter would be. And that is precisely why the truly virtuous person does not require constant conscious deliberation on his final end in order to act in accordance with it. His immediate responses will reliably direct him to act appropriately, at least in normal circumstances. The rest of us, who are at best on the way toward true virtue, cannot trust our immediate responses so completely. And yet, even those of us who are still only imperfectly virtuous will find ourselves responding appropriately at least some of the time.

If this line of analysis is correct, we can readily see why an account of virtue and the virtues should be so important to Aquinas' theory of morality that he structures his discussions of substantive matters in the *Secunda Secundae* around the framework of an analysis of the cardinal and theological virtues. It is true that in doing so, he is making use of traditional lists of the virtues, but he does not simply repeat or expand upon traditional material. Rather, as Otto Pesch points out, he combines the previously disparate frameworks of the cardinal and theological virtues into one unified framework that reflects his own overall theory of morality.[2] His careful reformulation of the traditions concerning the virtues reflects the importance that the notion of the virtues has for him as a means of providing a bridge between his understanding of the natural (and supernatural) human good, and the concrete ways in which persons attain their specific perfection as human beings.

In this chapter, we will begin our examination of Aquinas' theory of the virtues, focusing first on his general idea of what a virtue is, and then on his treatment of temperance and fortitude. Justice and prudence raise special issues that call for more detailed examination in subsequent chapters. When that examination has been completed, we will be in a position to understand his treatment of the traditional doctrine that some virtues are cardinal virtues.

The Concept of Virtue and Concepts of the Virtues

As we saw in the first chapter, the general topic of the virtues has become an important subject for Christian ethics, due in large part to Hauerwas' work. It will be apparent by now that Aquinas' own theory of the virtues is very different from Hauerwas' theory, if only because Aquinas, unlike Hauerwas, grounds his theory of the virtues in a general theory of goodness and the human good. For this reason, it would be misleading to assume that the dichotomies between virtue theory and other sorts of moral theories that Hauerwas emphasizes are also present in Aquinas' work.

A case in point is provided by the sharp distinction that Hauerwas draws between a theory that sees morality as primarily a matter of virtues, and a theory that emphasizes moral rules instead. On

Hauerwas' view, moral rules are precisely defined, rigid, and apply mostly to quandaries, whereas virtues are not precisely defined, are flexible, and apply to the whole of life. For this reason, he proposes a theory of virtues as an alternative to rule-oriented accounts of the moral life, although he admits that moral rules do have a subordinate place to play in the moral life.[3]

Whatever the merits of this sort of appeal to a theory of the virtues as an alternative to a theory of moral rules, it would be a mistake to turn to Aquinas for an early example of a moral theorist who offers a theory of virtues *rather than* a theory of rules. If one means by a morality of rules a theory of morality according to which certain concrete kinds of actions are identified as praiseworthy or blameworthy, then Aquinas certainly espouses a morality of rules as well as a morality of virtues. Indeed, his analysis of the moral value of actions and his analysis of the virtues fit together as two parts of one comprehensive theory of morality. Morally good kinds of actions are conceptually linked to the virtues, in that certain determinate kinds of actions are characteristic of particular virtues and tend to promote them in the individual (although any determinate kind of good action can also be done by one who has no trace of the corresponding virtue). For this reason, we cannot form concepts of particular virtues without some idea of the kinds of actions that correspond to those virtues, even though it is also true that a virtue cannot adequately be understood only as the tendency or capacity to perform a certain kind of action.

The connection between concepts of virtues and concepts of particular kinds of actions is obscured in many contemporary discussions by the relative lack of attention given there to the question of how we arrive at our notions of particular kinds of virtues.[4] Hence, this link may be more evident if we work through the notion of a particular virtue, asking what it is that we know when we know what it is to be virtuous in this particular way.

Let us, then, take the example of *gentleness.* We all know, more or less, what it means to be gentle, and we can usually recognize a gentle person, a gentle voice, a gentle action or manner or way of doing something. Yet just what is it that we know, when we know what gentleness is? Or if this question seems to be too general for a starting point, consider another one: Suppose that we have been asked to explain gentleness to someone who knows that it is a trait of character that we consider to be desirable, but not much else (a foreigner learning English, perhaps). How would we go about it?

Of course, we could begin by quoting a dictionary, or devising a verbal definition of our own. But this approach is likely to be unsatisfactory. At best, it will give our interlocutor only a very abstract notion of gentleness. We will have greater success if instead of or in addition to citing a verbal definition, we give examples of people and things that are gentle: gentle Anna, a gentle pony, gentle breezes, and so on. But our interlocutor may still ask what it is about Anna, the pony, and the breezes that justifies describing them as gentle. In order to answer this question, we will need to give examples of what Anna, the pony, and the breezes *do.* And in so doing, we will describe actions that exemplify gentleness, in short, gentle actions. This brings us to our first observation on what is involved in developing a concept of a particular virtue: Such a concept will be tied to a notion of a certain kind of action in such a way that our concept of a particular virtue will be inseparable from the concept of an action typical of that virtue.

But are matters really that simple? It might seem that I have just made a rather silly mistake, assuming falsely that we do indeed have one simple idea of what a gentle action (for example) is. But surely matters are more complex than that. In fact, we carry around with us a whole range of instances of gentle actions and things which may have little in common, except that they are all gentle. To consider Anna alone: We may think of her washing her baby, of her scolding her children in a particular reticent way, of the way she speaks to her employer and fellow-workers, of her demeanor when she had to tell a friend that his sister had died, and so on. In other words, our ability to recognize gentle actions does not depend on a capacity to identify some trait or quality of gentleness that they supposedly all have in common. It would appear that Wittgenstein is right: We just pick out certain kinds of actions as falling under this description, without being able to point to some one thing that they all have in common and in virtue of which they fall under this common description.[5]

I will argue that there is indeed a basis, beyond linguistic convention, for our classification of certain things as gentle, but our present line of criticism serves the most important purpose of identifying what that basis is *not*. It does not lie in some supposed quality or characteristic of gentleness that can be found in every act or thing that is gentle, in just the way that whiteness can be found in everything that is white. Rather, "gentle" is a formal description by which any number of things, having perhaps no one specific concrete trait in common, can be classified together as exemplifying one formal notion.[6]

In what, then, does this formal notion consist? I will suggest that as a formal notion, the concept of gentleness cannot be identified adequately except by giving some account of how this notion is grounded in recurring features of our common experience. More specifically, the notion of a gentle action, which is central to the concept of gentleness, will turn out to be dependent on a sense of recurrent contexts in which we are faced with a choice of acting or not acting, or else of acting in this or that particular way.

What sort of recurring context gives meaning and point to the concept of gentleness? It would seem that this notion is inseparably connected with situations in which it is possible to do damage in some way by our manner of acting. For example, in an emotionally charged situation, a clumsy or thoughtless word can give great pain, whereas a gentle word is spoken in such a way as not to hurt, or at least not to hurt more than is strictly necessary. When one person must touch another, with all the vulnerability that such an action implies, it is all too easy to insult or hurt if the manner of one's touching is rough or careless, whereas a gentle touch is so delicate as not to do damage to the other. Hence, we speak of a gentle medical examination, gentle sexual contact, even a gentle spanking. Similarly, because the tone of one's voice may hurt the ears, the harshness of colors may hurt the eyes, and the strength of one's perfume may offend the nose, we speak of a gentle voice, gentle colors, or even of a gentle perfume.

Note that in forming the concept of gentleness, we correlatively shape the concepts of the contrary vice, or rather, vices, since, as with most of the virtues, the situations calling for gentleness allow for more than one sort of failure. Hence, gentleness as a desirable way of acting is associated with roughness, harshness, and abruptness, to name three of its most obvious correlative vices.

So far, we have focused on the task of identifying the boundaries of gentleness as a concept applying to particular actions, because without some notion of what counts as a gentle action, we would find it impossible to form a concept of gentleness at all. But at the same time, it will be apparent that the concept of gentleness, as applied to a person, will include more than a notion of gentleness sufficient to deal with particular actions. For a gentle act alone does not a gentle person make. In a particular instance, a person may be just pretending to be gentle, to name only one possibility. In order to expand the notion of gentleness as it applies to actions into a full concept of a virtue, it is necessary to add some account of what gentleness looks like as a pattern of behavior which characterizes a person's activities over time. (And the same observation applies to our concepts of particular vices.)

And how are we to spell out what it means to exhibit gentleness as a pattern of behavior? It is not enough to think of someone performing a succession of gentle actions, since each individual action might conceivably be feigned, or performed unwillingly. In order to meet our sense of what it is to be a gentle person, the concept of gentleness must incorporate two further elements. First, this notion must incorporate some assessments of reactions as well as actions. The person whose immediate response is to strike out, to speak harshly, to move roughly, can hardly be called a gentle person—*even if* she always manages to act, contrary to her impulses, in a gentle manner. We might well say that she is trying to become a gentle person, or else, if we put a different construction on her motives, that she is pretending to be a gentle person. But both of these conditions are very different from actually *being* a gentle person. Second, the notion of gentleness must be expanded to include some idea of what the life of a gentle person looks like over time. If gentleness is a trait of persons, then we must have a sense of how it is displayed in the patterns of activity that go to make up a human life, and we must also have some sense of the context of circumstances and motives by which we can distinguish true gentleness from its counterparts. For this reason, Hauerwas is right to insist that if we are to have a satisfactory concept of a particular virtue, we must be able to tell stories about persons whose lives exemplify that virtue.[7]

There is one further point to be made about concepts of individual virtues; this point will prove to be essential to understanding Aquinas' account of the cardinal virtues. Concepts of particular virtues remain somewhat indeterminate, even after we have given the fullest possible account of them in the terms sketched above. In other words, notions of particular virtues cannot be explicated fully on their own terms.

Consider once again the concept of gentleness as it applies simply to an action, and is accordingly correlated with concepts of different sorts of failures to act well. At first glance, it would seem that the various sorts of failures to act gently can be characterized straightforwardly enough. But on closer examination, it becomes apparent that our ideas of success and failure in situations calling for gentleness are more complex. For in addition to true gentleness and the obvious kinds of failures to be gentle, for example, harshness, we also recognize a way of failing in action through a sort of counterfeit gentleness. For example, what might seem at first to be a gentle action in Anna may prove, on further reflection, to be an excessively timid, or soft, or obsequious action on her part. She speaks to and touches her husband in a certain way because secretly, and without good reason, she is afraid of him; she hardly ever disciplines her little boy because she cannot bear to cause him even momentary pain; and she speaks mildly to her overbearing boss because she is afraid of losing her job, even though she knows that she could easily get another one that would be just as good. In cases like these, what we have are counterfeits of gentleness, distinguished from the real thing by a consideration of the motives and circumstances of the action.

But now consider a further case. Suppose that Anna, who, let us say, is a nurse, is asked by her patient, an ill old man, how sick his daughter really is. Let us assume that his daughter is very sick indeed, and the truth about her condition would make him very unhappy, and might slow down his own recovery. However, it would not kill him, or even do him lasting harm. All the same, Anna does not wish to give him even transitory pain, when he is already suffering so much. So she tells him less than the truth. His daughter is sick, she says, but not *very* sick. In fact, today she looked almost well. Is this an instance of true gentleness, or of something else, say, of squeamish dishonesty?

In order to answer this kind of question, it is necessary to ask further whether the behavior in question is directed toward genuinely good ends, and otherwise corresponds to the principles set by a wider context of moral beliefs. In this specific case, we cannot say whether Anna's response to her patient was an instance of true gentleness or not, until we have established whether justice toward her patient demands that he be told the truth, however unpleasant, or requires that he be protected from certain harsh realities. What this indicates is that concepts of at least some of the virtues are open-ended, in the sense that their content is incomplete unless filled in with principles taken from more comprehensive moral concepts.

So far, we have located four elements that go to make up a concept of a particular virtue: (1) a notion of a particular kind of action that is characteristic of the virtue (although not necessarily linked with it in every instance), which will include some idea of the kind of context in which this sort of action would be appropriate; (2) some idea of kinds of actions that are characteristically failures to act well, in the context that provides the setting for the virtue in question; (3) some idea of what it would mean, concretely, for a person to display this virtue through his actions and reactions over a substantial period of time; and finally, (4) some guidelines for distinguishing true from false exemplifications of the virtue in question, guidelines derived from a higher principle that will enable us to say whether in a particular instance this putative virtue is truly being exercised in such a way as to promote the true good of the human person. What indication do we have that Aquinas' theory of the virtues presupposes this line of analysis?

There are two sorts of indications that the analysis of the concept of a particular virtue developed in this section is in accordance with Aquinas' theory of the virtues. The first kind is found in his explicit remarks on the virtues. Hence, we read first of all that virtue is a habit: "The rational powers, which are proper to the human person, are not determined to one [particular kind of action], but are indeterminately open to many. These powers are determined to their particular actions by means of habits, as has been shown above (I-II.49.4). And therefore, human virtues are habits" (I-II.55.1). That is, they are enduring traits of character which incline the agent to act in one characteristic way rather than another. Furthermore, a virtue is always a good quality: "A virtue implies the perfection of a power. . . . Now, it is necessary that the end of which any power is capable is good, because every evil implies a certain defect, and hence Dionysius says . . . that every evil is a weakness. For this reason, it is necessary that the virtue of anything be said to be ordained to good. Hence, human virtue, which is an operative habit, is a good habit, and is productive of the good" (I-II.55.3). And so, Aquinas accepts (with minor qualifications) the definition of virtue derived from Augustine's writings: "Virtue is a good quality of the mind, by which we live righteously, of which no one can make bad use, which God brings about in us, without us," adding that the last clause ("which God brings about in us, without us") applies only to the infused virtues (I-II.55.4). Aquinas' remarks in this question suggest that he would at least agree that a virtue is a good quality of the person which is characterized by actions of a certain kind, and his subsequent remarks confirm that reading: "For since every virtue is a habit which is a principle of a good act, it is necessary that a virtue be defined through the good act concerning the proper matter of the virtue" (II-II.58.1).

A second and fuller indication that Aquinas' understanding of the virtues follows the lines laid out in this section may be found in an examination of the way in which he actually does analyze particular virtues. Accordingly, in the next section, we will look at Aquinas' treatment of the two cardinal virtues that concern the passions, namely temperance and fortitude.

Temperance and Fortitude

The best way to understand Aquinas' treatment of a particular virtue is to attempt to think through our notions of that virtue with him. In this way, we are more likely to capture the give-and-take between theoretical dicta and practical insights that characterizes his discussions of the virtues than we would be if we pursued a more strictly expository method. Therefore, rather than going directly to what Aquinas says about temperance and fortitude, let us begin by asking what comes to mind when we think of the concepts of temperance and fortitude. These, the standard English translations of *temperantia* and *fortitudine,* may have a misleadingly old-fashioned ring, and so it may be helpful to substitute modern equivalents, for example, self-restraint and courage, to see what kinds of action and demeanor come to mind. It does not matter, at this stage, that our modern equivalents are not likely to capture the exact meanings that *temperantia* and *fortitudine* have for Aquinas. What *does* matter is that we are sure to have at least rough equivalents of these concepts in our working moral vocabulary, whoever we are, by which we can recognize at least some instances of something like *temperantia* and *fortitudine.* It is on just such a mass of half-formed intuitions that Aquinas' own moral analysis depends.

And how can we be so sure that whoever Aquinas' interlocutors may be, they will have at least rough equivalents of temperance and fortitude? We are so assured because these virtues concern two of the ubiquitous situations of human life—namely, the experience of feeling a strong desire that tempts one away from one's sense of right or overall goals, and the experience of feeling a strong fear or aversion that tempts one in the same way (cf. I-II.60.4, 5).[8] As long as people feel that they must struggle with urges for more food and drink than is good for them, sexual pleasure with other people's husbands or wives, and fears that would lead them away from the bold activities that prudence or duty sometimes demands, there will be a place for some concepts roughly equivalent to temperance and fortitude. That is why these concepts seem to appear in some form in every culture.

Hence, it is easy enough to recognize the recurrent situations of human life that form the contexts for our notions of temperance and fortitude, and to formulate a first working definition of these terms on that basis. Let us say, then, that temperance and fortitude are qualities of character which are characterized by actions that exhibit self-control in situations in which one is tempted by desires (in the case of temperance) or aversion, especially fear (with reference to fortitude), to act contrary to one's overall aims or commitments. This preliminary definition is not dissimilar to some of Aquinas' own remarks on fortitude and temperance. For example, we read that "fortitude concerns fear and audacity, in that it restrains fear and moderates audacity" (II-II.123.3), and "Desire implies a certain impulse of the appetite toward what is desirable, which appetite lacks a bridle; which [function] pertains to temperance" (II-II.141.3 *ad* 2;

in addition, see I-II.61.2; II-II.123.1, 2; II-II.141.1-3). But as soon as this working definition is suggested, it immediately raises a question: Is self-control really the best way to characterize these virtues, either for Aquinas, or for ourselves?

Even though Aquinas does sometimes seem to speak as if the affective virtues are equivalent to self-control, nonetheless, he does follow Aristotle in distinguishing between the true virtues of temperance and fortitude, on the one hand, and self-control (*continentia*, often rendered "continence") or skill in facing dangerous situations, on the other (II-II.155.1; II-II.123.1 *ad* 2).[9] But this distinction itself depends on moving to the next stage in the construction of more adequate concepts of these virtues. For at first glance, our concepts of both of these virtues do seem to find their contexts in situations in which persons are called upon to exercise self-control. Or perhaps it would be better to say that in these sorts of situations, the ordinary person must exercise self-control, or she will give in to the cheerful but impractical imperative, "If it feels good, do it!" Nonetheless, we may well still ask: Is self-control really the ideal response to these kinds of situations?

The answer that Aquinas gives to this question is that it is not. It would be better, in these sorts of situations, if one's immediate responses were such that no self-control is necessary: "According to others, continence is that by which a person resists disordered desires, which are vehement in him. . . . Understood in this way, continence has something of the character of virtue, namely, insofar as the reason [of the continent person] stands firm against the passions, so as not to be led by them. However, continence does not attain the perfect character of moral virtue, according to which even the sensitive appetite is subordinated to the reason, so that vehement passions contrary to reason do not arise in it" (II-II.155.1; cf. I-II.58.3; II-II.53.5; II-II.141.3 *ad* 3). While I am to be commended for refusing a third brownie, even though I desperately want it, nonetheless it would be better and more praiseworthy if I did not desire a third (or possibly a second or even a first) brownie at all. In the former case, my act displays continence, which is good, but in the latter case, it displays the far more valuable and praiseworthy quality of temperance.

Many of us would take issue with Aquinas at this point. In our culture, there is a widespread sense that in matters of morality, effort counts for a great deal. Hence, we often assume that the temperate and brave actions of a congenital libertine and coward are worth more, morally, than the same actions performed by someone who is naturally or habitually abstemious and brave. Neither view is obviously correct or wrong. What matters most for us at this point is that each view depends on a particular moral psychology, by which the data of our experiences and intuitions can be organized and interpreted.

Specifically, Aquinas, like Aristotle before him, grounds his distinction between true virtue and self-control in his understanding of the passions and their relation to the intellect.[10] For Aquinas, the passions are grounded in that aspect of the human person that responds, consciously yet prerationally, as it were, to the world around us (I-II.22.2; I-II.23.1, 2). And yet, even though our passions are not rational, they do have what might be called a cognitive dimension (I.81.2, 3; I-II.24.1, 2; I-II.58.2). Like the will, they are expressions of our fundamental appetite for the goods that are appropriate to our nature. (At this point, Aquinas departs from Aristotle's analysis, since Aristotle has no concept of the will.)[11] Aquinas characterizes the will as a "certain rational appetite" (I-II.8.1), by which he means that the will, as such, is directed toward the good on the basis of a more or less well-formulated intellectual judgment that something really is good for the agent. The passions are not similarly grounded in an intellectual judgment of what is good or bad for the agent. We feel desire and aversion before we are able to think of such things, and as adults we may well find ourselves desiring what we know to be bad for us, and filled with disgust for what we know to be really good. Nonetheless, the passions are responses which, when they function correctly, draw the agent toward what is truly good, and incline him to avoid what is truly harmful, albeit on the basis of sensual pleasure or pain, rather than on the basis of an intellectual judgment (I-II.22.2; I-II.23.1). For this reason, the passions can either confirm or oppose the dictate of the will to pursue this object, judged by the intellect to be good, and to avoid that object, judged by the intellect to be harmful or evil. Hence, they are both subject to, and stand in need of direction by, our rational capacity to grasp the true good and evil for the human person, and to act accordingly (I-II.58.2).

The inevitable dichotomies into which we fall when talking about our capacities as embodied spirits will mislead us badly at this point, unless we attend to Gilson's reminder that for Aquinas, intellect, will, passions, and senses are all different aspects of one creature that engages reality in a complex yet fundamentally united way.[12] Just as intelligibility and goodness are two aspects of one reality, so intellect and will are two aspects of one knowing and desiring subject, who is drawn, as a willing agent, to the good that she grasps as an intellectual creature. She may well intellectually misconceive the character of the human good, and in that case, her will will be directed toward what is not in fact good for her. All the same, the will, by definition, is always directed toward something that is apprehended by the intellect as good. The passions are yet another aspect of the human person, by which she responds to reality through knowledge and love. But the passions, unlike the will, can be misdirected, as it were, in such a way as to perceive and respond contrary to the deliverances of the intellect. The mechanisms by which this happens are less important, for our present purposes, than the fact that it *does* happen, with distressing frequency (I.81.3, esp. *ad* 2). And clearly, this malfunction in the complex processes by which we respond and act within our world is in itself a misfortune for the individual who undergoes it (II-II.156.4). She will frequently find herself torn in two directions, as we say, between acting in accordance with her intellectual judgments as to what is really good, and following her contrary urges. As a result, she will sustain a consistent course of activity with difficulty, if she is able to do so at all.

Given this philosophical psychology, we can readily see why Aquinas holds that the person of true virtue, that is to say, virtue in the proper and unqualified sense, is characterized by harmonious unanimity among her feelings, judgments, and will (II-II.155.4). Because she wants to do what she knows she ought to do, she will act easily and readily, without the inner conflicts that impede less fortunate mortals. At the same time, she will stand a better chance of being in full alignment with reality, and with God, the ultimate source of all reality, than the person whose mind and will may indeed be at one with what is, but whose passions are oriented in another direction.

By now, it should be apparent that Aquinas' distinction between true temperance and fortitude, on the one hand, and self-control or continence, on the other, presupposes a distinction that our analysis in the last section would suggest that he would employ. That is, depends on a distinction between actions of a sort characteristic of a virtue, and the pattern of response and activity exhibited over time by a person who actually possesses the virtue. The actions of the continent person are of a kind that is characteristic of temperance or fortitude, and yet the overall pattern of the individual's life, including his responses as well as his actions, reveals that he does not truly possess those virtues—to his misfortune. Something similar can be said about the incontinent person, who has a correct understanding of his true good and who nonetheless consistently acts contrary to that understanding (II-II.156.1, 2). Such an individual performs the actions of a particular vice, for example, gluttony, without actually being a glutton.[13] What characterizes the truly vicious individual, on the other hand, is that he truly believes that his inordinate pursuit of the pleasures of the palate, or of sexual activity, or whatever, is necessary to his ultimate happiness (II-II.156.3). Hence, the incontinent individual is likely to be less comfortable, but more easily reformable, than the truly vicious individual.

Even though Aquinas holds that continence and, even more, incontinence are of less moral value than true temperance, he could nonetheless account for our widespread intuition that there is something praiseworthy about struggling to do the right thing when all one's desires and fears are pulling in the opposite direction. It is true that this struggle is praiseworthy for the person who is not yet virtuous in the full sense, and who therefore still experiences some conflicts between rationally informed and passionate desires. The continent individual, who acts rightly even though her passions urge her not to do so, does at least manage to realize genuine good through her actions, albeit less well than does the truly virtuous person (II-II.155; II-II.156; I-II.58.3). Even the incontinent person, who has a correct understanding of that in which true human happiness consists but suspends it under the influence of a contrary passion, is at least likely to come to his senses and repent once the passion is spent (II-II.156.3). Moreover, we can train our passions in such a way as to respond appropriately, that is, in accordance with what right reason dictates in a given situation, by taking the actions of a virtue even before we perfectly possess the virtue (I-II.63.2). Hence, the person of imperfect virtue, who struggles to do the right thing, has not yet achieved the ideal harmony of the fully virtuous person, but she is moving in that direction, and her struggles are themselves praiseworthy, precisely because they are directed toward a still better ideal of human excellence. If considerations such as these did not form our rationale for praising the person who struggles to do the right thing, we would find ourselves in the decidedly odd position of commending struggle and inner conflict as good *in themselves.* If it seems that those of us who struggle are nobler than those persons who act readily and easily, that is because perfect virtue is so rare, and most of us who aspire to it are perforce struggling much of the time.

The analysis of the preceding section would lead us to expect that in addition to identifying ways of failing to exemplify temperance and fortitude perfectly, Aquinas would also identify more drastic ways of failing to exemplify these virtues. And so he does. These sorts of failures are exemplified by actions characteristic of the multitude of vices that are contrary to temperance or fortitude. We will not be able to examine all that he says about the ways in which we can fail to act temperately or bravely, but it should be noted that all these ways of failing have one thing in common. They fail to observe the rational mean, that is to say, the mean of action relative to us (I-II.64.2). It is important not to be misled by Aquinas' terminology at this point. His discussion of the rational mean, which may or may not coincide with the real mean, can easily suggest that Aquinas is commending a condition in which we feel just a moderate amount of a given passion, neither too little nor too much of it. But the rational mean that is preserved by temperance and fortitude cannot be quantified in this way, because it is determined by the good of the agent himself:[14] "[These virtues] are dependent on the internal passions, about which it is not possible to establish the right in the same way [as the subject matter of justice, which concerns objectively ascertainable right relations among people], because of this, that persons are in different conditions with respect to their passions. And, therefore, it is necessary that the rightness of reason in the passions be established with respect to us, who are moved with the passions" (I-II.64.2). Hence, the vices contrary to these virtues are in fact harmful to the agent. On closer examination, we see that they are harmful to the agent because they incline her to act in some way that is seemingly good, but is in fact contrary to her overall good (as that overall good is outlined in I-II.94.2). For example, fear, as a vice opposed to fortitude, inclines the individual to shun some greater good in order to hold on to a lesser, but more immediately sensible, good (II-II.125.1, 2). Fearlessness, which is also opposed to fortitude, leads her to take less care than she ought to preserve her well-being (II-II.126.1, 2). Gluttony, which is opposed to temperance, leads the agent to pursue the pleasures of the palate in preference to higher goods, or in detriment to her overall well-being (II-II.148.1, 2). Even the act of fasting, which is generally characteristic of virtue, can be a vicious act if it is done in such a way as to harm one's body or to impede one's pursuit of higher goals (II-II.147.1 *ad* 2).

Because temperance and fortitude have an intrinsic reference to the good of the agent, the descriptions of the kinds of actions that exemplify these virtues, and usually (but not always) of the kinds of actions that exemplify their corresponding vices, will have an open-ended quality that will give them sufficient flexibility to be applied to persons in different conditions. Certainly, we will be able to identify kinds of actions that would be characteristic of temperance or fortitude for most persons, or that would be typical of the corresponding vice. Without such stereotypical notions of what it is to behave in a temperate or brave way (and to fail to do so), we could not form concepts of temperance or fortitude or their corresponding vices at all. But before we can judge a particular action to be a truly temperate or (to a lesser extent) brave action, we must know enough about the individual's proclivities and the circumstances of his action to be able to say that this action is truly in accordance with his overall individual good. (And even though we have ascertained that an action is truly temperate or brave, that is, truly in accordance with the individual's overall good, it still does not follow that the agent is a temperate or brave person, for he may merely be continent.) As we will see, the same cannot be said of the actions of justice, which are determined by objectively ascertainable right relationships among people (I-II.64.2).

What we may call the agent-referential character of the actions associated with the affective virtues is especially evident with respect to temperance, which is characterized by desiring what is good *for oneself* in the way of food, drink, and (to some degree) sexual pleasure (I-II.60.2; I-II.57.1; II-II.141.6). Of course, what that is, concretely, will vary somewhat from individual to individual. My diabetic father and I may both have attained perfect temperance, but I readily take the piece of pie that he just as readily refuses. There would seem to be less scope for agent-referential evaluations of actions in contexts calling for the exercise of fortitude, on the part of a person who perfectly possesses that virtue, since fortitude is preeminently characterized by holding on to one's true good in the face of the danger of death, which is likely to provoke fear in nearly all persons (II-II.123.4). Nonetheless, although Aquinas does not say so explicitly, his analysis of the affective virtues would suggest that there is considerable scope for agent-relative evaluations of putative actions of fortitude as well as of temperance for the person who (like the majority of us) is not yet perfectly virtuous. What would count as either a brave or a temperate action for the imperfectly virtuous person would be whatever it is that moves her toward the ideal of perfect virtue, and that may or may not be identical with what a perfectly virtuous person would do in the same situation. For example, if I have an unreasonable fear of driving, it may count as a brave action for me to force myself to take a spin on the freeway for the sake of some greater good, even though that would not be a brave action for the person who was not troubled by a similar fear. Similarly, I may refuse a piece of pie, even though it would be perfectly healthy for me to have some—suppose that it is a high-protein health food pie—if I am attempting to discipline a tendency in myself to overindulge in sweets.

At the same time, it is not true that Aquinas holds that all the actions associated with the affective virtues and their corresponding vices must be described in such a way as to refer to the agent's particular condition or situation. Notably, according to Aquinas the sins of lust, which consist of determinate and objectively ascertainable kinds of actions, are always vicious (II-II.154). It should be noted that the natural sexual sins, that is, those which involve standard sexual intercourse between a man and a woman, are violations of justice as well as temperance, since each involves a distinctive kind of violation of the claims generated by the structures of kinship and marriage (II-II.154.1). Even simple fornication, that is, sexual intercourse between a man and a woman who are each free of any familial obligations, is a violation of justice, since it jeopardizes the well-being of the child who might be born outside the normal protection of a family (II-II.154.2). And if we grant that actions of natural lust are sins against justice, then it is easy to understand why they can be recognized as such without any reference to the special circumstances of the agent. As we have already noted, the same thing may be said of all actions that violate the norms of justice. But what of the actions of a sort that Aquinas characterizes as unnatural sexual sins? These are not similarly sins against justice, and yet they, too, can be identified as sinful on the basis of an action-description that does not refer to any of the particularities of the agents involved. For example, in order to identify a particular action of homosexual intercourse as a sin of lust, it is not necessary, on Aquinas' terms, to inquire into whether this action is increasing the tendencies of the agents to prefer sensual pleasure to their true good. It is necessary to ascertain only that these are two persons of the same gender having sexual relations with each other (II-II.154.11).

There may be no part of Aquinas' substantive moral views that has generated more controversy and outright dismay in our time than his treatment of the sins of lust. Therefore, if we are to understand what this discussion adds to his overall understanding of the affective virtues, we must be especially careful to try to identify the principles that underlie this treatment.

On Aquinas' view, as I read him, the sins of unnatural lust have an especially determinate and fixed character, as compared to other kinds of sins against temperance, because the character of sexual desire is different from the character of other desires. In order to see why Aquinas holds this view, we must first of all note that he draws a general distinction between natural and non-natural desires: "Desire is twofold: natural and non-natural. Natural desire certainly cannot be actually infinite, for it is of that which nature requires, and nature certainly always aims at something finite and definite. . . . But non-natural desire is altogether infinite. For it follows reason, as was said above [I-II.30.3], and now reason is capable of proceeding to infinity. Hence, he who desires riches is capable of desiring them, not to any certain limit, but simply to be rich, as much as possible"

(I-II.30.4; cf. I-II.30.3). Not all non-natural desires are bad, but because they have no built-in check in the natural needs of the organism, they are insatiable, and must therefore be brought under some sort of reasoned governance if we are to live a human life at all. At the same time, because sexual desire is the most voracious of desires (as sexual pleasure is the most intense sensual pleasure [II-II.153.4]), sexual desire separated from the boundaries set by nature is more likely to disrupt the personality of the individual than any other unchecked sensual desire: "When the lower capabilities are vehemently moved toward their objects, the consequence is that the higher powers are impeded and disordered in their acts. And now, it is through the vice of lust most of all that the lower appetite, that is to say, desire [*concupiscibilis*], vehemently aims at its object, that is to say, the desirable, on account of the vehemence of the pleasure. And therefore, the consequence is that through lust most of all the higher powers are disordered, that is to say, reason and will" (II-II.153.5; cf. II-II.151.3 *ad* 2). Thus, Aquinas holds that all non-natural sexual desire is *un*natural in the pejorative sense, and the corresponding actions are absolutely prohibited.

Note that on this reading, Aquinas' specific sexual ethic is dependent on his empirical psychology. He holds that certain determinate kinds of sexual behavior are always vicious because he believes that as a matter of fact, they will always tend to be destructive to the individuals involved (cf. II-II.141.6 *ad* 2). And whether or not we agree with his particular understanding of sexuality, it is worth asking whether the principle by which he identifies some kinds of actions as intrinsically evil sins against temperance is sound. That is, would we agree that a kind of action having to do with the fundamental physical needs and desires of the human person may in fact be a vicious perversion of those needs and desires, if actions of that sort are in fact harmful to the individual who does them?

I am inclined to think that this principle is sound, and by appealing to it we can identify some determinate kinds of actions that would be intemperate for any agent, in any circumstances. For example, it would seem to me that starving oneself to the point of damaging one's body (which Aquinas identifies as a sinful action [II-II.147.1 *ad* 2]), or deliberately gorging until one vomits (which he seems not to have discussed, although see II-II.148.6 *ad* 2), would always be vicious actions contrary to temperance, whatever the particular situation of the agent. (It may well be that in a particular case, an individual may be so mentally unbalanced as not to be responsible for an action of this sort, but the same may be said of any other kind of vicious action.)

So far we have identified, in a general way, the kinds of actions that are characteristic of temperance and fortitude, and their corresponding vices, and we have commented on the relationship between performing actions of a virtuous or vicious sort, and being a virtuous or vicious person. But our analysis of the previous section would indicate that the concepts of temperance and fortitude are still incomplete so long as we explicate them without reference to any wider context. That is, even though we may be satisfied that a particular action is not a specimen of sham temperance or fortitude, in any of the standard ways in which these virtues may be shammed, we may still ask, "But is that *really* an instance of temperance, or of fortitude?"

One example of this sort of puzzle that is frequently cited is that of the Nazi soldier who braves every sort of hardship and danger in knowing defense of what is objectively an appalling cause. (I add the proviso that he knows what he is doing, since a different sort of question is raised by the case of the Nazi soldier who has no real grasp of the policies for which he is fighting.) Is such a man *really* brave? Or to take an example of Aquinas' that we have already mentioned, consider the individual who makes himself ill through fasting. Does such an action really exemplify abstinence, which is an aspect of the virtue of temperance (II-II.147.1 *ad* 2)?

According to Aquinas, the answer to these questions would be no, but a carefully qualified no: "Moral virtue may be taken either as perfect, or as imperfect virtue. Imperfect moral virtue, indeed, . . . is nothing other than a certain inclination in us to do some work of a kind that is productive of good, whether that inclination is from nature or from custom. And taking the moral virtues in this way, they are not connected. For we see one who, from natural affection or from some habit, is prepared to do works of liberality, who nonetheless is not prepared for the works of chastity. However, a perfectly moral virtue is a habit directed to a good work done well. And taking the moral virtues in this way, we ought to say that they are connected, as nearly everyone agrees" (I-II.65.1).

As we saw above, the basic concept of virtue implies that the character traits so described are good without qualification (again, see I-II.55.3; I-II.65.2). But a habitual orientation or a specific action that is in fact directed toward a bad aim cannot be called a good orientation or action without qualification, since whatever is in some way defective cannot be said to be good (I-II.18.4 *ad* 3). More specifically, when we say that something is a human virtue, we imply that it is a perfection that promotes the true good of the human person (I-II.65.2). But if a character trait or action is oriented toward what is at odds with that ideal (which is what it means for us to say that a given orientation or action is bad), then it can hardly be consistent with that ideal at the same time. To the contrary, it will ultimately prove to be destructive to, rather than perfective of, the individual. That is why Aquinas defends what we refer to as the thesis of the unity of the virtues, that is, the thesis that anyone who possesses any true virtue must necessarily possess all of them: "And, taking the moral virtues in this way [that is, as perfect virtues], we ought to say that they are connected" (I-II.65.1; cf. I-II.61.4 *ad* 1). To many, this thesis has seemed highly improbable, at best. For example, Hauerwas objects that Aquinas has failed to take account of the complexity of the moral life, which will necessarily lead us to attempt to hold together values and virtues that are really inconsistent.[15] Aquinas' response would be that the moral life will indeed be characterized by such tensions as long as a particular community, with its inevitable flaws and deficiencies, provides the highest norm by which the virtues of the individual are to be regulated and evaluated. That is why, on his view, the individual virtues of temperance and fortitude must be given order and more definite content by justice, which directs the individual toward the ideal order of equality rather than toward the customs of his particular society, and by prudence, which grounds all the actions and reactions of the individual in his vision of the human good.

A second objection to the thesis of the unity of the virtues simply points toward the seeming unreality of this thesis.[16] After all, don't we all know (or at least know about) brave criminals, faithful but unkind (or kind but unfaithful) husbands and wives, honest gluttons, loyal drunkards, and (just to complicate matters still further) persons who are scrupulously honest at work, yet cheat on their income tax?

Aquinas is well aware that there are plenty of people who are inconsistent in these ways. What he denies, nonetheless, is that the individuals in these examples are *truly* brave, faithful, kind, or to use his own example, liberal, insisting that, at best, they possess deformed rudiments of the virtues in question (again, see I-II.65.1). And we can now see why he would argue in this way. For one aspect of the true human good cannot be at odds with another, so long as the specific ideal of human existence is to be an intelligible ideal of a unified life. In particular, the good of individuals cannot finally be at odds with the true common good of the community, which is the informing ideal of justice (II-II.58.5, 6). Not only is it the case that the true good of the human person includes full membership in a community, which can only be achieved through justice on both sides, but as we will see, even the private goods of individuals cannot be attained apart from participation in a well-ordered commmunity. Moreover, even the most well-meaning individual, who intends to live in right relationship with her neighbors and her community, will fail to live in a way that truly promotes both her own well-being and that of others, if she lacks prudence (I-II.58.4).

But don't we admire and commend what Aquinas holds to be the seeming virtues of people who are not all that virtuous, overall? That is, don't we consider these virtues to have at least *some* moral values? Of course we do. But here again, the facts of our experience do not cause any embarrassment to the theory of moral knowledge being set forth here. To the contrary, they support it. For even though the seeming virtues of those who are not virtuous without qualification fall short of true virtue, nonetheless they have *something* of the character of true virtue, or they would not answer to our concepts of those virtues at all. Specifically, the person who is brave or faithful or truthful in this derivative sense is able to sustain some consistent course of activity in situations that would derail many of us, even if he is not sustaining the right course of activity. And since the human good is intrinsically connected with the ability to act and to sustain activity, clearly it is better, all things considered, to be able to pursue wrongheaded activities than not to be able to sustain a course of activity at all. The bravery of the Nazi soldier may not be true bravery, and yet it is more admirable, and better for the soldier himself, than cringing cowardice would be. And this point is significant, not only for understanding the complexity of our moral evaluations but also for directing our efforts at moral education (of ourselves as well as others). A person who possesses some virtues in a derivative sense is better off in that respect, from the standpoint of her (presumed) desire to become virtuous without qualification, than the person who does not possess those virtues in any sense. Some of the necessary work of shaping and disciplining her affective self has already been done and what she must now do is to learn to put the virtues that she has into good order, by redirecting her life as a whole toward morally desirable aims.

But that task cannot even be begun without some knowledge of the universal norms of justice that set the ends toward which true temperance and fortitude are directed. Hauerwas is quite right that the virtues proper to individuals cannot be understood apart from the wider context of communal life. However, the communal context within which individual virtues must be understood cannot be reduced to the life of any particular community; rather, this communal context must be understood in terms of the norms of justice, as they would be instantiated in a particular community. And so we are led by the logic of Aquinas' analysis of the virtues to a consideration of perhaps the most challenging part of his moral theory, his analysis of justice.

5

Justice

When we turn to Aquinas' account of justice, we quickly realize that this virtue cannot be understood in such a way as to put it on a par with temperance and fortitude. As we saw in the last chapter, these virtues are exhibited by actions that are evaluated primarily in terms of their congruity to the well-being of the agent herself. The virtue of justice, on the other hand, is exhibited primarily in external actions which embody right relations among individuals, or between the individual and the community. Hence, we read that "it is proper to justice, among the other virtues, to direct the human person in those things which pertain to another. For it introduces a certain equality . . . ; equality, however, is toward another" (II-II.57.1; cf. I-II.60.2). That is, justice, unlike temperance and fortitude, is oriented directly toward the good of others, and of the community as a whole, and not toward the good of the individual.

For these reasons, the virtue of justice must be located in the will rather than the passions. The will is the immediate source of the external actions that are the proper object of justice (I-II.60.3). Aquinas adds that because the will, unlike the passions, is naturally directed toward the overall good of the individual (as that individual understands it), it needs no additional orientation to direct it toward the pursuit of the agent's own good, but it does need the additional orientation of special virtues (justice and charity) to direct it toward the pursuit of the good of others (I-II.56.6). At the same time, it is precisely because justice orients the will, and thereby the whole person, to the wider goods of other persons and the shared life of the community, that it serves to set the norms by which true temperance and fortitude can be distinguished from incomplete or counterfeit forms of these virtues (II-II.58.5, 6). It takes its ultimate norms from prudence and charity, but since the former is, strictly speaking, an intellectual virtue, and the latter is a theological virtue, Aquinas says that justice is the greatest of the moral virtues properly so called (II-II.58.1, 2).

Our examination of Aquinas' account of justice will raise a number of issues that are central to his moral theory. At the outset, it raises a question that is as urgent for us as it was for him: What is the proper relationship between the good of the individual and the common good? As we shall see, Aquinas insists that the common good takes precedence over individual goods, so much so that he seems to be saying that in moral matters, the well-being of the individual is important only insofar as it fosters the good of the community. Must we conclude, then, that the ideal of individual flourishing that informs temperance and fortitude just gives way to the common good when we come to justice? No; for Aquinas, individual and communal good stand in a reciprocal relationship such that the good of the individual is intrinsic to the common good. But in order to see this, it will be necessary to examine the way in which Aquinas spells out his notions of harm, equality, and the just community. This examination will prove to have further implications for our understanding of Aquinas' moral theory and its relation to present-day concerns.

Common Good and Individual Good

As we saw in the first chapter, normative individualism, once so clearly the supreme moral norm for Christan and secular thinkers alike, has recently come under attack from more than one quarter. The Protestant thinkers analyzed by Outka and, more obliquely, the Catholic moral theologians discussed in the first chapter, may be taken as examples of those who still hold that Christian ethics is grounded in a sense of the irreducible worth of the individual. On the other hand, Gustafson and Hauerwas both insist, albeit on very different grounds, that the good of the community must be given more emphasis, or even complete priority over the good of the individual.[1] And at first glance, it would seem that Aquinas' moral theory lends unqualified support to the latter view. After all, Aquinas insists, as strongly as any Marxist, that the common good takes precedence over the good of the individual, just as the good of the universe as a whole is a greater good than the good of any one creature, however exalted (II-II.47.10; II-II.58.12; II-II.64.2). And yet, Aquinas is not in fact the one-sided communalist that these remarks, taken alone, would suggest, for, as we saw in chapter 2, he affirms the duty of self-love and the irreducible worth of the individual just as strongly. But for that very reason, if we are to understand Aquinas' theory of justice, we must see how he understands the proper relationship between the common good and the good of the individual. In order to do so, we must see why he gives the common good so much prominence in his theory of morality.

The central importance of the common good in Aquinas' moral thought flows naturally from his anthropology. For him, as for Aristotle, we are intrinsically social beings who can exist and flourish only within the context of a community (I.96.4; II-II.47.10).[2] And we can readily see why he follows Aristotle on this point. In the first place, the community is necessary for our material support. Human children need the care of their parents for several years, and the exigencies of pregnancy and nursing make it extremely difficult, at least, for a woman alone to care for herself and her children. Moreover, the family unit, even the extended household, is not really sufficient for maintaining the necessities of life. Food, shelter, and safety can more readily and securely be provided by an extended group of adults, who can take advantage of the benefits of strength of numbers and some division of labor. Hence, a social life is necessary to secure the material necessities of life to each individual and to bring the next generation expeditiously onto the scene.

And although Aquinas does not say so explicitly, it is clear that his theories of knowledge and language imply that some sort of social life is necessary to the exercise of the rational capacities that are distinctive to the human creature (cf. I.84-88).[3] Because we come to knowledge through a process of discursive reasoning (unlike the angels [I.79.1]), our mental processes presuppose a language and a shared body of knowledge, both of which are cultural artifacts. Moreover, the whole superstructure of human thought and action— language, culture, shared traditions and their informing histories— constitutes a good in itself that transcends the good of any individual who participates in and contributes to it.

These considerations make it easy to see why Aquinas says that the common good transcends the good of the individual. And yet, we have seen other indications in the *ST* that Aquinas is not the one-sided communalist that our observations so far might suggest him to be. In the first place, such an interpretation of Aquinas is difficult to square with his insistence that the proximate norm of temperance and fortitude is the good of the individual. As we have already noted, justice transforms and completes temperance and fortitude by orienting them toward a good that transcends the good of the individual. But if that wider good were not somehow congruent with the good of the individual, it would be hard to see how Aquinas could maintain his thesis of the unity of the virtues, or render even plausible his ideal of the virtuous person as one who lives an ordered and therefore unified life. We have also observed that Aquinas holds that each individual necessarily seeks his own perfection as an individual (as do all creatures), and correlatively, no one can deliberately will what is harmful as such (I-II.29.4). Indeed, Aquinas is so far from condemning this self-love that he insists that each person is under a serious obligation to seek his own good correctly, that is, by pursuing the fundamental inclinations of human life in a way that respects their intrinsic ordering (II-II.26.4). Finally, Aquinas' theological commitments to the importance of the individual are hard to reconcile with an assertion of the absolute priority of the common good. Each individual human being is a potential intimate friend of God, and as such, each individual merits our active love (II-II.25.1, 6).

It begins to appear that if we are to make sense of the full range of what Aquinas has to say concerning individual and communal good, we must take these remarks as implying that correctly understood, the well-being of individual and community are interrelated in such a way that what promotes one promotes the other, and what harms one harms the other as well. And that is indeed the clear implication of his theory of justice. This way of proceeding could easily lead to a sophisticated strategy for throwing a verbal blanket over all sorts of abuses of the individual by the community. It does not do so in Aquinas, because he employs this strategy in the other direction as well. That is, he also defines the good of the community in such a way that it is a necessary condition for the human good that individuals be protected in certain ways, and correlatively, he holds that when these protections are absent, the community may cease to have a claim on the allegiance of its members.

In order to substantiate this reading, it will be necessary to examine Aquinas' substantive theory of justice in some detail. Discussions of Aquinas' views on justice usually focus on his treatment of distributive justice, that part of justice which regulates the distribution of the common goods of a community, and of course some discussion of that treatment will be called for in this chapter as well. However, the principles that underlie Aquinas' theory of justice are in my view more clearly evident in his analysis of the norms of nonmaleficence and fairness, which according to him are all associated in some way with commutative justice, that part of justice which deals with interactions between individuals (I-II.60.3).[4] For this reason, in the next section we will look at Aquinas' treatment of the norms of nonmaleficence, beginning with his discussion of homicide and murder. That examination will then suggest a direction for further inquiry.

Murder and Other Maleficent Acts

The norms concerning homicide and murder in the Thomist tradition have been widely discussed in the course of the debate in contemporary moral theology reviewed in chapter 1. And no wonder, for these norms have to do with one of the most fundamental claims that persons can make, namely, the claim to life, without which nothing else can be enjoyed. Moreover, these norms, at least as they are developed in the *ST* itself (II-II.64), seem at first glance to offer tantalizing hints of support both for the views of Grisez and Finnis and for proportionalism. In fact, Aquinas' remarks in this question fit with neither understanding of moral norms, but an examination of the ways in which he fails to fit with each position will provide us with a useful entree into his actual view.[5]

Observe first of all that the proportionalists are clearly right to say that for Aquinas (or for the tradition that he shaped on this question), there are justifiable forms of homicide, namely, capital punishment and the killing of enemy soldiers in wartime (II-II.64.2; killing in self-defense should not be assimilated to these sorts of cases, for reasons that I will discuss later).[6] On the other hand, Aquinas also prohibits other kinds of killing that would seem, prima facie, to have proportionalist justifications as strong as those that he allows. Most notably he allows capital punishment by the state, but prohibits the killing of a criminal by a private individual (II-II.64.3). Moreover, he asserts in the strongest possible terms that there can be no moral justification for killing an innocent person, whatever the circumstances (II-II.64.6). Hence, the debate between the proportionalists and Grisez and Finnis would seem to result in a draw, as far as this question is concerned. It is difficult to see why there might be a proportionate reason for killing a criminal or an enemy soldier, but never for killing an innocent person; on the other hand, it is equally difficult to see why the life of a criminal is inherently any less an inviolable basic good than that of a babe in arms.[7]

There is no satisfactory way out of these quandaries so long as we limit ourselves to the understanding of good and the moral evaluation of actions to be found in contemporary Catholic moral theology. But if we ask instead what criteria Aquinas uses to distinguish prohibited kinds of killing (murders, in our terms) from permissible homicides, we find that he draws the line between them in such a way as to suggest the concepts of the human good and human harm that inform his theory of justice.[8]

Let us begin with the obvious: The moral rules concerning murder and permissible homicide are all about the same kind of action, considered from one standpoint, namely, the killing of a human person. Considered from a premoral standpoint, an action of this kind involves harming another person, in the most obvious and drastic of ways. Hence, this sort of action is never desirable in itself (II-II.64.6; II-II.122.6 *ad* 4). And yet, there are cases in which an act of homicide is morally justifiable, even praiseworthy, while in other sorts of cases, of course, homicide is morally wrong. But if some kinds of homicides are morally permissible, and other kinds are morally wrong, then as we saw in chapter 3 these cannot belong to the same species of action, described from a moral standpoint, even if they belong to the same natural species of action (I-II.18.5). Hence, "killing a human being," understood as a natural species of action, divides into two specifically different kinds of actions, morally considered, namely, justifiable homicide and murder, just as other natural kinds of actions (for example, sexual intercourse) divide into two or more kinds of actions when considered from a moral standpoint (for example, marital intercourse, fornication, adultery).

The question that now arises is: On what basis does Aquinas distinguish between murder and justifiable homicide? If we examine II-II.64 carefully, we find that he does so on the basis of two criteria, both of which must be fulfilled if an instance of homicide is to count as justifiable homicide. First, the killing must be done by the state, acting through its authorized agent.[9] Hence, both capital punishment and the killing of enemy soldiers in wartime can be morally justified if certain conditions are met (the criminal must have been legally tried and convicted, or the war must be just [II-II.64.2]). Correlatively, if a private citizen takes it upon herself to execute a criminal, or if the remorseful criminal commits suicide, the act is condemned as murder, because no private individual has authoriy over the life of a human being, including one's own life (II-II.64.3, 5). The one exception, to be discussed below, is killing in self-defense. And second, the victim must have forfeited the immunity from harm guaranteed to all members of a just community through his own free action of grievous aggression against the community or some individual. As we noted above, Aquinas insists that this proviso holds without exception: "In no way is it justifiable to kill the innocent" (II-II.64.6).

Killing in self-defense presents a special problem to Aquinas because it would seem to be justifiable, and yet it also appears to instantiate one of the two sufficient criteria for an action's being murder, namely, that the actor is a private citizen (II-II.64.7). How to reconcile moral intuition and moral theory at this point? Aquinas proceeds by arguing that in this case, there is another aspect of the action that is definitive, and which sanitizes the action, so to speak: The actor is attempting to preserve her own life. And why should this particular good intention be so important as to override the usually decisive criterion for murder that is also present? Aquinas' answer does not depend on a relative weighing and assessment of the goods at stake, nor on an analysis of the causal reaction between defending oneself and killing another, as different interpretations of this passage have held.[10] Rather, what he argues is that one may legitimately describe an act of killing in self-defense *as* self-defense, rather than murder, so long as the actor's intention is to preserve her own life, and not to kill the attacker for the sake of killing him. (Note that the actor's intention is determined by an objective criterion, that the force used to repel the attack is no more than is necessary to prevent one's own death.) And why? In terms that clearly refer back to his discussion of the fundamental inclinations of human life at I-II.94.2, Aquinas argues that the preservation of one's own existence is the most basic inclination of nature. For that reason, an act of self-defense fulfills the most basic criterion for a moral action, namely, that it be in conformity with a rational apprehension of the exigencies of human nature. And because no one has a duty to take more care of another's life than of his own, this criterion overrides the criterion that would ordinarily identify the action as murder.

What is the significance of all these distinctions? First of all, they make it clear that for Aquinas, there is at least one determinate kind of action, namely murder, that is intrinsically morally wrong. That is, Aquinas does not define "murder" in a purely formal way, as "wrongful killing," without further specification, as some interpreters have suggested.[11] Rather, he distinguishes between murder and permissible homicide on the basis of criteria that are clear, correspond to objectively verifiable states of affairs, and are not themselves formulated in moral terms. ("Innocent," in the context of this question, should be interpreted to mean "not actively engaged in, or guilty of, aggression," not, "free of all moral guilt.") However, it is equally apparent that he does not define murder as any sort of attack on human life whatever. Rather, Aquinas' distinction might best be described as juridical, even at the risk of calling up connotations of legalism that I believe to be absent from his thought. That is, the morally relevant features of an action that determine it to be either murder or justifiable homicide include not only *what* is done (the natural species of the action) but also the standing within the community of the individuals involved, with all that that implies about their distinctive relationships and responsibilities. A justifiable homicide can only be carried out *by* one who is designated as a representative of the state, and it can only be carried out *on* someone who has freely alienated herself from the community through some act of aggression against it or one of its members.

It might seem at first that the example of self-defense contradicts this interpretation, since what is decisive in this case is the appeal to a natural human inclination that the act instantiates. But as I read him, what Aquinas presupposes is that an act of self-defense, even one that involves killing, does not violate the boundaries of the community because it is not inconsistent with one of the chief aims of the community, namely, the protection of its individual members. Hence, not only does an act of self-defense fulfill a natural inclination, but it does so in a rational way, that is, in a way that also respects and fosters the higher inclination to live in community. (We will return to the more general question of what is involved in fulfilling the inclinations in a rational way later.) For precisely this reason, the other criterion for murder can never be overridden. It is always murder to kill an innocent person. And why? Significantly, Aquinas appeals to the raison d'être of the community. Criminals threaten the existence of the community, whereas innocent persons are the very point of its existence: "However, the life of the just preserves and promotes the common good, because they themselves are the more principal part of the multitude" (II-II.64.6).

The same general point appears again in Aquinas' discussion of other serious harms against the person (II-II.65). There we read that grave bodily harm (involving permanent injury or imprisonment) can be inflicted by agents of the state only *on* malefactors *for* the sake of the common good (II-II.65.1, 3). Lesser bodily harm, of such a kind as to cause pain but not injury, can be inflicted by one private individual on another, but only in the context of private authority: A master may beat his servant, or a father his child, so long as he does so for purposes of correction and does not do lasting harm (II-II.65.2).

Hence, we see that according to Aquinas, while the infliction of harm is always morally significant, it is not always morally wrong. There are some natural species of actions involving harm that divide into two (or more) moral species of actions, of which one is prohibited while the other is not. However, Aquinas also identifies other kinds of harms that *are* always morally wrong. These are the harms that involve some violation of the fundamental institutional structures of the community. Adultery violates the norms of marriage (II-II.154.8); lying undermines the very point of language (II-II.110.1); usury violates the institutions of commerce and property (II-II.78.1); and the various sorts of judicial offenses, such as perjury, violate the norms of legal justice (II-II.67-71). In each case, certainly, the violation of the institutional norm in question can generally be expected to harm someone, since these institutions exist to promote human well-being. Even if no one is directly harmed by a particular action of this sort (for example, a lie told to benefit another—a case Aquinas discusses, II-II.110.3 *ad* 4—or consensual spouse-swapping, a case he does not discuss, to my knowledge), the community as a whole is harmed because a useful institution is thereby undermined, and the actor himself is harmed by acting contrary to the intelligible order of justice that informs, or should inform, his community. But in cases of these sorts, the very possibility of the harm in question is created by the existence of the relative institution. For example, there would be no such thing as adultery if there were no institution of marriage. Correlatively, what characterizes a prohibited action of one of these kinds is simply and solely the objectively ascertainable fact that an institutional norm is being violated.

So far, we have distinguished between two main classes of moral prohibitions in Aquinas, namely, those that concern natural harms, so to speak, and admit of a distinction between legitimate and wrongful inflictions, and those that consist of violations of institutional structures, which do not admit of any such distinction. There is a third class of prohibitions that do not fit neatly into this dichotomy; nor do they follow the pattern of permitting the infliction of harm, if at all, only on malefactors. These are the rules concerning property, which are set out in the course of a discussion of theft and robbery (II-II.65).

On examining this question, we find that, of course, both theft and robbery presuppose the institutional context of property, in that they consist of taking what is not one's own secretly or by force (theft and robbery, respectively [II-II.66.4]). In that sense, they resemble adultery, lying, or usury. But like the harms against the person, the natural species of action labeled "taking what is another's without his permission" does divide into legitimate and prohibited moral species of actions. Specifically, property may legitimately be appropriated by force (or the threat of force) *by* a representative of the state acting *on behalf of* the common good (II-II.66.5, 8). But note that in this case, there is an important difference between what counts as defense of the common good with reference to harms against the person, and with reference to the seizure of property. There is no way, for Aquinas, that killing, maiming, or imprisoning an innocent person could serve to promote the common good. But a similar restriction does not apply to the seizure of property. Rather, Aquinas holds that public authorities can appropriate whatever is necessary to maintain the general welfare of society from anyone whatever, so long as they limit their appropriations to what is genuinely necessary to maintaining the life of the community (II-II.66.8, esp. *ad* 3). Finally, even private individuals may seize whatever is necessary to maintain their own life, or the life of another, in cases of urgent necessity (II-II.66.7).

How are we to interpret these remarks? I believe that they can best be understood as reflecting Aquinas' sense of the special characteristics of the institution of property. On the one hand, Aquinas is not prepared to say that ownership is purely a matter of convention. There is a sense in which human dominion over things is natural, but to be exact, what is natural to us is the general relationship between humanity and the subhuman creation ordained to our use, and not ownership per se (II-II.66.1). The institution of private property is an addition to the natural, which presupposes the dominion of humanity over creation and serves to implement it (II-II.66.2 *ad* 1). More specifically, it serves to implement the divine intent that *everybody* should be provided for out of the bounties of creation (II-II.66.2 *ad* 2). Hence, when the institution of property threatens its own raison d'être by preventing individuals or the whole community from having access to the necessary means of life, then the institution itself breaks down, or at least, the claims that it guarantees under ordinary circumstances must give way to more exigent claims. It is on this basis that Aquinas justifies the seizure of property by private individuals who are pressed to do so by urgent need (II-II.66.7):

> Those things which are of human law cannot restrict natural law or divine law. Now according to the natural order instituted from divine providence, lower things are directed to this, that from them, human necessities are to be relieved. And therefore, through the division and appropriation of things, which proceeds from human law, human necessities are not prevented from being met by these sorts of things. . . . [Aquinas goes on to say that ordinarily, human needs will be met through the alms of those who have more than enough.] Nevertheless, if the need be so urgent and evident that it is manifest that the immediate need must be relieved by whatever things occur, . . . then someone can licitly take another's things to relieve his need, whether openly or in secret. Nor does such an action properly have the character of theft or robbery.

Finally, it should be noted that for Aquinas not every moral species of actions is defined by reference to particular institutional contexts. The sorts of harms that arise in everyday social intercourse, for example, reviling, gossiping, and cursing (II-II.72-76), are not defined in terms of institutional contexts. And because no special institutional contexts are involved here, Aquinas generally allows more play for considerations of circumstances and motivation when distinguishing permitted and illicit moral kinds of actions of these sorts. For example, the natural kind of action of mockery, can be divided into two moral kinds of actions, justified correction and wrongful reviling, depending on the speaker's motivation and the overall circumstances (II-II.72.2). Even in these cases, however, communal considerations are centrally important for Aquinas, although more specifically institutional considerations generally are not. Thus, the harms involved in the sins of "extra-judicial speech" (reviling, gossiping, and the like) are harms to one's honor (II-II.72.1), reputation (II-II.73.1), or friendships (II-II.79.1), in short, to one's status within the community.

Precept and Principle in the Treatise on Justice

We are now in a position to spell out more exactly the principles that govern Aquinas' account of justice, and the way in which he relates the individual good to the common good.

Observe first of all that, as we would expect, institutional contexts, and more generally communal contexts, are centrally important to Aquinas. We have already observed that he defines the species of actions, justifiable homicide and murder, juridically, that is, by reference to the distinctive role or status within the community of the persons involved, as well as by reference to the natural species of action in question. The same pattern appears in his treatment of other centrally important species of actions, namely, those involving serious injury to the person or the appropriation of another's property. Still other species of actions are defined wholly in terms of the violation of some institutional norm. Even when moral species of actions are not defined juridically, Aquinas' discussions reveal great awareness of the communal contexts of the moral life, and more specifically, of the ways in which one can injure another through damaging her standing within the community.

And yet, it would be a mistake to characterize Aquinas as a moralist of social convention—that is, as one who holds that the actually existing institutions of society should be upheld at whatever cost in human suffering. His methodological emphasis on the institutional and communal contexts of moral reasoning does not commit him to the substantive moral view that the interests of the community always take precedence over those of the individual. To the contrary, he sets clear limits on what the community can do to the individual, even for the best of reasons. "However, no one must do harm to another unjustly in order to promote the common good," he says (II-II.68.3), and this acknowledgment informs all of Aquinas' remarks on the limits of the power of the community vis-à-vis the individual (see, for example, II-II.10.8, 12; II-II.64.3 *ad* 2; II-II.67–72; II-II.104.4).

The communal contexts of morality are of central importance to Aquinas because he sees the basic institutions of society as embodying the principles of justice, which guarantee right relations among individuals and between individuals and the community. And before we accuse him of naiveté, we must add that he *defines* these institutions in such a way that what seems to be an unjust instantiation of a given institution does not really instantiate it at all, with direct consequences for one's obligations as defined thereby. For example, as we have already remarked, an individual may take from another what is necessary to sustain his life, or even a third party's. The reason that Aquinas gives is not that this is justified robbery. Rather, he argues that in such a case, the institution of property has broken down, because it has ceased to fulfill its primary purpose (II-II.66.7). Similarly, he argues that an unjust ruler need not be obeyed, but may be opposed by force of arms if necessary, because an unjust ruler is not a lawful sovereign but a tyrant (II-II.42.2).

And what *are* the fundamental principles of justice, on Aquinas' account? In his treatment of the Decalogue (which for him is comprised of the basic norms of justice [I-II.100.1, 3]), Aquinas says that the Decalogue is grounded in the self-evident precepts of love of God and neighbor, which imply obligations to harm no one and to pay one's debts: "Toward his neighbors, one conducts himself well both in particular and in general. Indeed, in particular, [he conducts himself well] toward those to whom he is a debtor, in that he pays his debts. . . . In general, however, [he conducts himself well] toward all, in that he harms no one, either by deed, or by word, or in his heart" (I-II.100.5). Elsewhere, we learn that these two demands of justice are actually one, at least as far as the neighbor is concerned, since it is a form of harming another to withhold from her what is her due (II-II.44.8 *ad* 1). In other words, Aquinas' interpretation of the fundamental norm of neighbor love, insofar as it serves as the foundation for justice toward the neighbor, is very similar to Outka's account of agape as equal regard (see the section on Outka in chap. 1).[12] This similarity becomes even more apparent when we recall that at the beginning of his treatise on justice, Aquinas says that the basic principle of justice is equality (II-II.57.1). Aquinas spells out the meaning of equality through his interpretation of the fundamental norms of justice, in that one should do no harm to anyone and fulfill one's obligations to all. Specifically, for him normative equality is essentially an equality of immunity from harm and from certain kinds of coercion, together with a claim to fairness in one's dealings with others.

As we saw in chapter 1, a moral norm that is spelled out in terms of harm will necessarily remain indeterminate if it does not contain some account of what it means to harm another. Aquinas determines what counts as harming another, or coercing another in impermissible ways, on the basis of the fundamental inclinations, namely, to live, to reproduce oneself, to live in community, and to seek the truth about God, which are enumerated in I-II.94.2. The more basic such an inclination is, the more stringent the claims that it generates, over against both the community as a whole and other members of that community, presumably because one who is frustrated in pursuing one of the more basic inclinations will have much less, or no, opportunity to pursue the more distinctively human inclinations.

Hence, as we saw in the last section, each person without exception has a claim on his fellows and on the community for immunity from bodily harm, restraint of freedom of movement, and, to some degree, seizure of his goods against his will (although he may forfeit these immunities by his own aggressive actions). In short, he has a claim not to be deprived of his life, or of the material goods necessary to support life and to maintain a family. Significantly, Aquinas remarks that anyone who harms another in these fundamental ways "dishonors him by depriving him of some excellence on account of which he has honor" (II-II.72.1). That is, someone who harms another in one of these ways disregards her fundamental excellence as a human being, in virtue of which she has a claim, equal to that of anyone else, to the most basic conditions for attaining natural human perfection, namely, life itself and the means to sustain and reproduce one's life. Correlatively, she may seize what is held by another in order to preserve her life, or that of a third person. Moreover, she has a claim not to be told lies, or to have her standing in the community impaired without grave reason, both of which would interfere with her participation in the common life of her society.

In addition, each person has a limited but real claim on freedom from forms of coercion that would interfere with her efforts to attain natural happiness through attempting to fulfill the fundamental inclinations of her nature. According to Aquinas, no person may demand obedience from another with respect to those commonalities of human nature in which we are all equal. For this reason, no one may force another to marry or to enter religious life (II-II.104.5; however, those under the authority of another may be prevented from entering religious life, according to II-II.88.8).

Most important of all, Aquinas interprets the natural law commitment to equality in such a way as to determine which institutional context is the morally relevant one for determining the moral description of a given action. We have already noted that he defines the different moral species of actions having to do with killing, serious injury, and appropriation of goods partially in terms of whether the actor is an agent of the state or not. And yet, why should it matter, morally, whether an executioner (for example) is an agent of the state or a private citizen? In either case, the victim is just as dead. I believe that for Aquinas, the significance of this distinction lies in the fact that when the state, through its duly chosen representatives, punishes, wages war, or levies taxes, it does so precisely as a collectivity that transcends any one individual (II-II.64.2; II-II.65.1, 3; II-II.66.8; II-II.67.1). That is why the state is the only proper agent for the conservation and promotion of the common good, just as the individual is the proper agent for the conservation and promotion of his private good (II-II.64.3). Thus, only the state can inflict serious harm or loss on individuals without violating the essential equality that all individuals have with respect to the fundamentals of human nature (cf. II-II.64.3; II-II.65.1).

What is the rationale for Aquinas' commitment to equality? To my knowledge, Aquinas does not pose that question in those terms, and (not surprisingly) does not answer it in so many words. And to make our attempts to reconstruct his rationale still more difficult, there are at least three different sorts of justifications for some kind of normative equality in the sources on which Aquinas draws. In Aristotle, whom Aquinas quotes at one point in defense of his claim that justice is informed by a commitment to equality (III.85.2), the equality in question appears to be essentially a moral/political application of the principle of sufficient reason: Persons should not be treated unequally unless they really are unequal in some relevant respect. However, as is well known, Aristotle also held that identifiable classes of persons are indeed unequal in ways which justify a complex system of different sorts of subordination.[13] On the contrary, the main lines of the pagan/Christian natural law tradition that dominated the moral and political thought of Aquinas' own time based its commitment to equality on the assertion that all mentally normal adults are in fact equal with respect to the critically important capacity to attain moral virtue.[14] In its Christian versions, the commitment to equality was strengthened and expanded by specifically theological arguments: All persons are equal in the sight of God, equally his creatures, and equally in need of his grace.[15]

One way in which we can reconstruct the rationale for Aquinas' commitment to equality will be to proceed by eliminating what he does not adopt from his sources' justifications for this commitment. First of all, it is clear that while Aquinas does adopt some of Aristotle's formulations of justice as equality, he does not adopt the Aristotelian anthropology that gives concrete content to the latter's own political theory. Aquinas does not even consider the possibility that there is such a thing as a class of natural slaves. He does assume that children are not fully capable of either moral virtue or the management of their own affairs, but he is hardly alone in that assumption, and, at any rate, the resultant inequality is not permanent. The obligation of children to respect and honor their parents *is* permanent, according to Aquinas, but that obligation is grounded in the debt of gratitude that we owe to those who were the means of giving us life, and does not seem to extend to a lifelong obligation to *obey* one's parents in matters that touch the individual's private affairs (II-II.88.8 *ad* 2; II-II.101.1, 2).

The only other natural division of humanity that Aquinas considers to be morally significant is the division between male and female. Aquinas' understanding of gender roles is complex, and must be pieced together from widely scattered remarks. But at least we may say that, contrary to Aristotle, Aquinas holds that women and men are equal with respect to what is essential to the nature of the species of humanity, namely, the possession of an intellectual nature. He asserts that all persons, men and women alike, possess the image of God, that is, an intellectual nature enabling the individual to know and to love God: "The image of God, with respect to that in which the character of the image principally consists, that is, with respect to the intellectual nature, is found in the man and in the woman. Hence, Gen. 1:27, after saying, 'to the image of God he created him,' that is to say, the human person [*hominem*], adds, 'male and female he created them.' It says 'them,' in the plural, as Augustine says, lest it should be thought that the two sexes were united in one individual" (I.93.4 *ad* 1). A little further on, he remarks, "Scripture, after saying, 'To the image of God he created him,' adds, 'Male and female he created them,' not inasmuch as the image of God is considered to follow the distinction of the sexes, but because the image of God is common to both sexes, since it is in accordance with the mind, in which there is no distinction of sexes" (I.93.6 *ad* 2). He does say that men generally tend to be better at rational thought than women, justifying the subordination of women within marriage for this reason (I.92.1 *ad* 2), but he explicitly adds that this difference of capability is a difference of degree and not of kind (I.93.4).

Aquinas also does not adopt at least one of the theological rationales for equality that we might have expected him to produce. That is, he does not argue that all persons are strictly equal before God. Not only does he believe in a form of predestination, he also holds that even among the elect, some are predestined to a greater degree of charity, and a more profound vision of God, than are others (I.12.6; II-II.26.13). These claims are the logical consequences of his stringent doctrine of grace, according to which not only the bestowal of grace, but the degree and intensity of the individual's love for God, cannot be attributed to any human attainments or distinctions whatever, but depend solely on the unconstrained will of God (I-II.109.4; I-II.112.1, 4).

Moreover, Aquinas denies that we are obliged by charity to love all persons equally, in the face of Augustine's assertion to the contrary (he reinterprets Augustine rather than contradicting him outright, as is his wont, but clearly the two are at odds here [II-II.26.6 *ad* 1]).[16] To the contrary, Aquinas argues that we are positively obliged by charity to love some persons more than others, and he then goes on to spell out, in disconcerting detail, who should be loved more than who. For example, one ought to love one's father more than one's children, if he is considered as the principle of one's origin, but in another respect, one's children should be loved more, since they are more closely connected to oneself considered as an agent (II-II.26.9); similarly, a man should love his parents more than his wife, if he considers them as his origin, but from the standpoint of the union between the spouses, he should love his wife more (II-II.26.11; in general, see II-II.26.6-12).

On close examination, we see that these gradations of charity do not affect the normative equality of immunity from fundamental sorts of harm and coercion. They are grounded in our special obligations to parents, family members, benefactors, and countrymen, which Aquinas holds to be deliverances of natural reason that are not abrogated by charity; they are also grounded in our obligation to love more those who are better, that is, more charitable (and since the latter distinction depends on the free will of God, it cannot be made the basis for identifying a privileged class of persons within society [I-II.109.4]). At any rate, the gradations proper to charity are expressed through differing degrees of our obligations to come to one another's assistance, so that, for example, I have a greater obligation to support my needy mother than to give alms to strangers. These obligations do not affect the more fundamental and stringent obligations to assist any person in a case of urgent necessity, and not to harm another in the ways specified by the basic norms of justice (II-II.31.3). However, if Aquinas' account of charity does not undermine the normative equality that is fundamental to his account of justice, neither can that account be taken as the basis for his commitment to equality.[17]

What remains as the basis for Aquinas' commitment to equality is the anthropological thesis, common to pagan and Christian expositors of the natural law, that all persons are equally capable of moral virtue, because they possess those capacities of knowledge and will that are proper to humanity as a specific kind (I-II.94.4–6; II-II.47.12). This claim is entirely consistent with the belief that some people are in fact more intelligent than others. Being more or less bright is relevant to many of the practical affairs of life, but in Aquinas' view, which he inherits from the natural law tradition, it is not directly relevant to the attainment of moral virtue, on which human happiness depends.[18] In other words, in order to be a morally good person, it is only necessary that one be able to reason and to will the good accordingly. One need not be capable of an especially high quality of reasoning. Aquinas then goes on to interpret this fundamental capacity of the human person in terms of his theology, specifically, his doctrine of creation, arguing that this capacity for rational self-direction is precisely the quality in virtue of which persons are said to be in the image of God (I-II, Introduction).

Much more could be said about Aquinas' notion of equality and the philosophical and theological grounds on which it is based. I do not imagine that I have fully justified that account, and indeed, I would not attempt to defend Aquinas' theory of justice in every detail. For example, he is certainly wrong about the relative mental inferiority of women, and therefore the subordination of women to men in marriage that he justifies on the basis of women's mental inferiority cannot in fact be defended. More generally, it is fair to say that Aquinas does not go far enough in the direction of extending his commitment to equality into a critique of the institutions of his society, although he is apparently aware of the problematic character of some of those institutions (I.96.4). In this section, I have simply attempted to show that Aquinas' account of justice is in fact based on a commitment to normative equality.

Even though we cannot hope to address every question that Aquinas' theory of justice raises, there is one set of issues that is very germane to the purpose of this study, and therefore merits a more detailed treatment here. These are the issues posed by Aquinas' assertions that there are some determinate kinds of actions which are always sins against justice, and are therefore never morally justifiable. For example, as we have seen, he holds that it is always morally wrong to kill the innocent, to injure them, or to deprive them of liberty. It is always wrong to lend money at interest, deliberately to say what is untrue, or to have sexual intercourse with another person's wife. To add yet another example, it is wrong to baptize infants without their parents' consent, even though withholding baptism from these children, in Aquinas' view, would necessarily put their salvation at risk (II-II.10.12). These sorts of actions are never consistent with justice because they always involve harming another person in such a way as to violate that fundamental equality between one person and another that is integral to justice. Hence, actions of these sorts are intrinsically evil.

Having said that, we still feel that Aquinas' claim that some species of actions can never be morally justified calls for further discussion. This claim raises two sets of issues for us, which we might characterize, roughly, in terms of two leading questions: Might the individual not find herself in a situation, however bizarre, in which she (morally) can or even should commit an act of a sort for which Aquinas says no moral justification would be possible? And might we not find that the specific catalogue of intrinsically evil kinds of actions varies from time to time and culture to culture? It will turn out that our efforts to address each of these questions will raise considerations that are critical to Aquinas' moral theory. The first will call upon us to consider further the relationship between individual and community, and the way in which the good of each is integrally bound up with the good of the other. The second will raise the difficult question of whether the concrete norms of justice are different for different cultures, or change over time.

Intrinsic Evil, Part One:
Individual and Community

The claim that some sorts of actions are intrinsically morally evil is one of those assertions that we seem unable either to accept or to do without. On the one hand, it seems unrealistic, and therefore harsh, to say that one ought never, ever to do certain kinds of actions, no matter what the results of doing otherwise might be. Anyone with the least flash of imagination can easily come up with any number of cases in which this stricture would lead to seemingly horrendous conclusions. On the other hand, once we admit that seemingly evil kinds of actions can be justified in extraordinary circumstances, a whole set of embarrassing questions arises from the other side. Does this mean that it might sometimes be permissible, for example, to torture someone, or to rape her, or to perform scientific experiments on her without her consent? No matter what position we take in these discussions, it would seem that we will inevitably be embarrassed and perplexed.

At the outset, it will be important to distinguish two sorts of challenges to the claim that some kinds of actions are intrinsically evil. Often, it is said that some supposedly intrinsically evil act really is not such. For example, we frequently read that the direct killing of innocent persons who would otherwise suffer through a lingering and painful dying process is not morally wrong, or perhaps, that sexual activity between two persons of the same sex is morally innocent and even desirable. The point of such objections is this: The traditional catalogue of intrinsically evil acts has been misformulated in such a way as to stigmatize as morally evil some kinds of actions that are actually quite permissible. And there is no reason, in principle, that Aquinas could not admit the possibility that the traditional list of intrinsically evil actions does indeed sometimes call for some revision. In fact, it would be odd if it did not, since this list depends in part on our knowledge of what it is to be human, which is itself imperfect and subject to revision. At any rate, certain questions raised by this line of inquiry—that is, questions about the cultural invariability, or otherwise, of the precepts of justice—are better deferred to the next section.

The issues that we will consider in this section can best be focused by considering this question: Granting that we can identify some kinds of actions that we would generally condemn, might it not still be the case that in extraordinary circumstances, someone might be morally justified, or even obliged, to commit an action of one of these kinds?

For example: While driving on an isolated country road, Dr. Jones comes upon the scene of an accident and realizes, to his horror, that there is a living woman trapped in a flaming car. He realizes that neither he nor anyone else can possibly reach her in time to save her. And so, in order to spare her an agonizing death by burning, he takes his rifle (he had planned to go hunting) and shoots her dead. How are we to characterize his action: as an act of mercy, or as murder?

Let this example suffice. The reader can surely come up with a few more, all equally difficult. Note, however, that painful as this scenario is, it is not impossible, or even terribly improbable. Hence, it does suggest the sorts of strains that the notion of intrinsically evil kinds of actions can undergo when put into practice. How are we to deal with these difficulties?

Let us begin by noting that, no matter how we characterize Dr. Jones' action, it would seem on its face to involve the infliction of harm on the woman. It is possible to argue that under the circumstances, her death is not a *real* harm (indeed, that is a large part of what makes this a hard case), but the very fact that such an argument would be in place indicates that this action does at least involve the infliction of what we would ordinarily count as a harm. And if we examine the kinds of actions which, according to Aquinas, can never be morally justified, we find that nearly all of them share that same characteristic.[19] That is, what characterizes actions of these kinds is the fact that they involve the infliction of harm, either on the agent herself, or on another individual or the community as a whole. As such, they would seem to fall under the prohibition that Aquinas identifies as one of the foundations of the natural law, namely, "Do no harm."

But of course, matters are more complex than that. Certainly, there can be no intelligible reason to harm someone or something if the act in question is described and considered *simply* as a harm, without reference to any of its good consequences. The difficulty is that no true human action can be understood solely in terms of being a harm. As we saw in chapter 3, unless it is possible to identify some good toward which a putative action is directed, the item of behavior in question cannot be said to be an action at all. Even a seemingly senseless act of destruction, a random killing, for example, must be describable in terms of some good if it is to count as an action. (One might say that a random killing is an act of asserting one's power, which is at least arguably a desirable aim in itself.) Hence, for any harmful action, it would seem to be possible to say that this action is justifiable, because it has this particular good aim, even though, were we to consider it solely as a harm, it would not be justifiable. Of course, this line of argument invites the response that in this particular case, the seemingly good aim in question either is not a true good, or it does not justify the infliction of this particular harm. At that point, the question becomes one of deciding which sorts of good aims (if any) justify the infliction of harm. And as our example serves to remind us, this question presupposes that we have addressed the prior problem of determining what counts as a true harm.

In order to address these difficulties, Aquinas appeals to his account of the human good, on the basis of which he separates real from supposed harms and distinguishes aims which legitimate the infliction of harm from those which do not. We have already begun to see how this account gives substance to his account of justice. Let us now carry that examination further.

We have already observed that for Aquinas, the fundamental

human inclinations are permissive. That is, an action that is truly in accordance with one of these inclinations is morally permissible, and is *therefore* defined in terms of the good of the inclination toward which it is directed. Hence, as we saw above, killing in defense of the community, when carried out by authorized agents of the community in accordance with fair norms of public procedure, is an act of justice; the use of lethal force as the only possible way to defend one's own life is a legitimate act of self-defense; and the act of taking what is held by another, if that is necessary to preserve one's own life, is a legitimate means of self-preservation. But correlatively, a putatively harmful action that does not truly promote the aims of one of the fundamental inclinations falls squarely under the prohibition, "Do no harm." Therefore, an action of this sort must be categorized morally in terms of the harm that it inflicts, and for this reason, this sort of action can never be justified morally.

Of course, the sting in this proviso is contained in the qualification, *"truly* accords with, or promotes, a fundamental inclination." How are we to decide whether a particular action is genuinely in accordance with one of these inclinations, or not? After all, it would seem to be at least possible to argue that any action whatever is truly aimed at one of the objects of these inclinations, in some way or another. But for Aquinas, it is not enough to say that a particular action promotes or enacts an inclination in some way or other. If an action is to pass muster, morally, it must be possible to show that it is *genuinely* directed toward one of the basic inclinations. That is, we must be able to show that it seeks to fulfill the inclination in a way that respects the overall structure of human fulfillment outlined in I-II.94.2, and moreover, that it takes account of what we know of the empirical conditions necessary for attaining that fulfillment. Specifically:

First, it is most significant that *the inclinations are hierarchically ordered.* In chapter 3, we saw that this ordering implies that if one is to attain one's specific perfection as a human being, it is necessary to subordinate the pursuit of the lower inclinations to the pursuit of those that are higher. But when applied to the norms of nonmaleficence that apply to individuals, this ordering cuts in the opposite direction. The more fundamental an inclination is, the more absolute are the claims that it generates regarding respect on the part of others. Hence, even though we ought to live for the sake of enjoying higher aims, still, claims that stem from the necessities of human life are the most exigent of the claims to mutual respect that we have on one another.[20] A private individual may threaten the life of another only if that other is posing an immediate threat to his own life. Similarly, the urgent need of one person for the necessities of life overrides even the normally legitimate claims of another to possess a share of the material means of life, if the latter is not similarly in imminent danger. Correlatively, if an individual attempted to pursue one of the higher inclinations by killing another, or harming her in some other fundamental way, his action would be unjustifiable. That is, it would properly be described as a harm, not as a legitimate pursuit of human well-being.

Just as the individual is the natural and proper agent for his own self-preservation, so the state is the natural and proper agent for the preservation of the common good, and that is why the state may act through its lawful agents in defense of the common good in ways that would not be morally permissible for the individual. But in relations between state and individual, too, the hierarchical ordering of the inclinations determines (among other factors) what the state may do, even for the sake of the common good. If, on the one hand, the good of the individual and the family must give way to the common good in some circumstances, on the other hand, the good of the community itself depends on preserving the well-being and integrity of the individuals and families that go to make it up. The latter are not *means* to the common good. Rather, the well-being of the individuals and families within the community are a necessary *component* of the common good. For this reason, it is never possible to justify an act of harm *simply* by appealing to the common good, on Aquinas' terms. It is necessary, in addition, to show that this sort of action respects the integrity of individual identity and the structures of family life. For example, not even the state can authorize the killing of innocent persons, for any reason whatever; nor can it condemn even the guilty except through a fair judicial procedure (II-II.67-72). As we noted above, the infant children of Jewish parents cannot be baptized against the parents' will, since that would violate the precept of natural justice that gives parents the right to determine how their children should be raised (II-II.10.12).

Second, *our moral evaluation of actions will necessarily be determined in part by our empirically grounded knowledge* of what it is to be human. A particular action, or a given species of action, that might seem at first to be in accordance with our basic inclinations might well turn out not to be such, once we take into account the full range of our knowledge of the exigencies of human life. Let one example suffice.

If any action in accordance with the basic inclinations is morally licit, then what is wrong with simple fornication, if it is conducted (as it seldom is, but could be) with the aim of having a child? (Recall that simple fornication is sexual intercourse between a man and a

woman, neither of whom is married or has any other relevant juridical obligations to a third party [II-II.154.1].) Aquinas does not formulate precisely this question, but he does ask, "Whether simple
fornication is a mortal sin?" (II-II.154.2), and his answer indicates
what he would have said to our question as well. He argues that a
child born outside marriage will lack the protection, support, and
stability necessary to rear a child properly, and for this reason, simple
fornication is an act of injustice to the child that might be born of
such a union. In other words, simple fornication is not a *rational* acting
out of the inclination to reproduce. While such an action may well
result in a baby, it is at odds with the practical exigencies of human
reproduction, which demand not only the production of a baby but
also its continued care.[21]

If the preceding line of interpretation is correct, we may conclude that Aquinas distinguishes those sorts of actions that are never
morally justifiable from licit ways of doing harm on the grounds that
the former are not definable in terms of fulfilling one of the fundamental inclinations given at I-II.94.2. Hence, they must be defined
precisely as harms, which fall under the prohibition, "Do no harm."
Granting that, however, we may still ask whether the norms implied
by these distinctions are literally exceptionless. After all, these distinctions have a rationale which, it would seem, may cease to apply
in some unusual situations. They are meant to prohibit harms, but
if, in very unusual circumstances, the harm in question is not a true
harm, must we still judge that an act of the prohibited kind must be
prohibited in these circumstances? Or, even if harm must be inflicted
in a given case, might it not be justifiable to do so in order to prevent
a much greater harm? The case described at the beginning of this
section illustrates the issues that are being raised here. Does it really
count as harm to deprive a woman of a last few, pain-filled moments
of life? Or, even if it does, might it not be justifiable to inflict harm
in this particular case, since that is the only way in which much
greater harm to her could be prevented? If we find ourselves in a
situation like this, then might we not conclude that we may, or even
must, do what would ordinarily be an intrinsically evil action? Aquinas does raise the question of whether a particular instance of an
action that is intrinsically evil in kind might be permitted in abnormal circumstances, and he answers negatively (II-II.154.2; cf. II-
II.64.6). Is it possible to make sense of this denial, or do we here come
up against an inconsistency in his thought?

In order to understand Aquinas' reasoning on this point, we
must go further into the implications of his view that the norms of
justice comprise a law, that is, the natural law. In his discussion of

simple fornication, he observes that simple fornication would be wrong even if the partners were careful to provide for the welfare of the child to be born, because, he says, a law is formulated with respect to what generally happens, not with regard to the odd exception (II-II.154.2). In other words, Aquinas apparently bases his claim that some kinds of actions are always morally wrong on the grounds that the moral law is a law in a proper, not just a metaphorical, sense. As such, it exercises a binding force that goes beyond the rationale that went into its original formulation.

And why so? It does not appear that Aquinas grounds the moral law in the authority of God as supreme legislator.[22] He does not hold that the natural law is promulgated by God independently of human reason. Rather, the discernment of the moral law by human reason *is* God's promulgation of that law (I-II.90.1 *ad* 2; I-II.90.4 *ad* 1; I-II.91.2; I-II.94.1). (In the same way, God illuminates the intellect of each person in and through God's creation of that intellect, but not through some special intervention over and above the act of creation and sustenance by which every creature comes to be and continues in being [I.84.5].) Moreover, Aquinas explicitly says that sin is an offense against God not because it injures God, but because it is self-destructive in some way or other (and therefore contradicts God's absolute will that creatures should exist and flourish [I.103.1]). Hence, it would seem that Aquinas holds that there is something intrinsically self-destructive in violating the moral law, over and above the sort of harm that an act of that kind normally brings about, and for that reason there are some kinds of actions that are not permissible, even in those abnormal circumstances in which they would not be harmful in the ordinary way.

In order to understand why Aquinas holds this view, it is necessary to realize that the natural law as he understands it is not just a source of private morality, but the basis of a rational public order. To put it another way, the natural law is to the community what humanity is to a human being. That is, it represents the rational character of the community, according to our best understanding of it. Of course, we can expect to find gaps between ideal and real on both sides, so to speak. Our grasp of the natural law will always be imperfect, and no community will instantiate the natural law completely. Nonetheless, we do have some knowledge of the natural law. Moreover, the natural law, as it would be perfectly instantiated in this time and place, is finally equivalent to the ideal rational character of any particular community, insofar as it is a just community, and any community, however wretched, must retain some degree of justice, if it is to continue to exist at all. To violate the rational character of the community, as expressed in the prohibitions of natural law, is therefore to undermine it. Moreover, because the good of the individual consists in part in her harmonious relationship with a well-ordered community (and therefore with her actual community, insofar as it is well-ordered), her violation of the ideal norms of such a community, that is, the norms of the natural law, will be harmful to her as well, by putting her at variance with her community as it should be. (At the same time, allegiance to a specific community as it should be may require violation of the norms that it actually follows, if it is in fact seriously unjust in some way.)

At this point, two related objections must be considered. Even if we agree that a community has an ideal rational structure, it may be argued that an action that does not actually harm anyone cannot plausibly be said to violate that structure. Or if it does, then, we may say, so much the worse for the rational structure of the community. Surely there are circumstances in which it would be better to sacrifice our ideal of what a just community should be to the urgent needs of the real persons before us.

These objections have undeniable force, and yet, in my view, they are not decisive against Aquinas' claim that some kinds of actions are never morally justifiable. What they presuppose is that the good of the individual and the good of the community can be neatly separated and set over against one another, at least in some cases. If Aquinas' understanding of justice were more abstract, we might well conclude that that is his view. But as we have seen, Aquinas has a substantive theory of justice, according to which the just community is characterized by relations of equality among all its members with respect to the fundamentals of life. Actions that violate justice do so not only by harming individuals in obvious ways, but by harming them in such a way as to violate the relationships of equality that structure the life of a just community. And for this reason, a violation of the norms of justice undermines the relationships of equality that characterize the just community, whatever other harms may or may not result from it.

Given this substantive account of justice, the distinction between the good of the individual and the common good of a just community is not so clear as the objection described above presupposes. Whatever our other interests in a given action may be, we all do have a stake in preserving the interrelationships of equality which safeguard both the conditions for individual well-being and a harmonious common life. Moreover, the individuals directly involved in a given action arguably have an obligation, on the one side, and a just claim, on the other, to relate to one another in such a way as to preserve the relationship of equality with respect to the fundamentals of life that transcends their obligations and claims not to harm or be harmed in more obvious ways. In other words, the violation of the relationship of equality in fundamentals that should exist among all persons is arguably a harm to the individual who suffers it, as well as to the community as a whole, even when circumstances are such that it might be possible to argue that he is not truly harmed otherwise.

Even if this line of argument is accepted, we may still find ourselves perplexed by cases like that of Dr. Jones. We may not be able to say that the action described there is just or even permissible, and yet it may seem unduly harsh to characterize Dr. Jones as a murderer. Let me suggest a way of looking at the issues raised by cases of these sorts that may at least help to make sense of our remaining perplexities.

The questions that are raised in the course of moral discernment are complex because they reflect the diverse interests and purposes that we bring to that task. So far in this section, our reflections have been informed by the sorts of considerations that come into play when we evaluate actions, including a set of considerations that might be described, very roughly, as community-oriented concerns. That is, we have emphasized the issues that are raised when we attempt to determine the boundaries of a just community, as expressed (in part) in the kinds of actions that it prohibits. It would appear that these considerations force the conclusion that Dr. Jones' action is an action of an intrinsically evil kind, specifically, murder, and therefore it cannot be morally justified.

On the other hand, if the primary concern guiding our reflections has to do with the stance that we are to take toward the persons who do the sorts of actions that we identify as intrinsically evil, then a somewhat different set of considerations arises. In ordinary cases, an individual who knowingly and freely does an action of this sort may fairly be said to have a malicious will, in that she knowingly violates the essential equality that should exist between herself and her neighbors. But in a case like that of Dr. Jones, it is more difficult to stigmatize the agent as malicious. "Anyone might have done what he did," we say, or else, "No one can deny that he intended to do the right thing." In other words, we acknowledge that in some extraordinary cases, the situation is so painful or ambiguous that it would have been heroic to have acted in accordance with what morality strictly demands. And since most of us are not heroes, the fact that someone fails to act heroically, in an especially difficult situation, does not indicate that he is ordinarily malicious, and not to be trusted in everyday social intercourse. A man who would kill his aged, suffering grandmother in order to get her inheritance is repugnant to most of us, although it is the beginning of moral wisdom to know that under the right circumstances, we might do the same. A man who would kill someone in order to spare her seemingly pointless, extreme suffering is not nearly so repugnant, but he still bears watching, for who among us is not vulnerable to what another would judge to be pointless suffering? Even so, the action of the latter would seem to be *excusable* in a way that the action of the former is not. (Both actions are *forgivable*, but that is another sort of judgment.) In each case, it should be noted, we make a judgment as to what we are to say about the agent himself, as he reveals himself in and through what he does. It does not follow that in the latter case we commend the action, which must still be classed as murder. We would not advocate that others, in a similar situation, should act similarly. Nonetheless, our evaluation of the agent, and his subsequent standing in the community, will reflect our sense that there are circumstances in which it is difficult for any of us to reproach another, even for doing what is morally wrong.[23]

Intrinsically Evil Acts, Part Two: Are the Norms of Justice Culturally Invariant?

We now return to a consideration of the question that was raised, and bracketed, at the beginning of the last section. Might it not be the case that the traditional catalogue of intrinsically evil actions is misformulated, in that it stigmatizes as morally wrong some kinds of actions that are actually innocent, and/or fails to stigmatize some kinds of actions that ought to be condemned? If this question simply raises the possibility that the traditional list is mistaken at some points, then it can be readily answered. Of course the traditional list can be—indeed, almost certainly is—in need of revision. After all, discernment of moral norms depends in part on our assessments as to what does and does not promote human happiness. And since those assessments depend in turn on our knowledge of what it is to be human, which is as subject to mistake and correction as the rest of our knowledge, then it would be surprising indeed if our list of intrinsically evil actions were not in need of periodic correction.

However, a more difficult and theoretically interesting question is often raised in this context. Might it not be the case that the traditional list of intrinsically evil actions is not so much mistaken, as outdated? That is, might it not be the case that some kinds of actions that truly were violations of justice, hence intrinsically evil, in different cultural contexts, are not such today, in our very different context? Lending money at interest, which Aquinas stigmatizes as the intrinsically evil action of usury, may be the most commonly cited example of a kind of action that has changed its moral character in such a way. Of course, the opposite possibility must also be acknowledged. Some kinds of actions that were once morally permissible may now have become intrinsically evil. For example, it is sometimes argued that today no form of warfare is morally licit because of the danger of escalation to nuclear war that is now inseparable (it is said) from any military action.

For some time now, scholars of Aquinas have recognized that he does indeed acknowledge that specific kinds of actions may change their moral value in this way.[24] That is, Aquinas recognizes that some precepts of the natural law appear to express what justice and human happiness demand in a particular set of circumstances, and therefore appear to be subject to change (I-II.94.4, 5). Odon Lottin provides a very striking example of this aspect of Aquinas' thought in his analysis of all of Aquinas' writings that touch upon the norms concerning marriage.[25] As Lottin shows, Aquinas knows quite well that the norms of marriage have varied widely from society to society, and so he is reluctant to say that those peoples who practice (for example) polygamy are morally corrupt. (He is not always unwilling to judge a people as morally corrupt, however. The barbarian Germans, who were said to commend thieving, *are* stigmatized by him as a corrupt society [I-II.94.4; cf. I-II.94.6].) Instead, Aquinas attempts to make sense of these variations by observing that just as the institution of marriage has both primary and secondary purposes, relative to human well-being, so the norms of marriage are of primary or secondary importance. On these grounds, he argues that polygamy does not depart from the natural law so radically as to be wholly unacceptable. This institution impedes the secondary purpose of the institution of marriage, that is, the mutual companionship of husband and wife, but not its primary purpose, namely, the propagation and rearing of the next generation in a stable family structure. Moreover, he suggests that the secondary precepts of the natural law may change in part because the needs of human communities vary, so that, for example, polygamy may well have been the only workable form of marriage when the world was new and sparsely populated.

This line of analysis suggests what Aquinas says in the *ST:* "The natural law is something constituted by reason, just as a proposition is also in a way a work of reason" (I-II.94.1). That is, as we have already seen, the concrete norms of justice (and more generally, of morality) are not self-evident to us. They must be discerned through a process of ongoing reflection on the meaning of the fundamental norms of morality, that one should fulfill one's special obligations and do no harm to anyone, in the context of the concrete conditions of a particular time and place (cf. I-II.92.4, 5). And since both our knowledge and our circumstances are in flux, the exact content of the natural law as we discern it will also be in flux.

Nonetheless, it would be a mistake to conclude that the concrete norms of justice are wholly subject to revision and change from one culture to another. It is sometimes suggested that justice is a formal norm that can be filled in with any particular set of concrete norms whatever.[26] But this claim is absurd. A concept of justice that would be consistent with any set of specific norms whatever would be empty rather than formal. What gives the concept of justice its formal meaning, for Aquinas, is the notion of equality with respect to the fundamentals of human life outlined above. That is, for Aquinas, justice in its most formal sense requires allowing each person to pursue happiness by acting on the fundamental inclinations of human life, unless an individual forfeits her claim to act within the community through her own wrongdoing. While this norm is consistent with a great deal in the way of specific content, it is not consistent with every institution that has existed or could be imagined. For example, some forms of servitude—working for wages, for instance—can allow individuals enough freedom to be consistent with justice. On the other hand, chattel slavery does not allow sufficient freedom to individuals to be consistent with justice in any society, although it has been practiced in many corrupt societies (including, of course, our own). Moreover, there are some kinds of harms that strike so radically at the core of human dignity and freedom that they can never be consistent with justice, such as rape, torture, or, to take Aquinas' paradigmatic example, the killing of innocent persons.[27]

Distributive Justice

The reader may be surprised that so little has been said so far about Aquinas' treatment of distributive justice. However, our consideration of this aspect of his theory of justice has been delayed in the interests of clarity for two reasons. The first is that Aquinas himself has so little to say about distributive justice; II-II.61.1-3 and II-II.63 contain almost all his remarks on the subject in the *ST*. The brevity of his treatment of distributive justice does not at all indicate that he considers this topic to be unimportant, but it does render that treatment less useful for our first efforts to understand his overall theory of justice than his much more extensive discussion of commutative justice and the sins opposed to it. Second, it will be especially illuminating to examine Aquinas' treatment of distributive justice in conjunction with our investigation of his doctrine of prudence (an investigation we will take up in the next chapter). For justice, like temperance and fortitude, is essentially open-ended and must be completed by the higher virtue of prudence. Of course, the open-ended quality of justice will also be sometimes manifested in the interactions between individuals which are the special province of commutative justice, especially in those interactions which involve buying and selling. But when we turn to those questions that are the special province of distributive justice, we find that in this area, the dependence of justice on prudence is especially evident.

In II-II.61.2, Aquinas asks, "Whether two species of justice are suitably assigned, that is, commutative and distributive?" He argues that this division is indeed correct, because these two parts of justice concern two different kinds of interactions, reflecting the two ways in which individuals are related to others. The proper matter of commutative justice concerns exchanges between private individuals; whereas the proper matter of distributive justice concerns the distribution of the common goods of society to its individual members, including spiritual goods, honor and respect, as well as material goods (cf. II-II.63.2, 3). Both forms of justice are grounded in the general norm of equality (II-II.61.2 *ad* 2), but they reflect two different forms of equality. Commutative justice preserves equality of exchanges (broadly understood to include any sort of interaction between private individuals), and therefore it is maintained when whatever is exchanged between two persons is equal, that is to say, when neither one suffers at the other's expense (II-II.61.2). Distributive justice, on the other hand, preserves the proper proportion between what an individual deserves from the community, and what he receives from it (II-II.61.2).

So far, Aquinas' account of distributive justice would seem to be straightforward enough, although we might have wished for a fuller treatment. However, two qualifications must be added to this account.[28] The first is that Aquinas does not appear to distinguish between desert and merit in assessing what an individual deserves from the community. When he addresses the question of what it is in virtue of which citizens deserve more or less from the community, he simply observes that the specific criterion for desert depends on the organizing principle for the community: In an aristocratic community, desert is determined by personal worth (at least in theory);

in an oligarchy, by wealth; in a democracy, by liberty; and so on (II-II.61.2). He does not indicate which, if any, of these distributive principles he considers to be the most appropriate. Moreover, when we turn to his discussion of the vice opposed to distributive justice—namely, preferring one person to another in the distribution of common goods without adequate cause—we find that what counts as an adequate cause for preferring one to another varies with respect to the sort of good that is in question, and concerns an individual's merit or abilities to hold a particular post at least as often as it concerns her desert in the sense of general worthiness (II-II.63; cf. I-II.63.1, 2 and I-II.63.3). Hence, it would be more accurate to say that distributive justice as Aquinas understands it is grounded in considerations of both merit and desert.

Second, Aquinas' assertion that individuals have a fundamental claim to receive the necessities of life implies that he would also accept need as an appropriate criterion for just distributions (cf. II-II.66.7). That is, he implies that each individual in a just community would be guaranteed the necessities of life, and beyond that, individuals would receive from the common wealth of their community in proportion to their merit or desert.

Even amended in these ways, it is clear that taken by itself Aquinas' account of distributive justice is far too abstract to provide for much substantive guidance. Once we begin to consider the practical questions that arise when we attempt to assess desert, merit, and need, and to distribute the goods of society equitably on the basis of these criteria, we find ourselves confronted by a host of nice discriminations, delicate judgments, and gray areas in which we must decide without the benefit of detailed rules to guide us. Aquinas' sketchy treatment of distributive justice provides little or no guidance when we attempt to negotiate these waters.

And yet, the relative sketchiness of Aquinas' account should be seen as an indication of his wisdom, rather than of his lack of foresight. He recognizes that we will never be able to formulate guidelines that will settle in advance all the practical questions that arise when we enter into the realm of distributive justice (II-II.120.1, 2). That is why a legislator, or indeed, a private citizen, cannot be truly just unless he also possesses the virtue of prudence, which gives determinate content to the principles of justice in the concrete circumstances of our lives. We now turn to a consideration of that virtue.

6

Prudence; Cardinal and Theological Virtues

Just as the virtue of justice exhibits features that set it apart from temperance and fortitude, so the virtue of prudence cannot be put on a par with justice, temperance, or fortitude. In the first place, prudence, unlike the virtues we have considered so far, is strictly speaking an intellectual virtue (I-II.57.4, 5; II-II.47.1), although it requires the moral virtues for its exercise (I-II.58.5) and is accordingly ranked among them. Furthermore, even though prudence is the highest of the cardinal virtues, it does not stand in precisely the same relation to them as justice does to temperance and fortitude.

We have already noted that the norms of justice provide definite content to the otherwise open-ended notions of temperance and fortitude; those norms do so by directing the good of the individual, toward which the affective virtues are directed, to the common good that transcends and guarantees individual good. That is why Aquinas says that justice directs the other moral virtues to its own proper end, that is, to the common good (II-II.58.5, 6). When we turn to Aquinas' remarks on prudence, we would expect to find that just as justice directs the other moral virtues to its own higher end, so prudence directs justice and the affective virtues to the (naturally) highest end of all, that is, conformity with reason. And yet, that is not what Aquinas says. To the contrary, he denies that prudence determines the end of the moral virtues, which is already set by synderesis, that is to say, the habitual knowledge of the first self-evident principles of practical reason (II-II.47.6; I.79.12). Nonetheless, prudence may be said to regulate the other virtues by directing them toward their true end, and in that sense it is the highest of the cardinal virtues (II-II.47.7).

In order to make sense of Aquinas' account of prudence and its relation to the other cardinal virtues, it will be necessary to arrive at some understanding of the way in which, in his view, prudence directs the other virtues to the end which is set for them by synderesis. This effort will in turn provide us with a confirmation and summary of the interpretation of Aquinas' moral theory developed up to this point. For as will become apparent, Aquinas' account of prudence and its relation to the other virtues both presupposes and extends his account of the specific human good, which serves as the proximate norm of morality.

When we have completed our discussion of prudence and its relation to the other cardinal virtues, we will be in a position to understand the significance for Aquinas' overall theory of morality of the claim that certain virtues are cardinal (that is, primary) virtues. We will then consider how his treatment of the theological virtues both presupposes and resolves certain difficulties raised by his treatment of the cardinal virtues.

The End and the Mean

It is surprising, given our analysis so far of Aquinas' treatment of the virtues, to find that prudence does not determine the end of the cardinal virtues, as justice determines the end of temperance and fortitude. But Aquinas' justification for this conclusion, spelled out at II-II.47.6, is straightforward enough:

> The end of moral virtues is the human good. Now, the good of the human soul is to be in accordance with reason. . . . Hence, it is necessary that the ends of the moral virtues preexist in the reason. Just as there are certain things in the speculative reason which are naturally known, of which there is intelligence, and there are other things which are known through them, namely, conclusions, of which there is knowledge, so in the practical reason there are some principles known by nature, and such are the ends of the moral virtues. . . . And certain things are in the practical reason as conclusions, and among these are those things which are directed toward an end, at which we arrive from a consideration of the ends themselves. And these belong to prudence, which applies universal principles to the particular conclusions of operations. And hence it does not pertain to prudence to preestablish the end of the moral virtues, but only to dispose of those things which are directed toward that end.

He adds that it is natural reason functioning as synderesis which determines the end of the moral virtues (II-II.47.6 *ad* 1; cf. I.79.12).

In what sense does prudence determine what, concretely, con-
duces toward the attainment of the end set by the first principles of
practical reason? It would be natural to assume that prudence functions in this capacity by determining the appropriate means, in any
given set of circumstances, toward the attainment of the end set by
synderesis, and this is in fact how the translators of the widely used
1947 translation of the *ST* do read this text: "Certain things are in the
practical reason by way of conclusions, and such are the means which
we gather from the ends themselves. About these is prudence" (II-
II.47.6).[1] But in fact, Aquinas' Latin is not that specific. It reads: "Et
quaedam sunt in ratione practica ut conclusiones, et huiusmodi sunt
ea quae sunt ad finem, in quae pervenimus ex ipsis finibus. Et horum
est prudentia, applicans universalia principia ad particulares conclusiones operabilium" (And certain things are in the practical reason as
conclusions, and among these are those things which are directed
toward an end, at which we arrive from a consideration of the ends
themselves. And these belong to prudence, which applies universal
principles to the particular conclusions of operations). In other words,
the statement that prudence determines the means toward the end set
by synderesis is an interpretation of Aquinas' meaning that is not
necessarily warranted by the text. And in fact, as I shall argue, this
is an inaccurate interpretation. Aquinas does not intend to say that
the primary function of prudence lies in determining appropriate
means toward preexisting ends, although that is undoubtedly one of
the subordinate functions of prudence.[2]

What is the point of pressing a distinction between discerning
the means toward an end, and making some more general sort of
determination of what pertains to that end? In order to appreciate the
significance of this distinction, it must be noted that the expression
"the ends of the moral virtues" is ambiguous, taken by itself. If we
interpret Aquinas to be saying that the primary function of prudence
is to determine appropriate means toward these ends, then that
would imply that he understands these ends to be fairly determinate,
at least on the conceptual level, prior to the workings of prudence
itself. After all, if we are to determine the means to attain some goal,
we will need a fairly definite idea of what sorts of things might bring
the desired goal about, and what sorts of things would be likely to
hinder it. Such an idea presupposes that we have a definite idea of
what the desideratum is and how it might be causally related to
events and circumstances that are more or less within our control.
Moreover, given that we are starting with this sort of determinate
notion of the goal at which we aim, it is very likely, at least, that we
will be able to devise more than one set of means that would serve

to achieve that goal. Since the goal at which we aim is by hypothesis a determinate good, it can be identified as such independently of an account of the specific chain of events that brings it about, and for that very reason, we can envision more than one way in which it might be attained.

For example, say that I want to be granted tenure in the university at which I teach. I can envision this goal in a reasonably determinate way. It is a status, granted by the dean of my department upon the recommendation of my colleagues, which would confer certain privileges that are spelled out in the faculty handbook. And because I know at least that much about tenure, I know, at least generally, what has to come about in order to achieve that goal. Specifically, my colleagues and, above all, my dean have to be persuaded to confer the desired status. Knowing that, I can begin to take definite steps in order to get tenure. The most obvious route to this goal would be to publish several solid articles and a book or two, while maintaining a decent quality of teaching and participation in committee work. But if that route seems impractical, there are other ways in which I might also attain my goal. For example, I could resort to bribery. My point is that, having a concrete goal in mind, I can devise the means to attain that goal, and I will most likely be able to devise more than one means to the goal.

It will probably be apparent by now that it is very difficult to think of doing a virtuous deed or living a virtuous life as the kinds of goals that would ordinarily lend themselves to this sort of means/end analysis. Suppose that, in addition to achieving tenure, I want to conduct myself among my fellow workers and students in a virtuous way. It is difficult to see what an analysis of the means by which I could reach this goal would even look like, because "behaving virtuously" does not name the sort of determinate outcome of a causal chain that "getting tenure" does. Indeed, if I am to attain the goal of behaving virtuously in my department, I must first of all decide what, concretely, would count as virtuous behavior in my particular circumstances. For example, I may resolve to be fair to my students, and courteous but not obsequious to my colleagues, as expressed by doing this in that situation, and carrying myself this way rather than that in the presence of this individual . . . and so on. Having made these determinations, I can then carry out the course of activity that I have identified as the path of virtue, but it would not be accurate to say that in so doing, I am executing the means to attain a predetermined end. Not only would it be impossible to say in advance exactly what would count as a virtuous action in any situation that might arise, but even more important, my specific actions are not the means toward my goal of attaining virtuous behavior. Rather, they *are* the virtuous behavior, assuming that I am in fact successful in my attempts to act virtuously.

My point is this. The goal of acting virtuously is not the sort of goal that lends itself to means/end analysis, because this goal cannot be specified independently of some specification of the kind of action or actions that would bring it about. Certainly, the individual who wants to act virtuously in a given situation will presumably have a formal idea of what the virtues mean and will therefore have a general idea of what virtue would require in this particular situation. But formal notions of the virtues relevant to a given situation will not necessarily be sufficient to determine what sort of action, concretely, will embody the virtue or virtues in question. For this reason, the person who wants to act virtuously must first of all determine what sort of action would count as an act of virtue in this particular situation. Once that determination has been made, then there may be room for a calculation of the best means to bring about the end of acting in that way. Such calculations would often be necessary when the virtue in question is justice, which demands that certain objectively ascertainable sorts of relationships between individuals be maintained if its demands are to be satisfied. But this sort of means/end reasoning will be secondary to a determination of what sort of action is required in a particular situation in order to meet the demands of the relevant virtue. Indeed, means/end reasoning will not always be necessary. What sort of means/end reasoning do I need to undertake once I have determined that in order to meet the demands of temperance I need to refuse to take a third brownie? All I need to do is to refuse the brownie.

These considerations suggest very strongly that when Aquinas says that prudence determines the things that are directed toward the ends of the moral virtues, what he is saying is that prudence determines which courses of activity and specific actions would instantiate the virtues in the specific situations that make up our lives. And this line of interpretation is confirmed in the next question, II-II.47.7, "Whether it belongs to prudence to find the mean in moral virtues?" He answers that it does. He explains that while it belongs to the very nature of virtue to seek the mean, so that this, the end of virtue, sets a goal prior to prudence, nonetheless the nature of virtue does not suffice to determine what, concretely, *is* the mean of a particular virtue. This latter determination depends on the operation of prudence, through which the virtuous person is able to discern what sorts of activities and actions will best instantiate the mean of a given virtue.

In every case, as Aquinas reminds us in II-II.47.7, the mean of a virtue consists in conformity with reason. At the same time, conformity with reason is specified in different ways for the different virtues (I-II.64.2). In the matters that directly concern the affective virtues, conformity to reason is secured when the individual's desires and aversions are in accordance with her reasoned grasp of what promotes, and what hinders, her attainment of the true human good. Hence, the mean of these virtues is said to be the rational mean, which is determined by reference to the individual's own overall good. On the other hand, the conformity to reason proper to justice is secured when an individual's actions preserve the relationships of mutual equality which characterize the just community, and therefore, the mean of justice is said to be the real mean. But whether the mean of the virtue in question is the rational or the real mean, that is, whether it refers primarily to the individual's own good or the preservation of right relations in community, it is the task of prudence to determine what, concretely, the mean of the virtue is. That is to say, synderesis determines the formal end of virtue, namely, correspondence to the mean, whereas prudence determines the substantive ends of the virtues (cf. II-II.47.7 *ad* 3).

At this point, it may be objected that Aquinas' remarks in II-II.47.6 contradict the interpretation of his account of the human good developed in the third chapter. It was argued there that while Aquinas holds that the principle that good is to be done and evil is to be avoided is self-evident to all, the substantive meaning of the human good is not self-evident, but calls for theoretical reflection on human experience. But how can this interpretation be reconciled with his claim at II-II.47.6 that the specific human good is naturally known by the reason? In order to answer this question, we must look further into the meaning of the phrase, "Bonum autem humanae animae est secundum rationem esse" (Now the good of the human soul is to be in accordance with reason) (II-II.47.6).

The meaning of the expression "to be in accordance with reason" must be understood in the context of Aquinas' dictum, very familiar to us by now, that what is proper to the human person is to pursue his specific good in and through rational activity directed toward that good, intellectually comprehended *as* his perfectly fulfilling and satisfying good. When Aquinas says that the good of the human soul is to be in accordance with reason, he is simply drawing out the implications of one of the fundamental claims of his anthropology. If the human person is to attain her good at all, she can only do so in and through her own rational activity. Thus, the good of her soul, which is the principle of all her activity, is to be, to exist, in accord-

ance with reason. Further, from Aquinas' claim that synderesis includes the principle that the human good consists in acting in accordance with reason, we should not conclude that Aquinas holds that all
persons naturally know the substance of his anthropology. This principle is universally known in the same sense as the first principle of
practical reason is universally known. Not everyone could formulate
it (that would indeed presuppose theoretical knowledge that not
everyone shares), but everyone necessarily acts upon it. That is,
everyone who acts at all necessarily does so out of the intellectual
apprehension of something as a good, and therefore embodies, as it
were, the principle that the good of the human soul as the source of
all properly human action is to be in accordance with reason.

Indeed, the first principle of practical reason, and the dictum that
the good of the human soul is to be in accordance with reason, are
really two ways of expressing the same first principle from different
perspectives. The first principle of practical reason expresses the necessity, built into the very nature of rational action, that anyone who
acts at all must necessarily act for some good. The dictum of II-II.47.6
reminds us that if the human person is to attain any good, his soul,
considered as the principle of his actions, must be rational, at least
in the minimal sense that it must be able to direct his external actions
toward the attainment or preservation of whatever he intellectually
apprehends to be good.

If that is so, why should Aquinas offer two different formulations of one first principle? He does so because these formulations
lend themselves in different ways to the different implications that
he wants to draw out. At I-II.94.2, he wants to call attention to the
different sorts of goods that human persons naturally seek, in order
to indicate what substantive kind of life is good for the human person
as such. In II-II.47.6, on the other hand, he is pointing to the link
between the fundamental good of the human person and the virtues.
In order to do so he reminds us that the human soul must be rational
if the individual is to attain any good at all, and rationality, in turn,
is secured by the moral virtues, which direct the various desires of
the human person to be in accordance with what she intellectually
apprehends as good (II-II.47.7).[3]

We are now in a position to see why Aquinas' analysis of prudence and its relation to synderesis does not call into question the
interpretation of his moral theory developed in chapter 3. In that
chapter, it was argued that while Aquinas holds that it is self-evidently true that the good is to be pursued, and evil is to be avoided,
this principle does not take on substantive content apart from an
account of what the concrete specific good of the human creature is.

And that account is not self-evident to us, because it presupposes a particular theory of goodness in general. Aquinas' remarks on the relation of synderesis to prudence are entirely in accordance with what we would have expected, given that the interpretation is correct. Natural reason, functioning as synderesis, generates the principle that the good of the human person is to be in accordance with reason. Prudence, which takes account of the specifics of an individual's own character and circumstances, determines what, concretely, it means for this individual to be in accordance with reason; prudence does this in and through determining the mean of the virtues relative to the individual and to the demands of equality and the common good. That is to say, prudence determines what amounts to a substantive theory of the human good, at least as it applies to this individual in his particular setting, although of course the individual may not be able to formulate that theory in any systematic way.

The Function of Prudence and Its Relation to Justice

How does prudence function in order to set the mean of the virtues? Aquinas' treatment of prudence follows Aristotle's treatment of practical wisdom very closely, so much so that we can apply to Aquinas' prudence what one commentator has said about Aristotle's practical wisdom:

> Whatever other roles practical wisdom may or may not play, I suggest that one role is this. It enables a man, in light of his conception of the good life in general, to perceive what generosity requires of him, or more generally what virtue and *to kalon* [the noble] require of him, in the particular case, and it instructs him to act accordingly. A picture of the good life will save him from giving away too much or too little, or to the wrong causes, in particular instances.[4]

Hence, we read that there are three actions of the reason, as it is applied to action, which ought to be regulated by prudence, namely, to take counsel, to judge what one has discovered, and to command, that is, to put the results of one's deliberations into action (II-II.47.8). We have already been told that counsel is an inquiry into the best way to bring about a given end (I-II.14.1, 2); in a given matter it leads the will to choose whatever specific course of action has been identified as conducing in some way to whatever the will has fixed on as its end (I-II.13.1). If the counsel in question is an act of true prudence, then the individual deliberates and chooses in the light of her desire to attain her true good by leading a certain kind of life (II-II.47.13). This deliberation leads in turn to the command of the reason, which results immediately in action, whether internal to the agent or an external act (I-II.17.5-7, 9). Indeed, there is no real distinction between the commanded act and the action which is commanded. That is, the command of the reason to take a walk, for example, and the agent's actually walking are two components of one unified action (I-II.17.4). In the case of the prudent person, successful deliberation as to the appropriate way to act out of one's desire to live a certain kind of life results directly in the agent's acting in that way. Because command is the act of prudence which is most directly connected to action, Aquinas identifies it as the chief act of prudence (II-II.47.8).

Moreover, only an action which proceeds from prudence in this way can be called a fully virtuous action (I-II.63.1). The actions of the truly virtuous person express his settled, intellectually informed commitment to live the sort of life that is a good life for human beings. It is sometimes possible for a person who does not have this sort of settled commitment to perform the sorts of actions that a truly virtuous person would perform, but her actions will not be truly virtuous actions precisely because they do not flow from an intellectual commitment to live in a virtuous way (I-II.57.5; I-II.58.4). It does not necessarily follow that her actions will be bad. They may well conform objectively to the demands of morality, and they may even be praiseworthy as the efforts of someone who is still immature in virtue or who is struggling to remain at least continent (cf. I-II.57.5 *ad* 5). At the same time, even the good actions of a well-disposed beginner, who has a natural inclination to behave in a virtuous way, are prone to deviate from the objective criteria for goodness in actions, since his actions are not regulated by an overall grasp of what the good life requires (I-II.58.5 *ad* 3). For example, think of a naturally generous young man who gives away his livelihood to unscrupulous persons who play on his sympathies. The truly prudent person, on the other hand, will bring her settled commitment to lead a good life to bear on all her actions and activities, thereby ensuring that her actions are truly in accord with her overall ideal, and her life is unified by her consistent pursuit of that ideal. Hence, Aquinas says that prudence is necessary if the individual is to lead a good life (I-II.57.5).

Aquinas' claim that prudence and the moral virtues properly so called will necessarily function together in a truly virtuous individual was anticipated in chapter 4, when we examined the basis of his commitment to the thesis of the unity of the virtues. Since he holds that the moral virtues are open-ended, and can only be completed through a consideration of higher principles, he is bound to hold that true moral virtue is possible only to the individual who habitually acts on the basis of a consideration of the human good as such. Prudence completes and unifies the virtues in and through directing all the actions of the individual toward the true human good.

At the end of the last chapter, it was suggested that prudence directs the moral virtues to their proper end in a more specific way as well, by giving definite shape to the notion of the common good toward which justice, temperance, and fortitude are directed (the latter two virtues being directed toward the common good through justice). While Aquinas does not make this claim explicitly, to my knowledge, it is implicit in his treatment of political prudence, which directs the activities of the individual toward the common good of his community (II-II.47.11).

In order to appreciate the full significance of political prudence, it is important to recall that the virtue of justice demands that objective relationships of equality be maintained among individuals and between individuals and the community itself (II-II.58.2). It is relatively easy to determine what those relationships should look like, concretely, among individuals. But the right relationship between desert, merit or need, and the distribution of the shared goods of the community is a more difficult question, and calls for delicate assessments of a number of particular variables. Hence, those who are responsible for the distribution of shared goods, to say nothing of the management of the other affairs of the community, must clearly possess prudence. Without it, they will not be able to maintain an objectively just society, all their good will notwithstanding. Indeed, the very substance of distributive justice is so intimately linked with the determinations proper to political prudence that it would seem that political prudence and distributive justice are in effect two components of one virtue by which rulers govern wisely and well.

Further on, at II-II.50.1 and 2, Aquinas adds that, properly speaking, the species of prudence which is concerned with the common good is divided into regnative prudence and political prudence properly so called. Regnative prudence is properly the virtue of rulers, since it is the ruler above all who directs the affairs of the community toward the common good (II-II.50.1). However, since all persons, being rational agents, are able to participate in the affairs of the community, all the members of the community can and should participate in the virtue of political prudence (II-II.47.12; II-II.50.2). Of course, the specific way in which this virtue is expressed will depend on the form of political life in a particular community. In a monarchy, which Aquinas himself believed to be the best form of government (II-II.50.1 ad 2), subjects will exercise political prudence by obeying the laws of their ruler willingly and intelligently, so as to cooperate with her in the maintenance of the common good. In a democracy, there will clearly be more scope for all the citizens of the community to participate in framing laws as well as carrying them out. We may conclude that the nearer a community comes to being a true democracy, the less basis there will be among its citizens for a distinction between regnative and political prudence.

Finally, although to my knowledge Aquinas does not mention it specifically, there will also be need for political prudence on the part of citizens of an unjust community. While Aquinas does not discuss the function of political prudence in an unjust community, he clearly envisions the legitimacy of recognizing that a particular ruler is unjust, and deposing him, even by force of arms, in order to reorient the community toward the common good (II-II.42.2 *ad* 3). Clearly, such a reorientation could not take place except through the efforts of persons who possess regnative/political prudence. Indeed, those who strive to be men and women of virtue in an unjust community may have an even greater need of political prudence than others who are better situated, since in order to live a life of virtue they must envision what their community could and should be, and participate in some way in efforts to bring it nearer to its ideal.

But whatever the specific form that it takes, regnative/political prudence will be necessary to the truly virtuous person, because it is this form of prudence which directs her to the common good on which her individual good depends (II-II.47.10 *ad* 2). In this way, the virtue of prudence completes its function of rendering the whole life of the individual good, at least in accordance with the natural good of the human person. In this way, it guarantees that the individual will enjoy that unity of life which is essential to the attainment of the human good.

The Cardinal Virtues

As we noted in chapter 5, the framework of the cardinal and theological virtues around which Aquinas builds his substantive moral treatise is built out of traditional elements. Nonetheless, he has interpreted and systematized these elements in accordance with his conception of the human good, thereby making the doctrine of the cardinal and theological virtues his own. Having examined his treatment of the four cardinal virtues (temperance, fortitude, justice, and prudence) in some detail, we are now in a better position to understand the role that the doctrine of the cardinal virtues plays in his overall theory of morality. In the next section, we will briefly examine his treatment of the theological virtues.

Aquinas' first systematic examination of the cardinal virtues

(I–II.61) begins with a question that may surprise us: "Whether the moral virtues should be called cardinal or principal virtues?" (I–II.61.1). He answers that they should indeed, since it is the moral virtues (including, in this context, prudence) that rectify our desires and responses as well as our actions, and which therefore deserve the name of perfect virtues.[5] What is startling in this question is that Aquinas assumes that the cardinal virtues can be equated with moral virtue simply speaking. Aren't there any other moral virtues besides temperance, fortitude, justice, and prudence?

Of course there are. However, as Aquinas analyzes the virtues, all other moral virtues can be understood as components of, or subsidiary virtues associated with, these four. His reasoning is made clear by his responses to the next two questions, "Whether there are four cardinal virtues?" (I–II.61.2), and "Whether any other virtues should be called cardinal rather than these?" (I–II.61.3). In answering these questions, he explains that the four cardinal virtues are the primary moral virtues because they represent the four fundamental modes, so to speak, by which the individual appropriates the human good as discerned by reason: *Prudence* appropriates that good directly by the action of the intellect, which determines how best to actualize one's specific good; *justice* directs external actions in such a way as to conform to reason—it does this by conforming the will to a wider good than that of the individual's own (cf. I–II.56.6); and *fortitude* and *temperance* moderate the irascible and desiring passions in such a way that the individual spontaneously desires what is truly in accordance with the specific good of the human person and avoids what is not in accordance with the human good (I–II.61.2, 3). Taken in this way, the cardinal virtues can be understood as general virtues, under which more specific virtues may be classed. For example, any virtue that rectifies external actions may be described as a kind of justice. It is also possible, Aquinas adds, to understand the cardinal virtues as particular virtues with a special matter, divided by that special matter from other, subsidiary virtues. Understood in this way, they are still to be called principal or cardinal, because they are concerned with matters of preeminent importance: *Prudence*, with that command by which the reason moves the individual to action (cf. I–II.17.1); *justice*, with right relations between equals; *fortitude*, with courage in the face of death; and *temperance*, with a right attitude toward the pleasures of touch (I–II.61.3).

How does this analysis reflect Aquinas' conception of the human good? Recall that according to him, we can only attain our specific good by means of rational activity, that is, by sustaining a lifelong course of activity that is determined by our rational grasp of that in which the true human good consists. Indeed, in one sense the natural human good *is* rational activity, since the natural human good can only be attained in and through the rationally directed pursuit of the individual's (correct) ideal of a good human life. And what is characteristic of the cardinal virtues as Aquinas understands them is that it is necessary that they all be present in some form if the individual is to sustain a course of activity directed toward a long-term goal. Temperance and fortitude enable their possessor to moderate her passions in accordance with her larger aims. Justice ensures that her external actions will be in accordance with the norms of a well-ordered community, which harmonizes her private aims with a larger good. Prudence enables her to use her practical intelligence to discern the most appropriate ways of living out her commitment to larger aims in the particular circumstances of her life. Breakdowns in the exercise of these virtues make it more difficult for the agent to carry out her aims, or to pursue them within her community. In extreme cases, the individual who lacks one of the cardinal virtues will not be able to sustain a course of activity at all.

At the same time, the cardinal virtues operate in such a way as to lay the foundation for what might be called the subjective appropriation of the human good in the character of the individual. We have already seen that the natural human good may be characterized as a life lived in the orderly pursuit of the fundamental inclinations; such a life will be unified. Correlatively, the individual who leads such a life will necessarily have, or be, a unified personality. That is, his soul "will be in accordance with reason" in the fullest sense (II-II.47.6), in that all the components of his personality will fit together harmoniously, being all informed by his commitment to lead a certain kind of life. And as Aquinas analyzes them, the cardinal virtues provide the foundation for this unification of the personality. "These four virtues can be said to designate one another through a sort of redundancy among them," he explains (I-II.61.4 *ad* 1):

> For that which belongs to prudence influences the other virtues, insofar as they are directed by prudence. And each of the others influences the rest, because whoever is able to do what is more difficult is also able to do what is less difficult. Hence, whoever can restrain his desires for the pleasures of touch, lest they exceed the proper mode, which is the most difficult mode, can for this very reason check his audacity when faced with danger of death, lest he go beyond the proper mode of daring, which is much easier, and in this sense fortitude is said to be temperate. In the same way, temperance is said to be brave, from

the influence of fortitude on temperance, insofar as he whose soul is strengthened through fortitude against dangers of death, which is very difficult, can more easily retain a firm soul against the attack of pleasures.

At the same time, the cardinal virtues only lay the foundation for a truly unified character. An individual can be fully one with herself and at peace with herself only through the theological virtues, above all through charity. Hence, it will be appropriate to close our investigation into Aquinas' moral theory by a brief consideration of his treatment of the theological virtues.

Faith, Hope, and Charity

The cardinal virtues are necessary to live a truly good life, and they do not cease to be necessary for the justified, who possess the theological virtues of faith, hope, and charity (I-II.65.3). But at the same time, Aquinas also holds that the cardinal virtues alone cannot now fully attain even the natural human good at which they aim, due to the universal corruption of sin which renders us incapable of attaining even our natural good without supernatural help (I-II.109.2, 4; cf. I-II.65.2).

Moreover, although he does not say so explicitly, Aquinas implies that even if we did not suffer from the corrosion of original sin, the individual who possesses the cardinal virtues alone would not be able to lead a fully unified life, even though that is the good to which the cardinal virtues are naturally directed. And why? Because even though the naturally good person directs all his actions and activities toward the ultimate goal of living the sort of life that is good for human beings, he can only do so in and through pursuing particular goods and assuming distinctive relationships, which involve specific duties to others.

As Hauerwas reminds us, there can be no guarantee that these particular aims and obligations will not sometimes clash, thus creating tension and disharmony in the life of even the best of us.[6] Aquinas holds that there will always be a way to resolve conflicts of aims and duties without sin, unless an individual is placed in a particular dilemma by her own prior sin (cf. I-II.19.6 *ad* 3). But often, the best possible resolution of such a conflict will still leave the individual with grounds for inner conflict and regret. Moreover, tensions, conflicts, and hard choices will inevitably be multiplied in even the best-run community, and since the natural good of the individual cannot be separated from the good of her community, it follows that all will be subject to the tensions and disharmony entailed by a shared life. As long as our happiness is found in and through the pursuit of finite aims and relationships—even though these are subordinated to, and unified by, the pursuit of the overall kind of life that is good for the human creature—it will inevitably be partial and vulnerable to tensions and regrets (II-II.29.1; cf. I-II.2.8; I-II.3.8).

Given the necessary limitations of the cardinal virtues, it is not surprising that Aquinas assigns to the theological virtues, and above all to charity, the unifying function toward which the cardinal virtues tend.[7] The theological virtues are distinguished from the cardinal virtues in that they direct their subject toward a personal union with God, whose personal revelations are accepted through faith, whose assurances of salvation are accepted in hope, and who is loved for himself in charity (I-II.62.1, 3; II-II.1.1; II-II.17.2; II-II.23.1). This sort of union utterly exceeds the natural inclinations of any creature, including the highest pure spirits (I.12.4; I-II.5.5). Hence, the theological virtues cannot be attained through human efforts, but must be infused in us by God "entirely from without" (I-II.63.1; cf. I-II.62.1). The highest of the theological virtues is charity, which inculcates the love of God for his own sake, and not as the source of benefits to us (II-II.23.6). As such, it directs the individual toward the one good that can truly satisfy all his desires (I-II.3.8), and for this reason, it is the one sure foundation of the inner unity that is the essence of peace (II-II.29.1, 3).

Hence, Aquinas holds that charity, rather than prudence, functions as the supreme organizing principle in the personality of the justified, by which not only all their actions but all their desires and impulses are directed toward God (II-II.23.3, 7). Through charity, the individual is enabled to participate in the very mind and will of God, not only to fulfill the precepts of the natural law (although those, the deliverances of reason, are not abrogated by charity [II-II.26.6]), but even to grasp intuitively what God's will is for the individual in any given situation. That is why wisdom is the gift of the Holy Spirit that corresponds to charity (II-II.45.1, 2). At the same time, charity transforms not only the behavior but the affections and the whole person of the justified. That is why the justified manifest the joy, peace, and compassion that are the marks of true happiness (II-II.27-30).

But charity does not just secure the inner unity that is the essence of peace. It is also the only sure foundation for that concord among individuals which is the basis for peace within the community. The connection between charity and the peace of the community is clearly indicated by the amazing fact that Aquinas analyzes charity in the terms provided by Aristotle's discussion of friendship.[8] Hence, at the beginning of his treatise on charity, Aquinas asks whether charity is a form of friendship (II-II.23). He affirms that it is indeed a form of friendship *with God,* as the words of Christ indicate: "Now I do not call you my servants, but my friends" (John 15:15).

It is tempting to take this statement as a poetic metaphor, especially given Aristotle's insistence that even the derivative kinds of friendship, and much more friendship in the most proper sense, presuppose equality and mutuality. In the *Nicomachean Ethics,* we read that if there is a very great gap between two individuals, they cannot enjoy even a limited sort of friendship.[9] For this reason, we most certainly cannot enjoy friendship with the deity. Nonetheless, for Aquinas the claim that charity makes us friends of God is no metaphor. He means it literally, his strong sense of the infinite gap between creature and Creator notwithstanding. In II-II.23.1, he assures us that charity is true friendship because it is based on mutual communication between God and the justified (cf. II-II.24.2). Of course, the friendship of charity is unique, not least because one party alone creates the very possibility for its existence. That is, God creates friendship with the justified by so transforming the human soul that it becomes, in some sense, connatural to God (II-II.23.2) and is united to God without intermediary (II-II.23.6; II-II.27.4; I-II.66.6). Elsewhere, Aquinas speaks even more strongly. He asserts that through the theological virtues, we become partakers in the divine nature (I-II.62.1). Through charity in particular, we enjoy "a certain intimate conversation" with God (I-II.65.5). Still more strongly, the grace of God, by which faith, hope, and charity are bestowed, can be said to deify *(deificet)* us (I-II.112.1). In short, charity can be described as the friendship of women and men with God, because charity transforms its subjects into participants in the very mind and will of God.

But the friendship of charity is not limited to the relationship between God and the individual. Aristotle has already laid down the principle that the most perfect friendship is grounded in a communion in the true good, and so we would expect that charity unites in friendship all who share in the supreme good of friendship with God. In fact, Aquinas goes farther than that. He claims that charity unites us in friendship with all persons, since everyone is either an actual or a potential sharer in the grace of God which generates the primary friendship between God and the individual (II-II.25.1, 6, 8, 12). Admittedly, the friendship toward all that is proper to charity cannot secure peace in the human community, because in the present condition of the world, no community will be characterized by universal charity. Nonetheless, the friendship of charity that the justified bear toward their neighbors will tend to promote peace, because it will tend toward the removal of the clash of wills that generates so much discord: "Insofar as we love our neighbor as ourselves, it follows that the human person wishes to effect the will of the neighbor as if it were his own will" (II-II.29.3). Hence, Aquinas associates with charity all those virtues which express themselves in active concern for the neighbor, such as beneficence (II-II.31), acts of mercy and almsgiving (II-II.32), and fraternal correction (II-II.33).[10] And significantly, although Aquinas defends the possibility of fighting a just war, he classifies the sin of fighting an unjust war as a sin against charity rather than justice (II-II.40, esp. 40.1).

At the same time, Aquinas is careful to point out that while charity transcends the rationally discerned obligations of justice, it does not abrogate them (II-II.26.6). More generally, he insists that while, on the one hand, the cardinal virtues are finally inadequate without faith, hope, and charity, on the other hand, the theological virtues could not operate in an individual who lacked the proximate principles of human goodness, namely temperance, fortitude, justice, and prudence (I-II.65.3). While the justified individual, who possesses faith, hope, and charity, enjoys a relationship with God of a sort that exceeds all natural aspirations, nonetheless she remains human, an inhabitant of the world and subject to its due claims.

7

The Permanent Significance of Thomas Aquinas

The history of Aquinas' influence in the ecumenical church is filled with ironies. In 1879, Aquinas' intellectual authority was held up by Leo XIII, in his famous encyclical *Aeterni Patris,* as "a singular safeguard and glory of the Catholic Church," because "with his own hand he vanquished all errors of ancient times; and still he supplies an armory of weapons which brings us certain victory in the conflict with falsehoods ever springing up in the course of years."[1] The effect of this encyclical was mixed, by any standards. It helped to foster the brilliant flowering of Thomistic studies earlier in this century, and yet it also fostered a kind of rigid scholasticism which discredited Aquinas in the minds of many intellectuals, both in and out of the Catholic church. But the ironies do not end there. Today, Aquinas' influence among Protestant theologians may be as great as or greater than it is among Catholic theologians, in spite of the historic resistance to Thomism within the Protestant churches. Certainly, no one at the turn of the century would have foreseen that the most prominent common denominator among Catholic thinkers and major strands of Protestant thought, as represented in the work of Outka, Gustafson, and Hauerwas, would be a shared indebtedness to some aspect of Aquinas' moral thought.

In the situation of the church today, shaped as it has been by ironies such as these, a claim that Aquinas' thought has permanent significance for the ecumenical church must be spelled out with some care. It would be easy to read this claim as a reassertion of *Aeterni Patris,* which at least implies that Aquinas is *the* Christian theologian, whose work can never be superseded. That is not at all what I want to claim. To the contrary, I will suggest that Aquinas' permanent significance lies precisely in the fact that his thought contains the seeds of its own transcendence.

As I understand it, the permanent significance of Aquinas' thought must be understood and defended within the context of our interpretation of the history of the Christian tradition and our best judgments about the challenges that that tradition must meet today, if it is to continue as a living tradition. That is, Aquinas' thought is of permanent significance for the Christian tradition for two reasons. On the one hand, his thought can be shown to address the tensions and problematics of that tradition, as it had developed up to his own time, more successfully than other attempts to do so. On the other hand, it can be shown to be capable of addressing the tensions and problematics of the Christian tradition in our own time in a satisfactory way, albeit through expansion and development that will take us beyond the limits of Aquinas' own system (as he himself transcended both Aristotle and Augustine).[2]

Those readers who are familiar with MacIntyre's book *Whose Justice? Which Rationality?* will recognize that my defense of the permanent significance of Aquinas' work is dependent upon MacIntyre's account of the rationality of traditions.[3] Moreover, MacIntyre himself argues "quite incidentally" that Aquinas' synthesis was superior within the context of the history of the tradition within which Aquinas stood; moreover, this superiority extended throughout that tradition as it developed beyond him, up to the emergence of liberalism as a tradition. As a result of his own account of the history of that tradition, MacIntyre concludes that he, MacIntyre, has exhibited

> an Aristotelian tradition with resources for its own enlargement, correction, and defense, resources which suggest that *prima facie* at least a case has been made for concluding first that those who have thought their way through the topics of justice and practical rationality, from the standpoint constructed by and in the direction pointed out first by Aristotle and then by Aquinas, have every reason at least so far to hold that the rationality of their tradition has been confirmed in its encounters with other traditions and, second, that the task of characterizing and accounting for the achievements and successes, as well as the frustrations and failures, of the Thomistic tradition in the terms afforded by rival traditions of enquiry, may, even from the point of view of the adherents of those traditions, be a more demanding task than has sometimes been supposed.[4]

In this book, I have attempted to develop another, far more modest part of a general case for the permanent significance of Aquinas' thought, understood in terms of its role in the development of an ongoing tradition. I have attempted to show that Aquinas' moral thought brings together concepts that, in the thought of

our contemporaries in the field of Christian ethics, provide the basis
for rival and incompatible theories of morality. If the interpretation
developed in this book is convincing, then Aquinas' theory of morality is of more than historical interest to us today, because it can
point to strategies for overcoming the fragmentation of contemporary Christian ethics.

As I indicated in the first chapter, I do not intend to argue that
Aquinas' theory of morality could be accepted as it stands today.
However, I do believe that some version of that theory, reformulated
in the light of contemporary problematics, would offer the best prospect for recovering a cogent account of human goodness and human
virtue from the chaos of contemporary moral discourse. In order to
defend this claim, it would be necessary to show how a Thomistic
theory of morality could meet the challenges which our contemporaries direct against Aquinas' thought, and that is a task for another
book. But even at this point, it should be possible to offer at least
some general indications of the way in which some of these challenges might be addressed in a Thomistic theory of morality, and that
is what I will now attempt to do. In addition to bolstering the case
that Aquinas' thought deserves serious consideration as a starting
point for contemporary Christian ethics, these reflections, sketchy as
they will necessarily be, may serve nonetheless to indicate the lines
along which a contemporary Thomistic theory of morality might be
developed.

Science, Rationality, and the Doctrine of God

Of all the contemporary ethicists we have examined in this
book, James Gustafson insists most strongly that if Christianity is
to continue as a living tradition, it must take account of the challenges of contemporary science. In my view, he is quite right. Furthermore, as he himself notes, his view is far more in accordance
with the Thomistic spirit than would be a cavalier refusal to consider the deliverances of modern science to be relevant to Christian
thought.[5] At the same time, if these challenges are to be met, it is
necessary to determine just where they lie. I would argue, contrary
to Gustafson, that the particular deliverances of modern science to
which he refers do not present significant new challenges to Christian thought. I do not deny in principle that some particular discov-
ery might present a new challenge to Christian thought, as the
theory of evolution in fact did. However, it does not seem to me
that the specific discoveries that Gustafson mentions raise serious
new challenges, as he thinks they do.

On the other hand, the philosophical theories of rationality that have developed under the impetus of modern science do raise serious challenges for Christian thought. In particular, the growing consensus around what was described in chapter 2 as the incommensurability thesis poses a very serious challenge to Christian claims for the universal truth of the central Christian beliefs. In that chapter, I indicated briefly how a Thomistic theory of the natural law might be developed in such a way as to take the incommensurability thesis into account. The reader will recall that I argued there that the incommensurability thesis does not necessarily raise internal difficulties for the philosophy of nature on which a Thomistic natural law theory must be based. However, it does imply that the universal validity of the natural law, so understood, could be established only in conversation with rival traditions, and indeed there can be no guarantee that its universal validity could be established even then. The aspiration—explicit in Catholic moral theology, and implicit in the work of those thinkers analyzed by Outka, and perhaps in the work of Gustafson as well—to establish an account of morality that would be rationally compelling to anyone whatever must therefore be abandoned. However, it does not follow, as Hauerwas argues, that there can be no rational grounds on which to promote and defend a Christian theory of the natural law over against rival theories of morality. As MacIntyre has shown, it is possible rationally to assess the rival claims of incommensurable traditions, and so it would be possible to defend a Christian theory of the natural law *so long as* it is understood and defended as part of a wider tradition of thought.

Ultimately, as Gustafson realizes, an adequate Christian response to the challenges of modern science must be grounded in the doctrine of God. Aquinas' thought offers an especially promising basis on which to develop a doctrine of God that answers the challenges of our times, not only because of the considerable merits of his own doctrine of God, but even more because his general theory of goodness presupposes the possibility and legitimacy of developing a natural theology as one component of a Christian theory of morality. Indeed, although we have not examined it in this book, I would argue that Aquinas' theological doctrine of God implies that Christians have reasons, implicit in their own tradition, to take the project of natural theology seriously. This conclusion would be especially significant because a sort of natural theology is emerging today among scientists themselves. While the details of this natural theology may not be compatible with a Christian doctrine of God, nonetheless, it would be foolish to deny that Christians can and should

attempt to learn from it and to incorporate its genuine insights into
Christian theology.[6]

The Social Dimension of the Human Person

A second challenge that a contemporary Thomistic theory of
morality would have to meet lies in the area of philosophical anthropology. This challenge might be expressed in rough terms by
asking whether Aquinas has fully grasped the social dimensions of
human existence. True, he is well aware that the human person is
a social creature, and he gives great weight to our obligations to
family and society. Nonetheless, it might be said that he still assumes that the human person is finally a self-contained individual,
capable of knowledge and free choice apart from the conditioning
influences of society. But in fact, this model of the human person
has been seriously undermined by philosophical work which seems
to show that the human person is a creature of the social matrix
within which she moves, and is radically conditioned by the structures of her society. In this country, this challenge is presented
most forcefully by American pragmatism, which has had a profound influence on Protestant ethical thought that is especially apparent today in Gustafson's writings.[7]

I would suggest that the tradition of American pragmatism offers
the same sort of challenge, and opportunity, to Christian theologians
of our own time and place as Aristotelianism offered to Aquinas and
his contemporaries. No modern school of thought offers a more radical challenge to Christian thought, and yet, for that very reason, there
may be no modern school of thought that is potentially more fruitful
for Christian theology. In order to address this challenge, it will be
necessary to deal with it as Aquinas dealt with Aristotle, by incorporating it as far as possible into Christian thought without compro-
mising what is essential to the Christian tradition. To be more
specific: I would argue that Christianity cannot surrender the claim
that human persons are capable in principle of knowledge and actions that are not radically determined by their social matrices. But
it can, and indeed must, show that this possibility is compatible with
the reality of a pervasive social conditioning, which initially determines the activities of all persons, and may well continue to determine the activities of some persons throughout their lives. And
arguably, Aquinas offers at least a starting point for such an analysis
of human freedom, in his acknowledgment of the degree to which
moral discernment is conditioned by the limitations of our knowledge of the human good, on the one hand, and by the particular
circumstances within which we must act, on the other.

Levels of Goodness: Individual, Communal, and Universal Good

It will be apparent that until the Thomistic tradition has developed further along the lines just indicated, it will not be able to offer a complete answer to one of the most important questions in contemporary Christian ethics, namely, "What is the proper relationship between individual and community?" And yet, the conclusions of chapter 5 suggest the direction that such an answer would take.

As we saw in our examination of Aquinas' account of justice, Aquinas does not address the tension between the claims of the individual and those of the community by collapsing one set of claims into those of the other—that is, by identifying the good of the individual without remainder with the good of the community, or vice versa. Rather, his account of the naturally good life for the human person enables him to offer a persuasive account of the way in which the well-being of individual and community are mutually interdependent. He recognizes that no individual is able to live, much less to lead a humanly good life, apart from the sustaining structures of the community. Moreover, he at least implies recognition of the existence of the goods of traditions, which transcend the good of any individual contribution to those traditions, however exalted. Hence, he can cogently insist that the common good is greater and naturally more lovable to the individual than his own individual good, and therefore it is rational for the individual to sacrifice some measure of his material goods and abilities, and even, in extreme circumstances, his life itself, for the sake of the community. But at the same time, the common good itself cannot exist without justice, and justice demands that the community respect and foster the well-being of all its members equally in certain fundamental ways, as indicated by a correct understanding of the good life for human beings. For this reason, while the community can legitimately ask a great deal of its members, it cannot arbitrarily sacrifice them to the common good (even though it can ask them to make sacrifices themselves). A community that attempts to do so, or allows some of its members to sacrifice the well-being of others to their private interests with impunity, forfeits its claim on the allegiance of its members.

In the last section, it was suggested that once the Thomistic tradition has incorporated the insights of American pragmatism and related philosophical movements, it will be able to deal more adequately with the paradox (but not contradiction) involved in the recognition that the human person is fundamentally shaped by the communal matrix out of which her life emerges, and yet is free before God, because freed by God. As a result, it will be able to address and incorporate the insights of liberation theologians that sin is not just a private affair. There is such a thing as collective sin, which corrupts individuals without their prior consent, and from which they must be freed before they can live in the grace of God.[8] Correlatively, the church will appear in a new light, as capable of profound corruption by society, or as capable of bringing a new hope to society, depending on its faithfulness to its own call.[9]

It is also possible to see in Aquinas' work some indications of the way in which the Thomistic tradition might be expanded to address a question which has taken on a new urgency in this century. That is, what is the proper relationship between humanity, individually and collectively, and the natural world on which we depend? There can be no doubt that so long as this question is answered within the framework of the Thomistic tradition, that answer must begin with a reassertion of the legitimacy of humanity's use of the subhuman creation for its own well-being. But it does not follow, within the parameters of this tradition, that we may treat the rest of the material creation with impunity in whatever way we like.

Apart from the requirements of a far-seeing prudence, the Thomistic tradition would suggest two parameters within which the human use of the material creation must fall. The first is that any such use must truly be directed toward the good of all persons concerned, since the material creation is seen within this tradition as intended for the well-being of humanity *as a whole.* Given the realities of global interdependence, it follows that our use of the resources of nature must be directed to the good of the whole human race, and not exclusively to the good of one nation or economic collectivity.

The second parameter is set by Aquinas' general theory of goodness, according to which all creatures, and not just rational creatures, possess an intrinsic goodness apart from their potential usefulness to anything else. The specific character of each creature bestows on it an intrinsic orientation toward higher goods, and that is why we may legitimately make use of nonrational creatures for our own ends. But that orientation does not annul the goodness that each creature possesses in and of itself. On the basis of that goodness, which after all is another participation in the goodness of God, all creatures deserve some form of respect, albeit not the sort of respect that we owe to one another. At the very least, this respect would ground a distinction between, on the one hand, legitimate use, and, on the other hand, waste, destruction, or (in the case of animals) wanton cruelty, which would rightly be condemned. Even in the thirteenth century, Aquinas recognized that while the lower orders of creation are directed to serve the higher, still, God also ordains that the lower should be preserved through the activities of the higher (I.64.4). Surely we in the twentieth century can say no less.

Ultimately, Aquinas' theory of morality is significant today because it is successful on Aquinas' own terms. That is, he offers an account of the moral life which integrates the central concepts of his metaphysics into a unified account of human goodness and the virtues. Although we can no longer accept that account as it stands, it remains an impressive achievement in its own right. And I know of no better starting point from which to develop a unified theory of morality that is both contemporary and Christian.

Notes

Chapter 1: The Purpose of This Study

1. For example, see Sallie McFague, *Models of God: Theology for an Ecological, Nuclear Age* (Philadelphia: Fortress Press, 1987), 1–6.

2. John Dedek, "Intrinsically Evil Acts: An Historical Study of the Mind of St. Thomas," *The Thomist* 43 (1979), 385–413; Louis Janssens, "Ontic Evil and Moral Evil," *Louvain Studies* 4 (1972), reprinted in Charles E. Curran and Richard A. McCormick, eds., *Readings in Moral Theology No. 1: Moral Norms and Catholic Tradition* (New York: Paulist Press, 1979), 40–93; Germain G. Grisez, "The First Principle of Practical Reason: A Commentary on the *Summa Theologiae* 1–2, Question 94, Article 2," *Natural Law Forum* 10 (1965), 168–201.

3. James M. Gustafson, *Ethics and Theology*, vol. 2 of *Ethics from a Theocentric Perspective* (Chicago: University of Chicago Press, 1984), 42–64.

4. James M. Gustafson, "A Response to Critics," *Journal of Religious Ethics* 13/2 (Fall 1985), 185–209, at 193.

5. Stanley Hauerwas, *A Community of Character: Toward a Constructive Christian Social Ethic* (Notre Dame, Ind.: University of Notre Dame Press, 1981), 5.

6. Alan Donagan, *The Theory of Morality* (Chicago: University of Chicago Press, 1977), 63.

7. James M. Gustafson, "Roman Catholic and Protestant Interaction in Ethics: An Interpretation," *Theological Studies* 50/1 (March 1989), 44–69, at 57.

8. Germain Grisez, *Christian Moral Principles,* vol. 1 of *The Way of the Lord Jesus* (Chicago: Franciscan Herald Press, 1983), 153.

9. Richard A. McCormick, "Moral Theology 1940–1989: An Overview," *Theological Studies* 50/1 (March 1989), 3–24, at 10.

10. Stanley Hauerwas, "Time and History in Theological Ethics: The Work of James Gustafson," *Journal of Religious Ethics* 13/1 (Spring 1985), 3–21, at 19.

11. Gustafson, "Response," 191.

12. Ibid., 198.

13. Alasdair MacIntyre, *After Virtue,* 2d ed. (Notre Dame, Ind.: University of Notre Dame Press, 1984), 1–5.

14. Besides Grisez's 1965 article (see above, n. 2) and 1983 book cited above (see n. 8), I have relied primarily on the following works in my summary of the Grisez/Finnis interpretation of the natural law: John Finnis, *Natural Law and Natural Rights* (Oxford: Clarendon Press, 1980); Germain Grisez, Joseph Boyle, and John Finnis, "Practical Principles, Moral Truth, and Ultimate Ends," *American Journal of Jurisprudence* 32 (1987), 99–151. The latter work presents a summary of this theory, including a detailed commentary on the earlier works through which it was developed, as well as responses to critics. I have also found Russell Hittinger's analysis √ and critique of this position in *A Critique of the New Natural Law Theory* (Notre Dame, Ind.: University of Notre Dame Press, 1987) to be very helpful.

15. Grisez, *Christian Moral Principles,* 178.

16. The list of basic goods is taken from ibid., 124, and from Grisez, Boyle, and Finnis, "Practical Principles," 107–8. Finnis' earlier list is somewhat different, but not, I think, fundamentally so; see Finnis, *Natural Law,* 86–90.

17. Grisez, *Christian Moral Principles,* 184.

18. Ibid., 186, 222–24.

19. Ibid., 191.

20. For a summary of these modes, see ibid., 225–26.

21. A number of Catholic moral theologians today may be considered to be proportionalists, but unlike the proponents of the Grisez/Finnis theory of the natural law, they have not collaborated closely to develop a unified theory. Hence, I have been forced to

generalize in my presentation of their views. In addition to McCormick, "Moral Theology," and the essays in Curran and McCormick, eds., *Readings in Moral Theology,* I have drawn primarily on the following works in my characterization of this view: Lisa Sowle Cahill, "Teleology, Utilitarianism, and Christian Ethics," *Theological Studies* 42 (1981), 601–29; Bernard Hoose, *Proportionalism: The American Debate and Its European Roots* (Washington, D.C.: Georgetown University Press, 1987); Brian V. Johnstone, "The Meaning of Proportionate Reason in Contemporary Moral Theology," *The Thomist* 49 (1985), 223–47; Philip Keane, "The Objective Moral Order: Reflections on Recent Research," *Theological Studies* 43 (1982), 260–78; Richard A. McCormick, "Ambiguity in Moral Choice" and "A Commentary on the Commentaries," in Richard A. McCormick and Paul Ramsey, eds., *Doing Evil to Achieve Good: Moral Choices in Conflict Situations* (Chicago: Loyola University Press, 1978), 7–53, and 193–267; Edward Vacek, "Proportionalism: One View of the Debate," *Theological Studies* 46 (1985), 287–314; James Walter, "Proportionate Reason and Its Three Levels of Inquiry: Structuring the Ongoing Debate," *Louvain Studies* 10 (1984), 30–40.

22. In "The Quest for an Adequate Proportionalist Theory of Value," *The Thomist* 53/1 (Jan. 1989), 56–73, Ronald H. McKinney argues that McCormick's understanding of basic goods is essentially the same as Finnis'. See Richard A. McCormick, "Notes on Moral Theology: April–September 1972," in *Notes on Moral Theology: 1965–1980* (Lanham, Md.: University Press of America, 1981), 422–23; see also idem, "Proxy Consent in the Experimentation Situation," in James Johnson and David Smith, eds., *Love and Society: Essays in the Ethics of Paul Ramsey* (Missoula, Mont.: Scholars Press, 1974), 209–88, at 217–18.

23. McCormick, "Ambiguity in Moral Choice," 38.

24. The qualification is necessary because the proportionalists all (as far as I know) insist that we are never justified in directly bringing about a moral evil, even to avert a seemingly greater premoral evil. But this is a narrow, although important, qualification, because "moral evil" is understood by them as a bad will, which is understood as explicit consent to (one's own or another's) sin as such, and nothing else; practically, this qualification amounts to a prohibition against direct scandal and formal cooperation in evil.

25. In his 1985 essay (see above, n. 21), Johnstone summarizes and critiques a number of different meanings that various authors have given to the phrase "proportionate reason." Bernard Hoose

also offers a summary of several different interpretations of this key phrase in *Proportionalism* (1987), 81–95.

26. For example, see Hittinger, *A Critique,* 30–48, and McKinney, "The Quest," 61–68.

27. Grisez, *Christian Moral Principles,* 159.

28. Gene Outka, *Agape: An Ethical Analysis* (New Haven, Conn.: Yale University Press, 1972), 13.

29. Ibid., 257.

30. Ibid., 274–85.

31. Margaret A. Farley employs this line of analysis to good advantage in her *Personal Commitments: Beginning, Keeping, Changing* (San Francisco: Harper & Row, 1986), see esp. 80–91.

32. Hauerwas, *A Community of Character,* 130.

33. In his review of Hauerwas' works, Outka makes the point that the concept of harm is ambiguous—see Gene Outka, "Character, Vision and Narrative," *Religious Studies Review* 6/2 (April 1980), 110–18, at 112–13. Also see Outka, *Agape,* 263–67.

34. See Outka, *Agape,* 260–74. For a second, excellent discussion of some of the central issues raised in this debate, see Bernard Williams, "The Idea of Equality," in Bernard Williams, *Problems of the Self* (Cambridge: Cambridge University Press, 1973), 230–49.

35. My summary of Gustafson's moral theory is based on the two volumes of his *Ethics from a Theocentric Perspective*—vol. 1: *Theology and Ethics* (Chicago: University of Chicago Press, 1981); vol. 2: *Ethics and Theology,* cited above, n. 3.

36. Gustafson, *Theology and Ethics,* 83.

37. Gilbert Meilaender, "Review of *Ethics from a Theocentric Perspective,* Volumes One and Two," *Religious Studies Review* 12/1 (Jan. 1986), 11–16, at 11.

38. Gustafson, *Theology and Ethics,* 113.

39. Ibid., 203.

40. Gustafson's discussions of specific moral questions are found in his *Ethics and Theology,* 153–278.

41. Gustafson, "Response," 202.

42. Gustafson, *Ethics and Theology,* 216.

43. Ibid., 245.

44. Ibid.

45. Ibid., 246.

46. Ibid., 248.

47. For an example of a Protestant feminist theologian who advocates a return to nature as a source of moral norms, see McFague, *Models.* Perhaps the most influential among the Catholic feminist theologians who adopt this position is Rosemary Radford Ruether; see her *Sexism and God-Talk: Toward a Feminist Theology* (Boston: Beacon Press, 1983), esp. 72–92, and 259–66.

48. Oliver O'Donovan, *Resurrection and Moral Order: An Outline for Evangelical Ethics* (Grand Rapids: Wm. B. Eerdmans Publishing Co., 1986), see esp. 31–52.

49. This criticism is offered by Meilaender, "Review," and Hauerwas, "Time and History," as well as by Richard A. McCormick, "Gustafson's God: Who? What? Where? (Etc.)," *Journal of Religious Ethics* 13/1 (Spring 1985), 53–70. For the record, I agree with this criticism and consider it to be appropriate. On the other hand, I also agree with Gustafson's countercharge that more traditional Christian thinkers have not, by and large, taken the questions that science raises for Christian doctrine with sufficient seriousness; see Gustafson, "Response," 193–94.

50. McCormick raises this question in his "Gustafson's God," 67–68.

51. Gustafson, *Ethics and Theology,* 215.

52. Hauerwas' most complete theoretical statements and defenses of his theory of morality are found in *A Community of Character* (see above, n. 5), and in *The Peaceable Kingdom: A Primer in Christian Ethics* (Notre Dame, Ind.: University of Notre Dame Press, 1983), and I have relied primarily on those works in my summary of his views, while also consulting the works cited below.

53. As Hauerwas says in the preface to *A Community,* x: "The debt I owe Alasdair MacIntyre is apparent on almost every page of this book. . . ."

54. Hauerwas, *A Community,* 98–99.

55. Ibid., 115.

56. Ibid., 148.

57. Hauerwas develops his sexual ethic in the second half of *A Community,* 155–229.

58. On this point, see the essays in Stanley Hauerwas, *Suffering Presence: Theological Reflections on Medicine, the Mentally Handicapped, and the Church* (Notre Dame, Ind.: University of Notre Dame Press, 1986), esp. "Reflections on Suffering, Death, and Medicine," 23–38, and "Suffering the Retarded: Should We Prevent Retardation?" 159–81.

59. A commitment to pacifism runs throughout Hauerwas' work. In his later works, this commitment is developed systematically in *The Peaceable Kingdom* and "The Reality of the Kingdom: An Ecclesial Space for Peace" (with Mark Sherwindt), in *Against the Nations: War and Survival in a Liberal Society* (Minneapolis: Seabury/Winston Press, 1985), 107–21.

60. James Gustafson, "The Sectarian Temptation: Reflections on Theology, the Church and the University," *Proceedings of the Catholic Theological Society of America* 40 (1985), 83–94, at 92.

61. Gene Outka, "Character, Vision and Narrative," *Religious Studies Review* 6/2 (April 1989), 110–18, at 111–14.

62. Hauerwas, *A Community,* 257, n. 17.

63. For example, see Hauerwas, *A Community,* 97: "At least part of what it means to call a significant narrative true is how that narrative claims and shapes our lives."

64. Gustafson raises this objection in "The Sectarian Temptation," 93.

65. Notably, in *The Peaceable Kingdom* Hauerwas seems to suggest that the narratives of Christianity are true in a more traditional sense, although the exact sense in which he uses "true" remains unclear to me; see, for example, 15–16, and 67–68. In a later essay, he says "I certainly do not wish that Christian theology would, nor do I think that it can or should, free itself from classical metaphysical concerns. . . . My emphasis on the narrative character of Christian convictions has not been an attempt to avoid truth claims but to understand better how claims about the God entail fundamental assumptions about the narrability of the world and our lives." See "Why the Truth Demands Truthfulness: An Imperious Engagement with Hartt," *Journal of the American Academy of Religion* 52 (1984), 141–48, at 145.

66. For example, Gustafson raises this point in "Response," 196.

Chapter 2: The General Theory of Goodness in the *Summa Theologiae*

1. Julius Kovesi, *Moral Notions* (London: Routledge & Kegan Paul, 1967), 1–2.

2. The literature generated by debates over the meaning of "good" over the past century is enormous. The following are especially important or illustrative statements of the various positions enumerated: G. E. Moore, *Principia Ethica* (London: Cambridge University Press, 1903); Henry Sidgwick, *The Methods of Ethics,* 7th ed. (1907; reprint, Indianapolis: Hackett Publishing Co., 1981), 391–407; R. M. Hare, *The Language of Morals* (London: Oxford University Press, 1952); Gilbert Harman, "Moral Relativism Defended," in M. Krausz and J. Meiland, eds., *Relativism: Cognitive and Moral* (Notre Dame, Ind.: University of Notre Dame Press, 1982), 189–204. For criticisms of some of these views, see Alasdair MacIntyre, *After Virtue,* 2d ed. (Notre Dame, Ind.: University of Notre Dame Press, 1984), 6–78; Kovesi, *Moral Notions,* 1–36.

3. Étienne Gilson offers a very good overview of Aquinas' doctrine of the transcendentals in *Elements of Christian Philosophy* (New York: Doubleday & Co., 1960), 149–78. For a more recent, and very fine, discussion, see Peter Simpson, "St. Thomas on the Naturalistic Fallacy," *The Thomist* 51/1 (Jan. 1987), 51–69. I agree with Simpson that the term "transcendental," correctly understood, captures the meaning of Aquinas' account of goodness, intelligibility, and being, although he does not use this term in the *ST* (see Simpson, 58).

4. On Aquinas' realism, see Étienne Gilson, *Réalisme thomiste et critique de la connaissance* (Paris: Librairie Philosophique J. Vrin, 1947), 184–239.

5. The use of the example of artifacts to illustrate Aquinas' teleology may give rise to some misunderstanding. It might be said that while artifacts have a function in terms of which their relative goodness can be evaluated, natural objects do not, and it is a simple mistake to attempt to apply the same sort of analysis to both. Hence, it might be argued that Aquinas, like Aristotle before him, has based his whole teleological analysis of nature on an illegitimate extension of the notion of functionalism from the world of artifacts to the world of natural objects.

It is true that Aristotle explains his understanding of happiness as the aim of human life in terms borrowed from the world of artifacts: Just as the lute has a function, he says, so does the

human person, and our happiness consists in fulfilling our function
(see the *Nicomachean Ethics* 1.1097b20–1098a20). Aquinas is more
reluctant to use the example of artifacts in this way, perhaps in
order to avoid the misunderstanding that the line of criticism described above reflects. (However, see I-II.13.2 *ad* 3.) In any case,
that line of criticism does indeed reflect a misunderstanding of the
way in which the example of artifacts functions for Aristotle. That
example simply provides an especially accessible way of explaining the general notion of the existence of a thing as acting for an
ideal final end, precisely because the final cause of artifacts is
clearly known to us, since it is constituted by the purpose for
which we made them. It does not follow that natural creatures have
a purpose *extrinsic to themselves.* For Aristotle, it is clear that the free
man, at least, does not have a purpose extrinsic to himself, since
what distinguishes the free man from slaves and women is precisely the fact that he himself is the sufficient purpose of his life.
With Aquinas, matters are less clear, since he sometimes seems to
imply that creatures are the purpose of God's act of creation (for
example, at I.65.2). But on closer examination, we see that this does
not mean that creatures are God's *instruments,* in the way that my
pen is an instrument of mine. God's purpose in creation is simply
that the creature *be,* as nearly in accordance with its specific perfection as is consistent with the overall good of the universe (cf. I.44.3,
4; I.65.2 *ad* 2). To turn matters around, natural creatures as they
would be in their perfection are their own purposes, the good for
which they strive in and through their dynamic existence.

6. I am grateful to Professor Alasdair MacIntyre for pointing this
out to me.

7. In "Aquinas' Definition of Good: Ethical-Theoretical Notes on
'De Veritate' Q. 21," *The Monist* 58 (1974), 151–62, Ronald Duska
argues that, according to Aquinas, the good must be consciously
desired, as well as perfective of some other whose good the
desideratum is. John Finnis cites Duska with approval in *Natural
Law and Natural Rights* (Oxford: Clarendon Press, 1980), 79. Duska
bases his interpretation of Aquinas on *De Veritate* 21.1 and 21.5, in
which Aquinas does indeed say that "something is said to be a
being insofar as it is considered absolutely; however, it is good, as
what was already said . . . makes clear, in accordance with its
respect to another" (21.5). However, even here he also says that all
existing creatures are necessarily good in some sense (21.5, esp. *ad*
1). Moreover, it should be noted that the relation to other things
in which good is properly said to consist at 21.5 is the proper

orientation of the creature toward the universe as a whole. What these texts suggest is that in the *De Veritate,* as in the *ST,* all things are said to be good insofar as they exist and have their proper place in an ordered universe. But in the *ST,* the primary sense given to goodness is associated with the existence or perfection of the thing in itself, and the secondary sense is associated with the thing in relation to others; logically enough, since on Aquinas' terms any-thing will be properly related to others if it is fully actual and therefore exercising its causality as it should be. Janice Schultz, in "Thomistic Metaethics in Controversy," *The Thomist* 52/1 (Jan. 1988), 40–62, also makes note of this shift at pp. 51–56.

8. Schultz, "Thomistic Metaethics," acknowledges that in the *ST* Aquinas holds that the good that all creatures desire is the fulfill-ment of a potency in the creatures themselves. But she does not believe that this is a fully cogent account, because nothing can desire what it already has, and therefore perfect creatures would not desire the good. Hence, she proposes the following definition as being more adequate, while still being consistent with Aquinas' overall doctrine: "a good X" is "an X suited to the desire that anyone might have for a complete X" (p. 55). But this definition does not really add anything to Aquinas' concept of the good, since on his account, a *complete* X, that is, an X which has perfectly actualized the potentialities proper to its species, is, by that very fact, a *good* X. Moreover, Aquinas clearly indicates that the love for its own good to be found in each creature includes tendencies to preserve what has been obtained and to resist corruption (II-II.64.5). That being so, we may assume that in the *ST* Aquinas intends that we understand that "desire" in this context includes a tendency to hold on to the degree of perfection that has already been obtained.

9. See Étienne Gilson, *The Christian Philosophy of St. Thomas Aquinas* (New York: Random House, 1956), 29–58.

10. Contrary to what D. J. O'Connor seems to think, our knowl-edge of the essences of things is not a sheer intuition, in the sense of a perception that has no necessary connection with sense experi-ence; see O'Connor's *Aquinas and Natural Law* (London: Macmillan & Co., 1967), 16. The classic treatment of Aquinas' epistemology is Bernard J. Lonergan's *Verbum: Word and Idea in Aquinas* (Notre Dame, Ind.: University of Notre Dame Press, 1967), see esp. 141–82. My understanding of Aquinas' epistemology has also been shaped by Anthony Kenny's *Aquinas* (New York: Hill & Wang, 1980), 61–81.

11. I have rendered Aquinas' *veritas,* usually translated "truth," as "intelligibility" in order to convey the idea that something is said to be true insofar as it is an appropriate object for the intellect. It should be noted, however, that things are said to be true/intelligible, according to Aquinas, primarily in virtue of their intelligibility in the mind of God, and only secondarily because they are apt objects of our own understanding (I.16.1).

12. Throughout the remainder of this section, I am especially indebted to James D. Wallace, who argues that our judgments that living creatures are creatures of a given kind have a necessary normative component; see Wallace's *Virtues and Vices* (Ithaca, N.Y.: Cornell University Press, 1978), 15–34.

13. On what is involved in recognizing that something is self-identical over time, see Richard Wollheim, "On Persons and Their Lives," in Amelie Oksenberg Rorty, ed., *Explaining Emotions* (Berkeley, Calif.: University of California Press, 1980), 229–322.

14. On the general idea of a hierarchy of being, see Arthur O. Lovejoy, *The Great Chain of Being* (New York: Harper & Brothers, 1936; Harper Torchbook, 1960); on its treatment by Aquinas, see 73–79.

15. Grisez's contention that Aquinas separates "is" and "ought" completely has been widely challenged. See, for example, Schultz, "Thomistic Metaethics"; idem, "Is-Ought: Prescribing and a Present Controversy," *The Thomist* 49/1 (Jan. 1985), 1–23; Simpson, "St. Thomas"; Ralph McInerny, *Ethica Thomistica: The Moral Philosophy of Thomas Aquinas* (Washington, D.C.: Catholic University of America Press, 1982), 50–62.

16. Germain G. Grisez, "The First Principle of Practical Reason: A Commentary on the *Summa Theologiae* 1-2, Question 94, Article 2," *Natural Law Forum* 10 (1965), 168–201; John Finnis, *Natural Law,* 36–48.

17. On the related but different claim that Aquinas commits the naturalistic fallacy, see Simpson, "St. Thomas."

18. Grisez, "The First Principle," 175.

19. Alasdair MacIntyre also makes this point; see MacIntyre, *Whose Justice? Which Rationality?* (Notre Dame, Ind.: University of Notre Dame Press, 1988), 172–73.

20. Grisez, "The First Principle," 194–95; note, however, that Grisez criticizes Hume for failing to be true to his own point, that

is, that " 'ought' *cannot* be derived" from statements about a given case; see n. 74, p. 195.

21. David Hume, *A Treatise of Human Nature,* ed. L. A. Selby-Bigge (Oxford: Oxford University Press, 1888), 469.

22. Alasdair MacIntyre, "Editor's Introduction," in *Hume's Ethical Writings,* ed. A. MacIntyre (New York: Collier Books, 1965), 13.

23. Ibid., 12–13.

24. It might be objected that some sorts of creatures do indeed have a natural inclination to do what is harmful to them. For example, the male black widow spider is inclined to mate with the female black widow spider, who then eats him (hence, the name). But even these sorts of creatures are not inclined toward what is harmful per se. They are inclined toward something that is good in itself, for example, mating (which may even be pleasurable to the spiders), and the evil to the individual that results is outside the intention of the act. Of course, in these sorts of cases, the individual male spider may be said to be sacrificed to the good of the species, and to that of the female and her offspring.

25. Gene Outka, *Agape: An Ethical Analysis* (New Haven, Conn.: Yale University Press, 1972), 56.

26. For an excellent discussion of Aquinas' treatment of the thesis that the human person is her own end, see Alan Donagan, *Human Ends and Human Actions: An Exploration in St. Thomas' Treatment* (Milwaukee: Marquette University Press, 1985), 6–17. I agree with Donagan that even though Aquinas places more emphasis on this thesis in the *Summa Contra Gentiles,* it continues to inform the moral theory of the *ST.* Jacques Maritain also discusses Aquinas' thesis that the human person is her own end at great length; for example, see *The Person and the Common Good,* trans. John J. Fitzgerald (Notre Dame, Ind.: University of Notre Dame Press, 1966), esp. 15–30. However, I would not agree with all the details of Maritain's analysis of Aquinas on this point.

27. James M. Gustafson, *Ethics and Theology,* vol. 2 of *Ethics from a Theocentric Perspective* (Chicago: University of Chicago Press, 1984), 55–56. For an example of a similar argument directed against Aristotle's metaphysical biology, see Ronald de Sousa, "Arguments from Nature," in David Copp and David Zimmerman, eds., *Morality, Reason and Truth* (Totowa, N.J.: Rowman & Allanheld, 1985), 169–92, esp. 172–74.

28. Gustafson, *Ethics and Theology,* 54, 55.

29. At p. 16 of *Aquinas and Natural Law,* O'Connor makes the argument, against Aquinas' account of specific kinds, that we impose classificatory schemes on things. However, he does not seem to realize the full implications of his claim for the philosophy of science.

30. For example, see Stanley Hauerwas, *A Community of Character: Toward a Constructive Christian Ethic* (Notre Dame, Ind.: University of Notre Dame Press, 1981), 89–110.

31. The literature generated by the debate over the incommensurability thesis is considerable. The version of this thesis that I accept is that developed by Alasdair MacIntyre in his *Whose Justice?,* 349–88.

32. At p. 16 of *Aquinas and Natural Law,* O'Connor uses the example of "water" as a category that Aquinas mistakenly applies.

33. MacIntyre, *Whose Justice?,* 349–69.

34. For example, Stanley Hauerwas makes this criticism; see Hauerwas, *The Peaceable Kingdom: A Primer in Christian Ethics* (Notre Dame, Ind.: University of Notre Dame Press, 1983), 60–84.

35. Again, see Lovejoy, *The Great Chain,* esp. 67–98. The claim that the universe as a whole is good may seem odd at first, until we recall that as Aquinas analyzes it, the notion of goodness is closely tied to the notions of intelligibility and unity. The universe as a whole *is* a whole, that is to say, a unity, and is intelligible as such, because it displays an internal ordering (I.5.5). Moreover, Aquinas argues that the orderly array of a variety of creatures reflects God's own goodness more nearly—or less inadequately—than a universe comprised of only the most perfect possible creature alone could have done (I.47.1, 2). This claim involves him in considerable theological difficulties, as Lovejoy observes, but fortunately they need not detain us here.

36. This line of criticism is widespread; for a typical and influential example, see Rosemary Radford Ruether, *Sexism and God-Talk* (Boston: Beacon Press, 1983), 72–92.

37. In *Innocent Ecstasy* (Oxford: Oxford University Press, 1985), 130–149, Peter Gardella provides very interesting examples of appeals to a kind of nature mysticism to justify the subordination of women.

38. Gustafson, *Ethics and Theology,* 57–58.

39. For a fuller discussion of this issue, see my *"De Ordine Caritatis:* Charity, Friendship and Justice in Thomas Aquinas' *Summa Theologiae,"* *The Thomist* 53/2 (April 1989), 197–214.

40. After considerable reflection, I have decided to retain the traditional usage of speaking about God in the masculine, for two reasons. First of all, any other usage would have been totally foreign to Aquinas himself, and it would be misleading to obscure that fact in representing his thought. Second, Christian language about God is, in my view, always at least implicitly Trinitarian, and our formulations of the doctrine of the Trinity are in turn inextricably bound up with the early church's tradition of Jesus as Son of the Father. For this reason, a usage of speaking of God *only* in the neuter seems to me to raise even more theological difficulties than the traditional usage.

41. The debate earlier in this century over whether the human person has a natural end involved complex theological as well as philosophical issues, and I have not tried to engage it in any detail here. For a good summary of that debate, see Kevin Staley, "Happiness: The Natural End of Man?" *The Thomist* 53/2 (April 1989), 215–34, esp. see 218–26. For examples of more recent thinkers who hold that Aquinas equates the end of the human person with the beatific vision and nothing else, see Donagan, *Human Ends,* 38–39, and MacIntyre, *Whose Justice?,* 192–93.

42. Cited in Staley, "Happiness," 226.

43. Staley, "Happiness," 226.

44. Ibid., 228.

45. Ibid., 229–30.

46. On this point, I follow David Burrell, *Aquinas: God and Action* (Notre Dame, Ind.: University of Notre Dame Press, 1979), 12–77.

47. I have argued for this thesis in more detail in my "Desire for God: Ground of the Moral Life in Aquinas," *Theological Studies* 47/1 (March 1986), 48–68.

48. For an illuminating and lovely development of this theme, see Josef Pieper's *The Silence of St. Thomas* (New York: Pantheon Books, 1957).

49. For a good discussion of the importance of the virtue of patience to Aquinas' overall project, see MacIntyre, *After Virtue,* 2d ed. (Notre Dame, Ind.: University of Notre Dame Press, 1984), 176–78.

50. I owe this point to Gilson, *The Christian Philosophy,* 3–5.

Chapter 3: The Human Good

1. Ralph McInerny, *Ethica Thomistica: The Moral Philosophy of Thomas Aquinas* (Washington, D.C.: Catholic University of America Press, 1982), 1.

2. John Rawls, *A Theory of Justice* (Cambridge, Mass.: Harvard University Press, 1971), 553.

3. Aristotle's discussion of incontinence comes in Book 7 of the *Nicomachean Ethics,* 1145a15–1152a35.

4. For good modern discussions of the distinction between actions and bodily motions, see Martin Hollis, *Models of Man: Philosophical Thoughts on Social Action* (Cambridge: Cambridge University Press, 1977), 107–22; Richard Taylor, *Action and Purpose* (Atlantic Highlands, N.J.: Humanities Press, 1966), 57–74.

5. I have taken the insight that a putative action must be intelligible in order to count as an action at all from Alasdair MacIntyre, *After Virtue,* 2d ed. (Notre Dame, Ind.: University of Notre Dame Press, 1984), 209–10. However, I would argue that an action is intelligible primarily in virtue of the good toward which it is apparently directed, and not primarily in virtue of its place in a narrative structure, as MacIntyre argues. If we are able to interpret an action as aimed at something that we readily acknowledge to be good, or even apparently good, nothing further is needed in order to render an item of behavior sufficiently intelligible to count as an action. We only need to attempt to construct a special narrative to render an item of behavior intelligible if it is not obviously aimed at something that we can recognize as at least seemingly good. At the same time, it is true that in order to recognize anything as a true good, we must have some normative account of what it is to be human, which will include an account of the course of a good human life. If that account is considered to be a narrative, then MacIntyre is correct that our judgments of the intelligibility of actions *ultimately* demand that we be able to place them in a narrative context. (On this interpretation, however, an action that is not directed to a true good is not fully intelligible. That is

Aquinas' view, but I am not sure that it is MacIntyre's.) As I understand him, Taylor, *Action,* esp. 99–264, makes essentially the same point as MacIntyre, that is, that a true action must somehow be intelligible.

6. The difficulties with a dominant-end conception of the end of human life are well-known; see W. F. R. Hardie, "The Final Good in Aristotle's Ethics," in J. M. E. Moravesik, ed., *Aristotle* (Garden City, N.Y.: Doubleday & Co., Anchor Books, 1967), 297–322, for a helpful review of these.

7. The terminology of dominant and inclusive final ends is taken from Hardie, "Final Good."

8. This account of social roles has been heavily influenced by MacIntyre, *After Virtue,* 121–29, and 181–255; idem, *Whose Justice? Which Rationality?* (Notre Dame, Ind.: University of Notre Dame Press, 1988), 1–87; Hollis, *Models,* 87–106; and George Herbert Mead, *Mind, Self and Society from the Standpoint of a Social Behaviorist,* ed. Charles W. Morris (Chicago: University of Chicago Press, 1934), esp. 135–226.

9. MacIntyre, *Whose Justice?,* 33–34. Also see Hollis, *Models,* 123–41; MacIntyre, *After Virtue,* 204–25.

10. Hollis, *Models,* 87–106.

11. MacIntyre, *After Virtue,* 211–19.

12. Ibid., 219.

13. The phrase "lifestyle enclaves" is from Robert N. Bellah et al., *Habits of the Heart: Individualism and Commitment in American Life* (Berkeley: University of California Press, 1985), 71–75.

14. However, he may have since changed his mind on this point; see MacIntyre, *Whose Justice?,* 402–3.

15. MacIntyre, *After Virtue,* 162.

16. It does not follow that we *earn* grace through attempting to lead a naturally good life. Rather, the life of grace includes the moral life as one of its necessary concomitant conditions (I-II.65.3).

17. My interpretation of Aquinas' analysis of self-evident principles, and more specifically, of the relationship between the first principle of practical reason and knowledge of the substantive human good, is deeply indebted to MacIntyre, *Whose Justice?,* 171–75.

18. I agree with Grisez that "good" in the first principle of practical reason should not be limited to the moral good, in the sense that any action whatever necessarily depends on this principle; see Germain G. Grisez, "The First Principle of Practical Reason: A Commentary on the *Summa Theologiae* 1-2, Question 94, Article 2," *The Natural Law Forum* 10 (1965), 168–201, at 183–84. Vernon Bourke has argued, contrary to Grisez, that a historical examination of the first principle of practical reason indicates that "good" and "evil" in the first principle of practical reason must be given a moral force; see "The Synderesis Rule and Right Reason," *The Monist* 66 (Jan. 1983), 70–82. It is true that for the agent who acts well, "good" and "evil" will be equivalent to the moral good and evil; it is also true, as Bourke points out, that "practical reasoning always has some moral overtones," in that a genuine action that fails to be morally good will necessarily be morally evil (I-II.18.9). These points are not inconsistent with the claim that even the person who acts immorally is employing the first principle of practical reason, albeit badly. The alternative to admitting that all action is grounded in the first principle of practical reason is to conclude that those who seem to act immorally are not really acting at all, and therefore, there is no such thing as an immoral action.

19. John Finnis, *Natural Law and Natural Rights* (Oxford: Clarendon Press, 1980), 65.

20. This appears to be Finnis' view; see ibid., 90–92.

21. MacIntyre also makes this point; see MacIntyre, *Whose Justice?*, 174.

22. At this point, my interpretation is indebted to ibid., 173–74.

23. The interpretation of I-II.94.2 developed by Grisez, "First Principle," and Finnis, *Natural Law*, is central to their theory of morality, and they refer to it throughout their writings. However, for that very reason it is sometimes difficult to discern when a particular point is meant as a reading of Aquinas, and when it is offered as part of an independent theory of morality. This is especially true of Grisez, who admits that he "freely parts company with Aquinas, usually without saying so" and without dropping Thomistic terminology; see Grisez, Joseph Boyle, and John Finnis, "Practical Principles, Moral Truth, and Ultimate Ends," *American Journal of Jurisprudence* 32 (1987), 99–151, at 148. For this reason, I have considered it safer to base my comments on Grisez's and Finnis' exegesis of Aquinas on these two sources, except where otherwise noted.

24. Alan Donagan, *The Theory of Morality* (Chicago: University of Chicago Press, 1977), 64–65.

25. What are we to make of the fact that Aquinas says that the precepts of the Decalogue are readily apparent to the natural reason of every person (I-II.100.1)? Note first of all that Aquinas does not in fact say that these precepts are self-evident to all; rather, he *distinguishes* them from precepts that are self-evident to all, on the one hand, and those detailed precepts which can only be discerned by careful reflection, on the other (I-II.100.3). Second, it should be noted that while the precepts of the Decalogue can be derived from the first self-evident principles of morality (that is, love of God and neighbor) with only slight reflection (I-II.100.1), it apparently takes further reflection to determine what, concretely, those precepts mean. Otherwise, Aquinas would not have to take such pains to distinguish legitimate homicide from murder (II-II.64), or legitimate seizure of another's possessions from robbery and thefts (II-II.66).

26. Louis Janssens, "Ontic Evil and Moral Evil," *Louvain Studies* 4 (1972), reprinted in Charles E. Curran and Richard A. McCormick, eds., *Readings in Moral Theology No. 1: Moral Norms and Catholic Tradition* (New York: Paulist Press, 1979), 40–93.

27. My account of the levels of descriptions of action is dependent on Eric D'Arcy, *Human Acts: An Essay in Their Moral Evaluation* (Oxford: Clarendon Press, 1963).

28. D'Arcy makes this point, although not specifically in reference to Aquinas, in ibid., 39.

29. This, as indicated above in n. 5, is how I would interpret the claim that actions can be rendered intelligible only by being placed in a narrative context.

Chapter 4: The Affective Virtues

1. I think this distinction between a discrete action and a course of activity may underlie Alasdair MacIntyre's distinction between a putative action and a true—that is, an intelligible—action, which can be recognized as such only by being placed in a narrative context; see MacIntyre, *After Virtue,* 2d ed. (Notre Dame, Ind.: University of Notre Dame Press, 1984), 207–11.

2. Otto Hermann Pesch, "The Theology of Virtue and the Theological Virtues," in *Concilium* 191: *Changing Values and Virtues,* ed. Dietmar Mieth and Jacques Pohier (Edinburgh: T. & T. Clark,

1987), 86–91. For another good discussion of the historical context of Aquinas' thought, see Alasdair MacIntyre, *Whose Justice? Which Rationality?* (Notre Dame, Ind.: University of Notre Dame Press, 1988), 164–82.

3. See, for example, Stanley Hauerwas, *A Community of Character: Toward a Constructive Christian Social Ethic* (Notre Dame, Ind.: University of Notre Dame Press, 1981), 111–28. However, on p. 114 he admits that "neither the language of duty nor of virtue excludes the other on principle."

4. I have not seen any discussion that focuses directly on the question of what is involved in forming a concept of a particular virtue, although there are a number of philosophical treatments of particular virtues which address this question obliquely; for example, see James D. Wallace, *Virtues and Vices* (Ithaca, N.Y.: Cornell University Press, 1978), 60–89. John Benson also addresses some of the issues raised in this section in a very interesting essay, "Hog in Sloth, Fox in Stealth: Man and Beast in Moral Thinking," in R. S. Peters, ed., *Nature and Conduct: Royal Institute of Philosophy Lectures, Vol. 8, 1973–1974* (New York: St. Martin's Press, 1975), 265–80.

5. Ludwig Wittgenstein, *Philosophical Investigations,* 3d ed., trans. G. E. M. Anscombe (New York: Macmillan Co., 1958), pars. 65–67, pp. 31–32.

6. My understanding of a formal notion is taken from Julius Kovesi, *Moral Notions* (London: Routledge & Kegan Paul, 1967), 1–65.

7. Hauerwas, *A Community,* 129–54. Anne Patrick also makes this claim in "Narrative and the Social Dynamics of Virtue," in *Changing Values and Virtues,* 69–80.

8. I have argued for the ubiquity of some notions of temperance and fortitude in more detail elsewhere; see my "Perennial and Timely Virtues: Practical Wisdom, Courage and Temperance," in *Changing Values and Virtues,* 60–68.

9. For Aristotle's discussion of continence and incontinence, see the *Nicomachean Ethics* 7.1145a15–1152a35.

10. For Aristotle's discussion of the relation of reason to the passions, see his discussion of continence and incontinence, cited above, and *Nicomachean Ethics* 1.1102a5–1103a15. For a good discussion of Aquinas' theory of the passions, see Mark Jordan, "Aqui-

nas' Construction of a Moral Account of the Passions," *Freiburger Zeitschrift für Philosophie und Theologie* 33/1–2 (1986), 71–97.

11. In *The Theory of Will in Classical Antiquity* (Berkeley: University of California Press, 1982), Albrecht Dihle argues convincingly that the modern conception of the will was invented by Augustine. For his treatment of Aristotle, see pp. 54–60.

12. Étienne Gilson, *Réalisme thomiste et critique de la connaissance* (Paris: Librairie Philosophique J. Vrin, 1947), 184–90.

13. It would be a mistake to assume that the incontinent individual acts directly on the prompting of his passions. Such behavior would not count as an action at all, on Aquinas' terms, since he holds that human action necessarily proceeds from the will, which pursues something apprehended by the intellect as being in some way good (I-II.6.1; cf. II-II.156.1). As I read him, Aquinas understands the case of the incontinent individual in this way: When the intellect and will are functioning as they should, in a person who has a true estimation of the human good, then the person naturally wills that which she recognizes as promoting human good in some way, on the basis of her grasp of the human good. But in the case of the incontinent person, the knowledge of the true human good is obscured by some contrary passion, in such a way that the person judges intellectually that the object of the passion is truly good, wills that (seeming) good, and acts accordingly (II-II.156.1 *ad* 2). In other words, at the moment of willing and acting for the seeming good proposed by an impulse of the passions, the mind of the incontinent person judges that this object is truly good, although she may recognize her mistake in the next instant. In other words, the incontinent person is really ignorant of her true good at the moment in which she acts, although she knows it potentially even then. The intemperate person, on the other hand, does not know, even potentially, what the true human good is (II-II.156.3).

14. My understanding of Aquinas' doctrine of the mean has been informed by J. O. Urmson's "Aristotle's Doctrine of the Mean," in Amelie Oksenberg Rorty, ed., *Essays on Aristotle's Ethics* (Berkeley: University of California Press, 1980), 157–70.

15. Hauerwas, *A Community*, 143.

16. Peter Geatch develops this criticism at some length in *The Virtues* (Cambridge: Cambridge University Press, 1977), 161–68.

Chapter 5: Justice

1. For a good summary of the development of the modern notion of individualism, including a discussion of some of the criticisms of this notion, see Steven Lukes, *Individualism* (Oxford: Basil Blackwell, 1973). In *Essays on Individualism: Modern Ideology in Anthropological Perspective* (Chicago: University of Chicago Press, 1986), Louis Dumont offers an excellent analysis of the development of individualism from its roots in classical Christianity to modern times, including an analysis of the ambiguities of this notion.

2. For Aristotle's affirmation of the social nature of the human person, see the *Politics* 1.1252a1–1253a35. My understanding of Aquinas' epistemology at this point is dependent on Alasdair MacIntyre, *Whose Justice? Which Rationality?* (Notre Dame, Ind.: University of Notre Dame Press, 1988), 172–75; I am also drawing on Bernard J. Lonergan, *Verbum: Word and Idea in Aquinas* (Notre Dame, Ind.: University of Notre Dame Press, 1967); Anthony Kenny, *Aquinas* (New York: Hill & Wang, 1980), 61–81.

3. My analysis of traditions is dependent on Alasdair MacIntyre, *After Virtue*, 2d ed. (Notre Dame, Ind.: University of Notre Dame Press, 1984), 181–225; idem, *Whose Justice?*, 326–403; and Edward Shils, *Tradition* (Chicago: University of Chicago Press, 1981).

4. The virtues annexed to justice, that is, its potential parts, are considered by Aquinas to resemble justice simply so called in that they regulate the individual's dealings with another, and yet fail to answer perfectly to the idea of justice, which consists in giving to another that which is his due in accordance with the norm of equality. Religion, piety toward parents and one's country, and the observance that honors exemplary virtue fall short of true justice, because one can never make an equal return to God, our parents and country, and the virtuous for what we receive from them. Truthfulness, gratitude, and revenge are necessary if we are to relate to others in a fully moral way, but they cannot be evaluated in terms of a precise equality of exchange. Liberality and affability are even less susceptible to such an evaluation, and furthermore are not strictly necessary to moral rectitude. Yet all these virtues, because they regulate our relations with others, are annexed to justice (see II-II.80).

5. This section and the next draw heavily on my "Moral Rules and Moral Actions: A Comparison of Aquinas and Modern Moral Theology," *Journal of Religious Ethics* 17/1 (Spring 1989), 123–49.

6. This argument is very frequently offered by proportionalists. For example, see Peter Knauer, "The Hermeneutic Function of the Principle of Double Effect," *Natural Law Forum* 12 (1967), reprinted in Charles E. Curran and Richard A. McCormick, eds., *Readings in Moral Theology No. 1: Moral Norms and Catholic Tradition* (New York: Paulist Press, 1979), 1–39; Louis Janssens, "Ontic Evil and Moral Evil," *Louvain Studies* 4 (1972), reprinted in Curran and McCormick, *Readings,* 40–93; Bruno Schüller, "Direct Killing/Indirect Killing," *Theologie und Philosophie* 47 (1972), under the title "Direkte Tötung— Indirekte Tötung," reprinted in Curran and McCormick, *Readings,* 138–57.

7. In fact, some of those who follow Grisez and Finnis do hold that no form of homicide is permissible, while others think that capital punishment, at least, may be permissible, considered as an act of justice. See John Finnis, Joseph M. Boyle, Jr., and Germain Grisez, *Nuclear Deterrence, Morality and Realism* (Oxford: Clarendon Press, 1987), 317–18.

8. Aquinas himself uses *occidere* (to kill) as the morally neutral term, and *homicidium* to denote wrongful killing; see, for example, II-II.64.1, esp. *ad* 3.

9. I use the term "the state" here to refer to the supreme political authority in a community, without intending to imply a particular form of that authority.

10. I cannot here engage the complicated debate over whether II-II.64.7 represents an early statement of the doctrine of double effect, but in my view, it does not. For two examples of the contrary view, see Joseph Mangan, "An Historical Analysis of the Principle of Double Effect," *Theological Studies* 10 (1949), 49–61; and Donald F. Montaldi, "A Defense of St. Thomas and the Principle of Double Effect," *Journal of Religious Ethics* 14 (1986), 296–332.

11. John Dedek, in "Intrinsically Evil Acts: An Historical Study of the Mind of St. Thomas," *The Thomist* 43 (1979), 385–413, argues that the sins against justice are to be defined formally as *undue* killing, taking, and so forth; see esp. 407–11. Knauer "Hermeneutic Function," suggests a similar conclusion; see pp. 18–21.

12. I have argued for this point in more detail in *"De Ordine Caritatis:* Charity, Friendship and Justice in Thomas Aquinas' *Summa Theologiae," The Thomist* 53/2 (April 1989), 197–214.

13. For Aristotle's treatment of justice as equality, see the *Nicomachean Ethics* 5.1130a10–1136a9 and the *Politics* 3.1282b15–1283a20.

14. Within the pre-Christian moral tradition the view emerged that all persons are equally capable of moral virtue; on this see Sir R. W. Carlyle and A. J. Carlyle, *A History of Mediaeval Political Theory in the West*, 3d ed., 6 vols. (Edinburgh: William Blackwood & Sons, 1923), 1:6–13.

15. For two excellent accounts of the development of the Christian natural law tradition from its classical roots, see Carlyle and Carlyle, *A History*, 1:81–193; and Ernst Troeltsch, *The Social Teaching of the Christian Churches*, 2 vols., trans. Olive Wyon (Chicago: University of Chicago Press, 1931; reprint 1981), 1:89–200, 280–445.

16. Aquinas himself quotes Augustine, *On Christian Doctrine* 1.28, to the effect that the love of charity should extend to all equally; he then argues that Augustine means that we should love all equally in the sense of wishing them the same good, but not in the sense that we love them all with the same intensity (II-II.26.6 *ad* 1).

17. For further discussion of this point, see my *"De Ordine Caritatis."*

18. Again, see Carlyle and Carlyle, *A History*, 1:45–62, 125–31.

19. There are in fact some kinds of actions which incorporate something morally problematic in their object (and are therefore intrinsically evil), but which nonetheless do not necessarily involve harm to the neighbor, for example, lies told for amusement or to benefit someone (II-II.110.3), hypocrisy (II-II.111.3), and boasting (II-II.112.1). However, it is significant that none of these kinds of actions is generically a mortal sin, because none of them necessarily involves either explicit rejection of God or harm to the neighbor (II-II.110.4; II-II.111.4; II-II.113.2).

20. Hence, Finnis is wrong to assume that because Aquinas would hold that one cannot take life in order to promote knowledge, then the ordering of the inclinations has no significance for his moral theory; see Johnny Finnis, *Natural Law and Natural Rights* (Oxford: Clarendon Press, 1980), 94–95.

21. It may be argued that Aquinas has misunderstood the character of the sex impulse, which should be seen as directed toward personal intimacy in addition to, or even instead of, reproduc-

tion. This line of argument is entirely in order, on Aquinas' own terms, since it amounts to a claim that he has misformulated a moral norm because of a misunderstanding of what it is to be human. But whether that is so or not, the fact remains that Aquinas' condemnation of simple fornication is justified by an appeal to what promotes the overall human good, based on his own best understanding of what that good is.

22. Hence, G. E. M. Anscombe is wrong to insist that a cogent doctrine of the moral law *must* be a divine command theory; see G. E. M. Anscombe, "Modern Moral Philosophy," reprinted in Anscombe, *Collected Philosophical Papers*, Vol. III: *Ethics, Religion, and Politics* (Minneapolis: University of Minnesota Press, 1981), 26–42.

23. I am indebted here to Alan Donagan, *The Theory of Morality* (Chicago: University of Chicago Press, 1977), 172–80.

24. The question of the exact meaning of "primary and secondary precepts" in Aquinas' moral theory was hotly debated some years ago; R. A. Armstrong provides a good summary and critique of this debate, together with developing his own views, in *Primary and Secondary Precepts in Thomistic Natural Law Teaching* (The Hague: Martinus Nijhoff, 1966). I have not attempted to address all the issues raised in this debate.

25. Dom Odon Lottin, *Le droit naturel chez saint Thomas d'Aquin et ses prédécesseurs,* 2d ed., rev. and enlarged (Bruges: Ch. Beyaert, 1931), 82–96.

26. Again, see Dedek, "Intrinsically Evil Acts," 407–11.

27. How are we to evaluate Abraham's willingness to kill his son Isaac in response to a divine command? As Dedek, "Intrinsically Evil Acts," 388–99, shows, this question was much discussed in Aquinas' time. Aquinas' own response is that Abraham's act of killing Isaac would have been licit since it would have been carried out at the explicit command of God, who has authority over all life (I-II.94.5 *ad* 2). It should be noted that Aquinas' analysis at this point is entirely in accord with his general analysis of homicide and murder at II-II.64. Just as it is not murder for an agent of the state to kill a convicted criminal, because the state (alone) has authority over the lives of wrongdoers, so it would not have been wrong for Abraham to kill Isaac at God's command, since God alone has authority over all human life. Nor would Abraham have violated the essential equality between himself and Isaac in this case, since he would be acting, not as an individual, but as God's agent.

28. In this analysis, I am indebted to William A. Galston's defense of an Aristotelian theory of justice in *Justice and the Human Good* (Chicago: University of Chicago Press, 1980), esp. 143–91.

Chapter 6: Prudence; Cardinal and Theological Virtues

1. *Summa Theologica,* 3 vols., trans. the Fathers of the English Dominican Province (New York: Benziger Bros., 1947), 2:1393.

2. Throughout this section and the next, I am indebted to Richard Sorabji's essay, "Aristotle on the Role of Intellect in Virtue," in Amelie Oksenberg Rorty, ed., *Essays on Aristotle's Ethics* (Berkeley: University of California Press, 1980), 201–20. I have also learned a great deal about Aquinas' treatment of prudence, and in particular, its relation to justice, from Alasdair MacIntyre, *Whose Justice? Which Rationality?* (Notre Dame, Ind.: University of Notre Dame Press, 1988), 183–208.

3. More exactly, the virtues of the truly virtuous person, who is fully rational, direct her desires and aversions in accordance with her true grasp of the human good, whereas the simulacra of the virtues possessed by the vicious person shape her desires and aversions in accordance with her false conception of the good. The soul of the vicious person is therefore not in accordance with reason in a proper sense. Nonetheless, in this case the soul is rational in the minimal sense that it is capable of directing the actions of the individual toward her desired (albeit bad) ends; otherwise, she could not act, or sustain a course of activity, at all.

4. Sorabji, "Aristotle," 206. Aristotle's remarks on practical wisdom are to be found throughout the *Nicomachean Ethics;* in particular, see 6.1140a20–1140b30 and 6.1143b15–1145a15.

5. Elsewhere, Aquinas reserves the name "perfect virtues" for the theological virtues, which alone direct the human person to his true ultimate good; see I-II.65.2.

6. Stanley Hauerwas, *A Community of Character: Toward a Constructive Christian Social Ethic* (Notre Dame, Ind.: University of Notre Dame Press, 1981), 143.

7. In the remainder of this section, I draw heavily on my *"De Ordine Caritatis:* Charity, Friendship and Justice in Thomas Aquinas' *Summa Theologiae,"* The Thomist 53/2 (April 1989), 197–214.

8. *Nicomachean Ethics* 9.1158b30–1159a10.

9. Ibid., 9.1166a1–1167b20; 1169b1–1170b20.

10. It may be asked whether these virtues should be associated with justice rather than charity, since they are other-regarding. In fact, Aquinas *does* associate them with justice (see II-II.44.8; cf. I-II.100.5), but he apparently considers them to have more of the character of charity than of justice. In the same way, he associates those aspects of chastity that concern heterosexual sexual relationships with the virtue of temperance, even though this aspect of chastity could also be associated with justice (see II-II.154.1–3, 6–10).

Chapter 7: The Permanent Significance of Thomas Aquinas

1. "The Encyclical Letter of Pope Leo XIII on the Restoration of Christian Philosophy According to the Mind of St. Thomas Aquinas, the Angelic Doctor" *(Aeterni Patris),* published in English in the 1947 edition of the *Summa Theologiae,* vii–xvi, at xiii.

2. Alasdair MacIntyre, *Whose Justice? Which Rationality?* (Notre Dame, Ind.: University of Notre Dame Press, 1988), 164–82.

3. Ibid., 349–403.

4. Ibid., 402–3.

5. James M. Gustafson, "A Response to Critics," *Journal of Religious Ethics* 13/2 (Fall 1985), 189.

6. For example, see Paul Davies, *God and the New Physics* (New York: Simon & Schuster, 1983); A. R. Peacocke, *Creation and the World of Science* (Oxford: Clarendon Press, 1979); and Robert Wright, *Three Scientists and Their Gods: Looking for Meaning in an Age of Information* (New York: Harper & Row, 1988).

7. The literature on pragmatism is extensive. For a good critical history of pragmatism, including a theological critique from the standpoint of African-American liberation theology, see Cornel West, *The American Evasion of Philosophy: A Genealogy of Pragmatism* (Madison: University of Wisconsin Press, 1989). Those who are especially interested in the influence of pragmatism on Gustafson should compare his work with the writings of H. Richard Niebuhr, who drew extensively on the work of the pragmatists, especially Mead. See H. Richard Niebuhr, *The Responsible Self: An Essay in Christian Moral Philosophy* (New York: Harper & Row, 1963); George Herbert Mead, *Mind, Self and Society from the Standpoint*

of a Social Behaviorist, ed. Charles W. Morris, (Chicago: University of Chicago Press, 1934).

8. For example, see Juan Luis Segundo, *Grace and the Human Condition* (Maryknoll, N.Y.: Orbis Books, 1973), 37–39.

9. See José Comblin, *The Church and the National Security State* (Maryknoll, N.Y.: Orbis Books, 1979), for an ecclesiology that develops along these lines.

Index of Names